Scribe Publications
FREELOADING

Chris Ruen, a Brooklyn-based freelance writer whose work has appeared in *The New York Times* and *Slate*, is a former contributing editor for *Cool'eh* magazine. He has covered music culture for *Tiny Mix Tapes*, a Minneapolis-based online music magazine.

Because of Emily

FREE LOADING

HOW OUR INSATIABLE APPETITE FOR FREE CONTENT STARVES CREATIVITY

CHRIS RUEN

SCRIBE

Melbourne • London

Scribe Publications Pty Ltd
18–20 Edward St, Brunswick, Victoria, Australia 3056
Email: info@scribepub.com.au

First published in the United States by OR Books, New York and London, 2012

Published in Australia and New Zealand by Scribe 2013

Typeset by Lapiz Digital, Chennai, India
Printed and bound in Australia by Griffin Press

The paper this book is printed on is certified against the Forest Stewardship
Council® Standards. Griffin Press holds FSC chain of custody certification
SGS-COC-005088. FSC promotes environmentally responsible, socially
beneficial and economically viable management of the world's forests.

National Library of Australia
Cataloguing-in-Publication data

Ruen, Chris.

Freeloading: how our insatiable appetite for free content starves creativity / Chris Ruen.

9781921844294 (pbk.)

1. Intellectual property. 2. Copyright and electronic data processing. 3. Internet–Law
and legislation. 4. Creation (Literary, artistic, etc.)–Law and legislation. 5. Open access
publishing.

346.048

www.scribepublications.com.au

"If we understand the revolutionary transformations caused by new media, we can anticipate and control them; but if we continue in our self-induced subliminal trance, we will be their slaves."

—*Marshall McLuhan*

CONTENTS

Introduction: The Future, On Repeat   001

Part 1: The Thicket   013

Part 2: Ground Clearing   079

Part 3: Restoration   143

Acknowledgments   257

Notes   258

INTRODUCTION

THE FUTURE, ON REPEAT

On a January morning in 2010, nervous congregants gathered in a San Francisco auditorium. They awaited revelation, if not rapture. Silicon Valley's far-flung diaspora joined the revival from afar, holding virtual vigil. With bent backs and glazed eyes, they stared at the live video feed streaming across their computer screens. Soon, the prophet of the information age would reward his followers and offer a new vision unto the people.

Inside the auditorium, eager eyes darted back and forth across the stage, straining to see their digital media savior. There he was! Applause thundered: dressed in his uniform of black turtleneck and blue jeans, Steve Jobs finally entered from stage left.

The oracle of Apple Inc. began to enumerate the many charms of his latest revelation: the iPad. The new tablet computer represented an entirely new category of digital device, splitting the difference between the smartphone's elegant mobility and the laptop's utilitarian power. Tablets took the totality of digital media consumption and made it truly mobile. Digital web browsing, email, photos, video, music, games, and books were hardly new, but having such an optimized, sleek, intuitive device with which to obtain and consume it all was revolutionary.

"Let me show you what it looks like. I happen to have one right here," Jobs said.

Like a postmodern Moses declaring new holy law, he walked to the lip of the stage and held out the diminutive iPad for its first inspection by his followers. They gave thanks, hooting and whistling up to the stage. Jobs stepped back to detail the features of his new brainchild, highlighting its big, beautiful touchscreen.

"Holding the Internet in your hands," he said. "It's an incredible experience."

But now that the prophet had offered the ability to hold the past, present and future of human expression in our hands—what would we do with it: create or destroy?

By 2010, the new age of digital media had already presented difficulties for traditional creative industries. With the iPad adding to the mix, would magazines, newspapers, books, television, and film reap sustaining profits from digital metamorphosis? Some believed the industries themselves would be reaped, sacrificed to the gods of progress. But not David Carr, media columnist for the *New York Times*.

In a column entitled "A Savior in the Form of a Tablet," Carr enthusiastically gushed: "The tablet represents an opportunity to renew the romance between printed material and consumer... somewhere between the iTunes model and the iPhone app store... there may be a model for print." In an issue of *Wired* magazine dedicated to the emergence of tablets, editor-in-chief Chris Anderson—otherwise an evangelist for "free" business models—proclaimed the dawn of a new age for digitized media, one where "tablets can show media in a context worth paying for." Rupert Murdoch temporarily suspended his battles against content aggregators and Google to call the iPad "a wonderful thing... If you have less newspapers and more of these... it may well be the saving of the newspaper industry."

But would consumers actually be willing to open their wallets for content after years of getting much of it for free online? The gale-force winds of technological change had already blown many media professionals to the precipice. Now the iPad threatened to push them over the edge.

Once the Internet became ubiquitous in the 2000s, newsstand, subscription, and advertising revenue dropped steadily as consumers migrated to the web for free news, information, and classified listings. Total paid newspaper circulation sunk by six million from 2005 to 2008, and print advertising revenues deflated by a whopping $13 billion—a contraction of nearly thirty percent. While newspars searched for an emergency parachute to ease their free fall, online advertising revenues offered little more than a cocktail umbrella. By 2008, merely eight percent of newspaper advertising revenues came from online content. Publishers, accustomed to the "analog dollars" of print, struggled to make due with online advertising's "digital pennies."

As if that were not ominous enough, in came the Great Recession of 2008.

Consumer budgets wilted. In the following year, overall print revenue dropped another twenty-eight percent. Even online ad revenues, modest but thought certain to grow, absorbed double-digit losses as total advertising revenue plummeted another $10 billion. Institutions of the news such as *The San Francisco Chronicle* and *The Seattle Post-Intelligencer* ceased printing. The *New York Times*, once thought invincible, became so cash-strapped that it took out a $250 million emergency loan from Mexican billionaire Carlos Slim, laid off employees, and axed sections. Magazine publisher Condé Nast shuttered historic titles and slashed its total budget by twenty-five percent in the face of sinking ad revenue.

Aside from optimists like David Carr, who had faith that new digital models would save us all, another school of thought emerged. Stewart Brand's famous edict "Information wants to be free" was its guiding light. For these people, the notion that any industry needed to be "saved" was misguided and pathetic. Technology was not responsible for *anything*, much less the salvation of old, inefficient industries rendered useless by the market. If historic institutions failed, even ones as important to society as robust journalism, it was the underlying industries' own fault for not adapting fast enough or for no longer serving a purpose in the eyes of the marketplace. Institutional death was a necessary cost of progress.

"Technology giveth and technology taketh away," BoingBoing editor Cory Doctorow declared. Others in this unsentimental sect adopted a more condescending and altogether nasty attitude. In the issue of *Wired* magazine devoted to the iPad, the editors gave "Fake Steve Jobs," a pseudonymous blogger well known in Silicon Valley, the last word on the iPad's potential impact for print industries. His entry, "Go Save Yourself," read:

> The *New York Times* sucks just as bad on Kindle as it does on paper. That, in fact, is the real problem with the *New York Times*: it sucks and everyone knows it, except, apparently, the dumb fucks who write for the *New York Times*... The iPad isn't about saving newspapers. It's about inventing new ways of telling stories, using a whole new language—one that we can't even imagine right now... the truth is you guys really need to die so we can clear the way for the new guys.

This endnote to *Wired's* exploration expressed a digital mob's readiness to drag old institutions to the village green for a good, old-fashioned stoning. But the mob never bothered to consider what these supposedly outmoded institutions would be replaced *with*. Instead, they blindly embraced the holy commandment that all digital content shall be open, free, and shared. Their vision of participatory, open-source digital creation and consumption (commonly called Web 2.0) preached that technology would bless us so long as we dutifully laid our offerings of labor and creativity before it for the good of the "hive." We would be rewarded, eventually, with progress and prosperity. The digital sect promised revelatory new business models, wealth creation hitherto unseen, an explosion in creative culture, and an evolution in modes of expression so fantastical we "can't even imagine" them.

"Now would be the time to embrace the Internet," Tech Crunch's Michael Arrington said of the iPad release. "But the *New York Times,* the *Wall Street Journal* and others are running in the opposite direction with (iPad) apps that have no hyperlinks and/or require a fee to get access."

Blasphemy!

The Web 2.0 crowd rejected the notion that consumers would ever pay for digital content, which after all could be easily copied and redistributed for free. It was an antiquated expectation to believe people would pay, pathetically out-of-touch with basic economic and technological reality.

The writer and BoingBoing editor Cory Doctorow openly mocked Carr's attitude: "Everyone in journalism-land is looking for a daddy figure who'll promise them that their audience will go back to paying for their stuff. The reason people have stopped paying for a lot of 'content' isn't just that they can get it for free, though: *it's that they can get lots of competing stuff for free*, too."[1] Doctorow had a point. In a worldwide Nielsen survey of consumers in 2009, seventy-nine percent said they'd avoid any website with a paywall, assuming they could find the same content free someplace else.

Whether idealistic notions of the Internet were being violated or not, pragmatists countered that publishers had a perfect right to charge for content and that consumers, regardless of what they might say in surveys, had already proved themselves willing to pay for their digital content.

"Five years ago," wrote David Carr, "almost no one paid for music online and now, nine billion or so songs sold later, we know that people are willing to pay if the price is right and the convenience is there."

But even *if* newspaper and magazine publishers could cajole their readers to pay for iPad subscriptions or submit to paywall fees, would the resulting model be sustainable? Not according to Australian media commentator Eric Beecher: "Like almost everyone else who works in the journalism industry, I desperately hope the iPad and similar devices will save newspapers from economic irrelevance." Upon studying the numbers, Beecher found minimal savings in eliminating printing and delivery costs, little to no profitability in low-cost digital subscriptions, and only modest increases in advertising revenues. "None of which," he concluded, "is to refute the idea that the iPad is a wonderful device that will bring joy and utility to millions of people. It just won't—and can't—save the economic fate of journalism."

"I fear the ship for most publications may have already sailed," wrote *Infoworld*'s Robert Cringely. "People are too used to getting subpar content for free.... The premium rates publications charge(d) for print advertising subsidized a great many things—like teams of researchers, fact checkers, copy editors, and multiple line editors—that online ad models simply don't support.... Does quality matter? Or have we passed the point of no return, where fast and cheap trumps fast and good, and everything else be damned?"

Media professionals assumed the digital revolution was unstoppable: a force of societal progress or doom. Another columnist from the *New York Times*, Tim Egan, managed to strike a middle ground between these factions. Egan tempered his excitement for tablets, reminding readers that, despite the iPad's potential, still another danger lurked amidst the shadows of digital content.

"There were nine million illegal downloads of copyright-protected books in the closing months of 2009," he wrote.

As eReaders took their first toddling steps toward widespread adoption in 2010, twenty-eight percent of eReader owners already admitted to downloading eBooks from illegal file-sharing services. In the days immediately following the release of iPad, when Apple had sold a mere 300,000 units, downloads of unlicensed eBooks via bittorrent protocols jumped by a whopping seventy-eight percent. In 2010, one company readied a "book ripper" that could automatically scan an entire book for eReader use in a few minutes, ostensibly making eBook piracy as easy as copying a CD and uploading it to a file-sharing service. File-sharing sites for books, based upon the same model as Napster, began popping up. With a quick Google search of a book's title, in most cases an unlicensed copy could be quickly had for free.

Though newspapers offered free (and legal) online content for years, the specter of piracy hung over that industry like an ashen cloud. A Pew survey found that seventy-five percent of newspaper executives, most notably those of the *New York Times*, were planning to institute paywalls for their digital content. "These days, print piracy is a trivial issue," said *The Economist,* "since most general news articles are given away free. If newspapers and magazines begin charging people to read their output, the pirates are likely to turn up, and quickly."

The pirating of large files like movies and television series was already a problem for entertainment studios and stood to accelerate as bandwidth and connection speeds exponentially increased. Downloading a season of a television show would soon be as quick and easy as downloading an MP3, while iPads and high-definition screens made the cinema a less sought-after experience.

Digitization threatened all content industries. The advent of the iPad opened the way to a world where digitized cultural content could be optimally consumed, illegally and conveniently, for free. What did this mean? The doors to the future, both exciting and ominous, flung open with such force as to altogether come unhinged, shattering commercial barriers between content creators and consumers forever.

The *Times's* Tim Egan tried to stay positive amidst the ongoing disruption. "I have to place my trust in readers," he said. "Tactile readers, e-readers: Save us all! Never give up on the power of the written word."

Nine years before unveiling the iPad, Steve Jobs had listed the many charms of another revelatory new product: the iPod. The new personal MP3 player turned consuming digital music into something hip and intuitive. The immensely successful CD format, which had taken music industry revenues to historic peaks at the turn of the millennium, became antiquated with the snap of Jobs's fingers.

If the iPod made CDs obsolete in the eyes of many, Napster turned the very concept of paying for music into something deserving to rot in the dumpster, along with yesterday's refuse like the 8-track and VCRs. Napster would go down in history as the first great peer-to-peer (P2P) service for uploading and downloading digital content outside the sanctioned realms of capitalist commerce. It also signaled the first battle in a perpetual war over the fate of digital content.

Multitudes adopted this paradigm shift. By early 2001, Napster claimed a membership of twenty-six million users. Though it was shut down by the Ninth Circuit Court of Appeals the following summer, other services like Grokster and Audiogalaxy filled the vacuum left by Napster's demise.

By further popularizing digital music consumption, many rightly feared the iPod would encourage file-sharing. Steve Jobs responded by categorically condemning music piracy. "Stealing music is not right," he told *Bloomberg Businessweek* in 2003, "and I can understand people being very upset about their intellectual property being stolen. But the stick alone isn't going to work."[2] He understood that any attempts at copy protections would only be decrypted by young hackers and rendered useless. Jobs rejected any digital lock-and-key restrictions, such as Digital Rights Management (DRM), which blocked content owners from indiscriminately copying files.

"Piracy is not a technological issue," Jobs said. "It's a behavior issue."

But it was also true that, by neglecting to block unlicensed content, the iPod made music piracy more desirable for consumers. In a world in which digital content was seemingly in infinite supply, Apple exploited the demand for hardware that could store thousands of songs and make them easily consumable. Steve Jobs played a starring role in the drama of music piracy. More than anyone, he destroyed the music industry as we knew it. More than anyone, he was actively trying to save it, too.

Jobs included a sticker on each new iPod that implored the customer: "Don't Steal Music." Translated into four languages, that plea did nothing to stem the tide or behavioral underpinnings of file-sharing. So, for his next attempt to assuage illegal MP3 consumption, Jobs offered what seemed to be a logical answer in 2003—the iTunes Store. Consumers *finally* had a reliable online store where they could efficiently sample and purchase individual MP3 tracks for 99¢ and albums for around $10.

"We're trying to compete with piracy," Jobs told the Associated Press at the time. "We're trying to pull people away from piracy and say, 'You can buy these songs legally for a fair price.'"[3]

Jobs trumpeted to *Fortune*, "It will go down in history as a turning point for the music industry. This is landmark stuff. I can't overestimate it!"

Monetization was achieved: the new model—discovered! Consumers were handed expanded choice, convenience and lower prices while record labels rejoiced over lower distribution costs and an expanded market of listeners. The dream of digital commerce finally found its path to realization. No more were we tied to point-of-purchase retail, wasteful packaging or shipping costs. In this world of digital commerce, anything seemed possible. And that proved to be its hazard.

Digital sales initially skyrocketed, leading to optimism from the music industry that profits from physical products would someday be supplanted by digital revenues. But the de-bundling of albums into the sale of individual tracks eroded the potential for such profits as physical sales careened into a free fall. After only ten years, US music industry revenues shriveled from over $14 billion a year to less than $7 billion. From 2000 to 2009, total US album sales (physical and digital) plummeted by fifty-two percent, from 785 million to 374 million units. When the Recording Industry Association of America analyzed the decade using 2011 dollars, the plight of the industry looked even worse. Per capita, Americans in 2009 spent just one third of the amount of money they devoted to recorded music in 2000, from an all-time high of $71 per consumer to a modern-era low of $26.[4]

Meanwhile, piracy expanded in scope and acceptance. David Carr may point to the ten billion songs purchased from the iTunes Store in its first seven years, but compare that to the forty billion tracks pirated worldwide in 2009 alone. Though numerous legal streaming services, subscription sites, and MP3 stores emerged over the years to offer digital consumers both convenience and affordable pricing, an astounding ninety-five percent of music downloads in

2010 were pirated (the same percentage as in 2009). And according to a 2009 study, only about three percent of the music found on the average person's iPod had been purchased via the industry-standard iTunes Store. Even aggregate digital music sales, thought destined for sustained growth, appeared ready to flatline in 2010.

"We are at one of the most worrying stages yet for the industry," Mark Mulligan of Forrester Research lamented in early 2011. "Music's first digital decade is behind us and what do we have? Not a lot of progress…. As things stand now, digital music has failed." [5]

The industry appeared to be locked in a downward spiral. No new business models had appeared to save the day. Record stores closed by the thousands. Record labels merged or went out of business. Chicago's Touch and Go Records, arguably the most influential independent record label of the '80s and '90s, abruptly closed down. According to a report conducted by the International Federation of the Phonographic Industry (IFPI), a global advocacy group for the music industry, the total number of people employed as professional musicians in the United States fell by seventeen percent from 1999 to 2009 as piracy migrated from the margins and into the mainstream. [6]

Even live concert tours, once considered "the savior of the music business," saw a historic downturn in 2010.[7] Across the world that year, despite the global economy gaining some steam after the Great Recession, live concert revenues, attendance, and the number of shows all declined by double-digit percentages. In North America, the concert business was comparably worse. The industry that supported one of humanity's greatest treasures crumbled before our eyes. After a decade of trying, no one knew what to do about it or even what to think.

As seventy-five million tablet computers, mostly iPads, were projected to be sold in the US alone by 2012, every creative industry had reason to cast a wary glance at the music industry and shudder at the prospect of their own digital doom. [8] Meanwhile, millions of technologically savvy consumers accepted piracy as the new norm. They enjoyed the bounty of free, high-quality entertainment waiting at the end of a few mouse-clicks, but what sort of future were they helping to build?

———————————

If we know an album or movie is for sale, but can be downloaded for free with a simple Google search; or a well-meaning friend links to an underground website where we can find a near-infinite supply of free digital music, books, film, or television shows, how to understand the resulting dilemma?

I'm here alone, you think, sitting at your computer or lounging on the couch with a tablet. *No one's watching. No one will know. So why would I choose to pay for this? What's the difference?*

To pay or not to pay? It is the existential crisis of the digital age. Today we all have the option to fall in line with the digital mob, passively sitting back, clicking, consuming, watching in awe as this great tool called "the Internet" refashions reality, seemingly in its own disruptive, brutally efficient image.

Newspapers are dying?

Well, shit happens.

New musicians have a harder time building sustainable careers than ever before?

A starving artist is a good artist.

How will writers make great works if no one will pay for them?

That's their problem, not mine. Who says artists deserve to make money anyway?

Can we perceive the dire consequences of P2P technology and find ways to lessen its damages?

You can't fight technology. Now, sit down, enjoy the spectacle with rest of us.

The fact is that no one knows where our use of rapidly advancing technology is taking us. We are like the pioneers of early America, ignorant of what waits around the next river bend. We may happen upon a spectacular vista, one that suggests a better world is indeed waiting. Or we may be suddenly jolted by a waterfall sending us to our death. There is no way of knowing what awaits us on this digital journey. For times such as our own, a healthy dose of caution may be the difference between human success and failure; metaphorical life and death.

As an example of the inherent clumsiness that has characterized our journey into digitization, let's revisit the Stewart Brand quote that "information wants to be free." The full quote reads:

> Information wants to be free. Information also wants to be expensive. Information wants to be free because it has become so cheap to distribute, copy, and recombine—too cheap to meter. It wants to be expensive because it can be immeasurably valuable to the recipient. That tension will not go away.

It leads to endless wrenching debate about price, copyright, 'intellectual property', the moral rightness of casual distribution, because each round of new devices makes the tension worse, not better.

"Information wants to be free" is little more than throat clearing for Brand's real aim, to elucidate the inherent paradox of the digital age. Though advances in technology allow all creative works to be digitized, copied and distributed easily for something resembling "free," does that mean we should carelessly treat it as such? The fact that content *can* be accessed for free doesn't somehow erase the immense value that professional creativity adds to our lives. Brand suggested we think seriously about this question by embracing its inherent tension.

Honestly embracing the ongoing digital tension is what this book serves to do. Hopefully, we will end in a better place than where we start, so that we can understand this tension. What does it mean to live with it, as individuals and as a society? What are the costs of lazily ignoring it, of hiding behind stilted ideologies?

———————————

To get at the essence of what the digital revolution means, we need context: a narrative. That is what the music industry's particular engagement with digitization provides.

A new approach is called for to more fully render the complexities of digitization. Silicon Valley technorati have presented their ideas with entrepreneurs, marketers, and media professionals in mind, rarely considering the two groups for whom this tension has greatest consequences: creators and their audience.

We need a strategy that hits the restart button on the discourse of piracy. We need new symbols, new ethics, and new prisms of understanding. Digital technology is nebulous and ever-changing, so it is crucial to ground our journey in honest, day-to-day experience as we search for enduring principles that can withstand the most violent winds of digital turbulence.

Welcome to FreeLoading.

PART 1

THE THICKET

Discovery

I spent the summer killing trees.

Kneeling down upon a grassy hillside under the searing heat of late July, sweat dripped down my forehead, stinging my eyes while I struggled with an eight-foot-tall eastern red cedar tree. Holding back its unforgiving bottom limbs, conifer needles and splintered bark clawed at my wrists and forearms. Reaching for a nearby hacksaw with a free hand, one briery limb broke free from my grasp and swung back in retaliation, burning as it scratched across the face and lacerated my cheek. Increasingly angry at this scurrilous plant, I seized the limbs once more and went about attacking the foundation.

A surprise awaited below the wide skirt of stiff branches. Not one, but three gnarled trunks spun out from the same patch of dry, bare soil. They grew furiously, spiraling in and out of one another. From a distance, eliminating the tree appeared to be a simple task; only by kneeling down to its source could I discover the organic dysfunction hiding below.

My amputation of the first trunk was crucial, severing one unit of outgrowth from its subterranean roots. I stood up to yank the marginalized gnarl from the tree's knotted body, then tossed it onto a burning pile of woody debris. Dried up, sterile earth hugged the lopped-off stump. Already, the tree appeared less formidable, begging to be undone.

Since childhood, I have visited my family's farmland in Southeast Minnesota, oblivious to the character of my surroundings, unmoved by nature. Neither the limestone outcroppings on the hillsides, the bluffs that towered over hemmed-in valleys, nor the gurgling trout streams that fed the rivers occurred to me as being out of the ordinary or special. Patches of cedar tree saplings rose unchallenged from the open meadows and tall glades of mature cedars dominated the hilltops, concealing dramatic limestone bluffs under shadow.

Growing older, I explored the many acres of farmland and my appreciation for it grew in kind. The proliferating cedars, I gathered, had rightfully outcompeted the neighboring plants and trees. They were a perfectly natural force of evolution, if unfortunate competition for the commanding oaks and the occasional maple tree that dotted the property.

My perception of the landscape fundamentally shifted in 2007. Researching this corner of Minnesota, I learned its true name: The Driftless. During the last Ice Age, glaciers that invaded from the north spared an ovular region of rolling hills, bisected by the Mississippi River. The area was left untouched by the glacial drift (rock and gravel carried by ice) deposited across the rest of America's flattened Upper Midwest. When the Ice Age ended, torrents of glacial meltwater carved narrow valleys and scoured the hillsides, exposing limestone bluffs and sculpting undulating land formations.

A unique landscape was born, the diversity of which was predicated on the natural forces and cycles. Whereas hardwood forests permeated the cool, north-facing bluffs that saw little direct sunlight, the rest of the land was characterized by oak savanna. Maintained by the wildfires that regularly swept through the open land, native prairie was graced by magisterial oak trees whose thick bark protected them from the wildfires. Beneath the oak canopies, tremulous light filtered in through permissive leaves. Rainwater drained through The Driftless's shallow soils and dripped through fissures in the underlying limestone into ice caves where waters cooled before emerging again as frigid freshwater springs. These springs collected as coldwater streams that meandered through the bottomlands, providing habitat for trout, birds, mammals, and reptiles. With rippling hills, craggy bluffs, open prairies, and massive savanna oaks, The Driftless was a land of magnificent depth and diversity.

When farmers began to settle the area, many of the centuries-old oaks were chopped down while the prairies were tilled for crops or converted into cattle pastures. Wildfires were abruptly suppressed. This allowed fire intolerant species—most notably the eastern red cedar—to move in and proliferate. They surrounded the oaks and gradually choked them off from water and sunlight.

The cedars' root systems and fallen needles altered the chemistry of the topsoil, making further degradation all the more likely; native plants withered into dormancy beneath the impenetrable branches. The barren understory soils that resulted were prone to erosion and runoff, dirtying the streams and filling the valleys with sediment. An erosive cycle began, with disturbed soils becoming more vulnerable to further invasion, leading to accelerated erosion, more cedars, and so on. With degeneration in full swing, land devalued. The cedars continued to rise up, threatening to transform a diverse habitat of color into one of dreary sameness and concealed potential.

Once I understood The Driftless, I no longer viewed the rise of the cedars as evolutionary. They were a regressive force, an opportunistic invader, a threat to development. I realized that, if I wanted to enjoy this land throughout my life, I'd have to do my small part to maintain it.

Having eliminated one small cedar tree, I looked out over the softly-cupped valley that surrounded me. Dozens more dirt-brown saplings were out there, blighting the hills. Though the trees appeared harmless and even decorative in their adolescent, shrub-like state, their degenerative implications for the future cluttered the horizon. Thick stands of cedars covered the ridges, trapping isolated oaks and killing off their low-hanging branches, imposing themselves as ineluctable evolution; a future that wasn't worth fighting against. The saw dropped from my hand.

This is a waste of my time.

That summer of 2007, I took two months off from my café job in Brooklyn and secluded myself on the farmland in order to type the first draft of a novel. There, I nailed a desk together from scrap wood, turning an empty late-19th-century barn on the property into the most inspiring of workspaces, if a dusty one. The novel went nowhere. Disappointment fueled distraction until writing became an afterthought. Most of my time was spent cutting cedar trees, taking self-guided hikes and—most surprisingly—writing an unplanned batch of songs and recording them onto my laptop.

A few weeks later, I returned from the bucolic scenes of the farmstead to a water-damaged, cockroach-infested apartment on a rat-run block of Williamsburg, Brooklyn. Rather than pass the time slaying cedars, I awoke at six each morning to sling espresso drinks at the Greenpoint Coffee House, a café in the Greenpoint section of north Brooklyn.

After fleeing from a post-collegiate stint at a Manhattan literary agency, I had settled into the life of a twenty-something barista, making rent each month on tips. For my writing, I exploited the flexible work schedule and the cafe's inspiring community of regulars. The place was one of many touchstones for north Brooklyn's concentration of established and emerging artists. Before the trip out to Minnesota, I made my writing plans perfectly well known to these customers, and with my fellow staff of actors and musicians. Upon my return, they asked how it all went.

Well, I did start the book. But I ended up recording an album instead.
Oh. (pause) You write music?
Apparently.

Satisfied with the preliminary recording experiments on the farm, I figured if I wasn't going back to New York with a book, I may as well return with an album. So, I wrote and recorded music during days and nights amid the cedar-strewn hills. Creating one surprising song after another, it numbed any disappointment or guilt from the failed novel. Melodies and chord progressions trickled out of my subconscious like groundwater discharged from the surrounding hillside springs.

Though unplanned, this newfound propensity for songwriting wasn't entirely surprising. Like many other lifelong music fans, I began participating in music culture during my adolescence. From the profits of a dog-walking job, birthday and Christmas money I bought my first CDs. A subscription to *SPIN* magazine exposed me to new artists and music journalism—and the high-stakes thrills of trusting a review enough to buy an album without having heard it. Music defined my self-image during those awkward periods of few friends and shapeless angst in the 1990s. So much so, that I soon thought myself to be one of music culture's loyal citizens; somehow responsible for maintaining its vitality. As my library of hip-hop, post-punk, and trip-hop grew, I amassed a parallel collection of crotchety opinions about which music was worthy of public consumption and which artists actually *deserved* careers. As is the case with many misfits of postwar suburbia, I cultivated a sneering suspicion for top-40 radio, major labels, or anything that smelled of "corporate America." Nothing stroked my self-righteous ego more than patronizing relatively obscure, small artists on independent record labels. I became, on some level, a music snob.

I grew older and began to engage with music as a writer and journalist, interviewing musicians and writing concert reviews as a college amateur and professional freelancer once I moved to New York City. Though friends with many musicians, I was content to play a writerly role: the outsider. I threw in my lot with the critics—leaning against a side wall of a rock club, straight-faced with folded arms— rather than with the creators themselves. I was entirely uninterested in humanizing musicians and didn't respect the work that went into making an album. Music was just "there," all around me, and waiting to be unearthed.

Because I had no way to appreciate the nature of recording, it was easy to disrespect musicians. If an artist I loved made a disappointing album, I acted as though I had been victimized by some criminal act. My subconscious separation from the artist became a matter of necessity. They were an "other" upon whom I depended to receive more of what I needed: good music. I put them on an inhuman pedestal when they made something I liked, and treated them like inadequate slaves when an album didn't please me.

Recording music on the Minnesota farm exposed the ignorance, entitlement and jealousy underlying my previous relationship with music as a fan and critic. I never accounted for the time, focus, inspiration, drudgery, and plain luck that writing music—even mediocre music—necessitated. I never understood the tedium of completing a decent recording. I had no clue.

My appreciation grew for all the music I had ever loved, the human labor and mysterious inspiration that brought it into being for my repeated enjoyment. To have any career in art was a sacred thing; to count on enough support from fans to devote oneself to creating new works, sharing them with the fans who made their creation possible in the first place. What a democratic cultural ideal, I thought.

When the file-trading service Napster was peaking in 2000, I was entering my freshman year at a university where each dorm room came outfitted with new, juicy broadband connections, ideal for transferring large digital files. Nearly all of my friends habitually used services like Napster, burning the digital songs to blank CDs. I knew very few people who still purchased music, even in 2000. Multiple record stores in my Minneapolis college district closed in my four years there.

I pirated hundreds of songs during my college years, but I sensed disposability and devaluation infecting my relationship with music. Logging on to a file-sharing service was part of an addictive cycle. The trembling high of infinite rewards captivated me as I searched for whatever band or song I could think of at the moment. At the end of each downloading session, the disappointment of a still unfulfilled and unquenched desire followed. "Free" music and its perfect abundance felt awfully cheap in the final analysis. Piracy turned my genuine love for music into just another fidgety online addiction. It was an exercise in hyper-consumption: quantity over quality, breadth over depth, entitlement over ownership. Intuiting that my classic relationship with music (paying for it) was indeed a more spiritually profitable enterprise, and a hell of a lot more interesting and fun, I mostly stopped pirating when my online service of choice, Audiogalaxy, was shut down in 2002.

Anyone in my generation who paid attention to the litigious battles between Napster, Metallica and the RIAA instinctively gleaned that *nothing* was less hip than getting uptight about music piracy. Doing so aligned one with multi-millionaire artists, greedy major labels, corporate scallawags and thick-skulled Luddites. I resolved to avoid that particular gnarled and futile debate.

While purposefully ignoring the controversy of digital piracy through the mid-2000s, I assumed new digital models were emerging to replace the revenues of physical music sales. They *had* to be emerging, right? Considering all the capital and brainpower invested in the industry's future, solutions would need to come sooner than later. In my mind, the controversy over piracy evidenced a perfectly healthy period of technological transition. As for the artists and industry heavyweights who predicted doom for the future of music: they were overreacting, obsessed with protecting their obscene profit margins. Piracy was arguably a positive development. It helped promotion-starved small artists connect with fans, threatening the unjust monopoly of bloated major labels. I didn't hear of any independent artists raising their voices on the issue. Plenty of great new records continued to be released each year. The industry seemed to be doing just fine. How bad could piracy be?

Years on, I realized it. Something was rotten in Brooklyn.

My Greenpoint café was frequented by members of various Brooklyn bands like TV On The Radio, The Hold Steady, Vampire Weekend, Yeasayer, and MGMT. From my traditional perspective of writer and fan, I saw the cyclonic press coverage of these artists, the breathless critical praise, and the sold-out dates around the country. In the sphere of indie rock, they were in the upper echelon—either one step away from being on a major label or already succeeding on one. These were the success stories of the Internet Age, supposed poster children for the triumphs of file sharing. But from my ground-level vantage point in Brooklyn—away from the *Rolling Stone* reviews, *SPIN* cover stories, and profiles in the *New York Times*—all was not as it appeared on the mediated surface.

After getting to know a handful of members from some of these bands, I was shocked by how little money they seemed to actually be making. As a measly young writer and part-time barista who had never even heard of a trust fund before moving East, even I had an apartment—that paramount symbol of fortune in New York City—as nice or nicer than those of some of these "rock stars."

Sure, I thought at the time, *multi-millionaire artists like Metallica don't really need me to help them finance that fourth house, but what could possibly be the rationalization for refusing to compensate working artists who desperately need the support?*

I suddenly observed the music scene in Brooklyn with both the perspectives of consumer and creator in mind, noting the music-buying practices of my friends, or lack thereof. My peers, twenty-something rock disciples and aspiring songwriters, obtained nearly all of their music by downloading unlicensed copies for free online, often well before album release dates. They rarely went to concerts or bought band merchandise like t-shirts or posters, rationalizations I'd heard others express for their downloading habits.

After purposefully ignoring the drama surrounding music piracy for years, I was shaken by its clear reality. Millions of fans, like my friends, had made up their minds that they no longer saw a reason to pay for the music they genuinely enjoyed and loved. Judging by the relative dearth of intelligent discussion I found on the subject online or in my immediate social circles, meaningful debate on the ethics of "taking" or "copying" one's music for free had effectively ceased. For such a recent technological phenomenon, packed with so many quandaries for consumers and creators, the lack of discussion was genuinely bizarre.

I saw that no moral high ground existed in the debate over music piracy; neither thankless consumers nor litigious major labels could claim it. "Free" music didn't discriminate between rich or poor, emerging or established artists. A growing class of consumers, spearheaded by my own generation, had been duped into believing that if it feels good to download your digital content for free, then it must be good. It was, somehow, the rest of the world's fault for not adapting to the noble practice. A new future was emerging; delirious, ominous, and liberated from timeworn social codes and responsibilities.

As the depressing realities of the digital music era sunk in, I remembered something my older brother Peter said to me years before when we shared an apartment in Jackson Heights, Queens. His words seemed innocuous at the time, but now simplified my thoughts on the consequences of piracy; why it might make sense to pay for content, even if you weren't being forced to do so.

One day, Peter and I sat on the E express train as it clattered and squealed down the track toward Manhattan. When it lurched to a halt at the Queens Plaza station, the silver doors slid open and a mariachi band squeezed into the train car. They collected themselves and struck up a resonant, bittersweet ballad. The train passengers around me looked up from their books and opened their sleepy eyes at the first few guitar strums. Soon, most everyone had craned his or her neck to watch and listen together. The passengers took a pause from worrying about their next month's rent, romantic woes, or defeated career prospects. My own frustrated inner monologue, about a day job in Manhattan I loathed, was silenced. Music made the trip endurable. The unheralded Mariachis collectively transported passengers' minds to a better place, one that reverberated subconsciously. The intent passengers shared the beautifully painted time—a few moments of life joined with an immediate community by the mystical power and beauty of music.

The brakes squealed. Passengers tripped forward and swung their bodies back in an effort to regain their balance. Before the silver doors opened again, one Mariachi frantically offered an overturned hat to the passengers. When he passed by our seats, I saw that his sombrero already held a few dollar bills and quarters. Yup, he seemed to be doing *just* fine. I decided against giving him any money, as there was no compelling reason to do otherwise. What value would I be receiving for my payment? I had already enjoyed the music. There was no logical reason to pay. For his part, Peter offered a dollar before the Mariachis moved on to the next car.

"Those musicians were pretty good, actually," I said to my brother as we later exited the train and took a staircase up from the bowels of Manhattan.

"Yup," he concurred. "The thing is, if you like having that music around the city... you've got to support it."

I instantaneously became defensive. What, was he trying to make me feel *guilty* or something?

No matter, after a few short minutes I realized the truth in my brother's simple observation.

On the basis of incentives, if a musician made a chunk of money off of performing and recording, one could realistically expect more music of similar quality to be made in the future as a result. The more consistently those Mariachis on the subway returned home with rent and grocery money, the more likely they were to perform in the future, and the more likely the weary passengers—including me— would enjoy the benefits. It wasn't merely a matter of incentivizing that particular Mariachi band, but of actively maintaining the health of a particular cultural ecosystem in the city that benefitted me, and the public-at-large, by association.

Aside from incentives, there was an ethical case that needed to be made in the context of digital piracy. By putting their music up for sale, musicians were tacitly requesting compensation for their work. Fans freely enjoyed the fruits of musicians' labor, but when it came time to show material gratitude they folded their arms, saying, "No, I'm not gonna," like a generation of spoiled, entitled children.

This was a sobering epiphany. Communities of artists and supportive fans offered organic bursts of cultural color and energy to balance and season the dreary dogmas of economics, politics and religion. The health and diversity of our creative industries mirrored the health and diversity of our culture, for better or worse. My eyes were opened to the pitfalls of digital piracy because of music, but I'd stumbled upon a much larger quandary, one in which individual consumers had gone numb to their own relationship to mass culture. They didn't feel their own impact upon society as consumers and, quite logically, assumed their actions and choices about whether to pay were meaningless. Who wouldn't choose "free" under such assumptions? But behind free content's superficial illusion of *more* lies a long-term reality of *less*. Sooner or later, it is something we all have to pay for.

KYS

As new thoughts on the nature of digital piracy percolated, I wondered whether there was good reason why no one had stepped up to credibly challenge consumers for their growing acceptance of piracy. Had I missed something fundamental about the issue during my period of blissful ignorance of the controversy? Had my still-developing arguments been judged obsolete years before? Regardless, intuition pushed me toward confrontation. I needed to know whether rampant piracy was something I could righteously change, or if it was, as so many assumed, a permanent side effect of technological advancement with no remedy, something we needed to just accept, adapt to and move on with.

I'd written in the past for a music website, Tiny Mix Tapes, that serviced precisely the young, music-obsessed, technically-savvy audience I now hoped to target. An old college friend of mine, Marvin Lin, managed the site and was happy to publish my first piece on the subject, called "The Myth of DIY: Towards a common ethic on piracy." My ideas were very much in a developmental stage, but my primary aim was to put consumers on the spot for their individual choices:

> If you find meaning and beauty from a musician's work and you want them to continue creating it—then you are obliged to support them. If you like the idea of record stores, the people they employ, the values and spirit they promote—then you are obliged to support them. If you're consistently doing one without the other, then on some level you, not Metallica, are the asshole. Out of basic politeness, I (probably) won't say any of this to your face and neither will your friends, your record store clerk, or your favorite band. But it is the truth.

Reader reaction was immediate… and immediately discouraging.

Message board threads soon popped up, including a particularly angry one on an online forum called Hipinion, under the pretense that I had written the worst article on piracy, ever. "Seems like this article was written by a whiney Brooklyn hipster, who is upset cause no one likes his music," one person anonymously posted. Small gangs of anonymous commenters devoted themselves to ripping me to shreds. The article's content became secondary as personal attacks reigned supreme. "The guy who wrote that is an idiot," another commenter wrote, "and i'm sorry i wasted time reading it."

Commenters that attacked me on the grounds of "pathetic sentimentality" didn't particularly surprise me; readers' efforts to rationalize away piracy did. They employed sloppy arguments based upon aesthetics ("Fuck recorded music. It further separates the listener and the musician. We need to return to a patronage system"), injustice ("who actually believes this nonsense? you think the music business is designed to help artists? the entire anti-piracy program is orchestrated by the record executives who have been ripping off musicians the longest and hardest"), and supposedly universal laws of technology ("Music is information. Information can be copied indefinitely, for a virtually null cost, without any means of regulating it. That's why information can be freely exchanged. It's a physical fact. Not a problem of law").

Consumers had each constructed a personalized cocoon of weird rhetoric to deflect any and all threats to their entitlement to unlicensed content. Addressing digital piracy was forever somebody else's problem or responsibility. These fans thought they deserved music for free. Speak of a responsibility to pay for the music one enjoyed and they defensively replied, "fuck recorded music"—even though their appetite for recorded music was self-evident. Suggest that artists needed support to live and create, and they countered that the music business and labels were never in an artist's interest—they "ripped off" musicians. Offer that a consumer still was obligated to follow basic guidelines of commerce and these folks retorted that, because some music could be illicitly downloaded for free, then all of it deserved to be free and the old world parameters of commerce were as outmoded as the player piano.

"It's all moot anyhow; can't 'uninvent' the Internet," another anonymous commenter wrote in regard to the piracy debate. Encountering that particular rationalization alarmed me—that our intellectual laziness was permissible, since we had zero agency in guiding technology anyway. At the same time, as more feedback to my writing came in, I was forced to reckon with the subtle spells cast by the Internet.

A few days after the article was published, I participated in my very own message board flame-up. It started off casually enough on a private site for contributors to Tiny Mix Tapes, where other writers offered feedback on my article. Some of this feedback was positive and some negative. I became uniformly obsessed with the negative, of course, and locked into a battle with another writer who, I sensed, was dismissing my arguments. I had never met the person; didn't know how old he was or what he looked like. This allowed my imagination to run wild with various opportunities for disdain. He was too young to understand what he was talking about, I reasoned, or he was simply "an idiot" for not seeing things my way. For a few days, I made it my mission to attack everything he said that I even remotely disagreed with. The stakes could not have felt higher, as if bending this one person to my argument meant life or death for my ideas and my sense of self. Minor differences of opinion became opportunities for amplified invective. Through the exchange, the protective, moderating forces of rationality, empathy, and good manners peeled back until my raw nerves were exposed to the hostile elements. I became defensive, angry and resorted to personal attacks.

My counterpart became more than just another person writing at his computer who genuinely shared my interest in a particular topic. He became a villain, embodying anyone and anything in the world that I was against or that I perceived to be against me. The debate continued to intensify until others stepped in to settle our disagreement. We had lost control of ourselves, arguing for argument's sake.

"I just read this entire thread and all of your posts," one outside observer wrote in, "and I don't think I read a single instance in which you two contradicted each other."

When I looked back at the exchange after the fact, it didn't read like an engaged argument at all. We were writing from our own little worlds, employing an imaginary foil to validate our complementary self-righteousness. We were, in fact, hallucinating that an enemy really existed on the other end of our broadband connections in the first place. No lessons were gleaned, save for the relative futility of online message boards and comment sections for resolving disagreements.

Some disconcerting feedback arrived in my inbox while the message board debate still raged. I clicked on the email subject heading that read, "Get a Life… End It:"

> Seriously, next time you feel the need to whine about something, get together a group of your closest emos, grab a box of tissues and talk about the deep void that has existed in your life since My Bloody Valentine stopped releasing new music….
>
> Chris, this message is a bit aggro. I know this. And I'm sorry if it frightens you. And you will most likely write off my comments as fanatical bullshit. But the bottom line is…no matter my opinions on you as a person… ignoring the fact that your emotion likely stems from the fact that you were born with no talent… regardless of piracy's existence, talented artists and musicians will always be dedicated to their craft and will always be spreading their ends. It's the no talent jerk-offs that will get weeded out by generational speedbumps like Internet piracy. No, you will never make it as an musician or writer…. But David Byrne and Jonathan Saffron-Foer (sic) will every time. That's what it comes down to. KYS.

The person accused me, first and foremost, of "whining." In his book *Snark, The New Yorker* film critic David Denby observes that "words, such as whiny or whiner… are often used to cut the ground under anyone with a legitimate complaint." Serving as a defense mechanism for any ideology, it is a tactic for short-circuiting debate, dodging empathy and dismissing critical perspectives without reason. The accusation of "whining" builds and maintains groupthink by efficiently stiff-arming contradictory threats. In the process, small, incestuous online minorities can convince themselves of just about anything, keeping the world at bay for as long as they wish to remain under an ideology's particular spell.

Tellingly, after I confronted this reader's basic duty to support his favorite musicians, he chose to sacrifice the very notion of responsibility rather than consider the meaning of his actions. So he wrote that talented artists "will always" have successful careers and make new works, even if consumers universally stopped paying for them. But if the assumption is true that the fruits of popular culture will persist undiluted despite our individual decisions to pay or not to pay, then what role did consumers even play in the first place? One can convince oneself that it is irrelevant whether we pay for content *only* if we first become numb to our own actions, believing our individual choices are meaningless; that our decisions never really mattered.

The dehumanizing subject line of the email also took me aback, along with the farewell: "KYS"—"kill yourself" in Internet speak. I didn't take this literally, of course, but the casual reference to suicide led me to wonder whether such dehumanized sentiments formed the logical terminus of the malevolent spirits often found online, such as the mantra of some hackers and digital pranksters, "I did it for the LULZ," or laughs at the expense of others. Getting your "LULZ" or telling someone to "kill yourself" in the analog world is the mark of an anti-social, maladjusted asshole. The consequential loneliness and alienation that normally constrains anti-social behavior can be ignored, when online, by communities of itchy digital discontents who reject the moral bounds of civilization as boring or passé. But such attitudes that gird the breezy acceptance of terms like "KYS" can have real world consequences... such as people who actually kill themselves.

There have been widely publicized cases of incessant online bullying over social networks, ending in real suffering and even suicide, but two particular precedents are a stark reminder of the numbness and lack of responsibility many of us feel toward our words and actions online—a numbness that challenges the assumed efficacy of digital communication. The digital revolution potentially sews the seeds for a new reality, one in which we forget the most basic notions of human decency as we grow giddy from careless anonymity and fool ourselves by thinking we can flee our common responsibilities.

Abraham Biggs was a teenager from Florida who struggled with depression and an unrequited romance, along with the normal anxieties and confusions of early adulthood. In 2008, he sought support in an online community, repeatedly posting about his feelings of depression and his suicidal thoughts. What support did this community provide? When sharing his feelings online, he received such sympathetic comments as "hahaha hahahahha hahahahahah ahhaha" and "Instant Darwinism."[1] When he logged on one day and announced that he had taken a fatal dose of prescription drugs and would be live streaming his death, a virtual audience of 1,500 voyeurs gathered. Many cheered him on.

"Fucking do it. Get on with it!" wrote one anonymous commenter. Others simply typed "LOL."[2] As Biggs laid motionless on his bed, those in the chatroom continued to pile on, accusing him of faking. For hours they watched, typing snarky comments and doing nothing as Biggs's dead, frozen body decorated their computers like just another screen-saver. By the time someone finally called the police, it was far too late. Biggs died at the age of 19.

A similar event transpired in 2007, involving a middle-aged, married father of two, named Kevin Whitrick in Shropshire, England. He too suffered from depression and announced his plans for suicide online, providing a live stream of the event. He too received taunts online as he prepared to hang himself.

"Fucking do it… get it round your neck," one wrote. "For Fuck's sake he can't even do this properly."[3] As with the case of Biggs, no one called the authorities until Whitrick had already ended his life. Even after the heinousness of the event had time to sink in, one blogger wrote:

> What an attention whore right till the end…. Normally, I do feel pity for people who rather take the easy way out due to depression. But no matter how hard I try I can't seem to squeeze an ounce of sympathy for Kevin Whitrick. Yeah, he's dead and he's left his two kids, likely traumatized for the rest

of their lives but really, how can you feel anything nice for
someone so fooking stupid?… Someone, please pass Mr. and
Mrs. Whitrick the Darwin Award![4]

Indeed, how *could* you feel anything nice for someone so stupid?
Conversely, how could you give any credence to the thoughts
of a "whiner"? How could you give a shit whether we're using
technology to advance our culture or degrade it? Why care, when
you can go on distracting yourself with the endless flurry of trivial
controversy or high quality pirated content online? Why bother
to be an aware, fully-functioning human being when it is easier to
accept whatever the imaginary "hive" mentality tells us is socially
acceptable behavior?

I wondered why it seemed to be the case that, when we log on to
the Internet, we are tempted to log off from our human selves.

———————————

"Thought is done in solitude and silence," says Pulitzer Prize-winning
journalist and social critic Chris Hedges, "and we live in a culture
where we fear any kind of solitude. We have created such powerful
systems of technology—most of us are hallucinating…. The Internet
and handheld devices have become tools which, if misused, make it
impossible to think and cut us off from what's real. We have to be very,
very careful with these technologies."

We convince ourselves that we are in control of our digital devices
and that our brains will naturally adjust to new stimuli and evolve,
as always. But the more we use technology, the more it controls and
manipulates us in turn. Marshall McLuhan, the radical media theorist
who taught us that "the medium is the message" and famously
validated Woody Allen in the film *Annie Hall*, agreed that the only
way to fully use a piece of technology, or "medium," is to surrender
oneself to it completely. But he didn't *advocate* for such a surrender,
because he knew it carried dire consequences.

In his 1964 book *Understanding Media*, McLuhan explored the
"messages" of various mediums, from books to phones to television
to clocks. McLuhan couldn't have predicted anything quite as grand
or pervasive as the Internet, but his essential observations remain
prescient. He noted that "hot" mediums—ones which concentrate

a "high definition" of information upon one sense and require little participation by the viewer, such as radio or cinema—tend to effect hypnosis. "Cool" mediums, like television and the telephone, are of "low definition" and demand participation by the user. When applied across multiple senses, cool mediums effect hallucination. The Internet, video games and forms of virtual reality seem to combine both hot and cold, tempting our consciousness with both hypnosis and hallucination. In his essay "The Gadget Lover," McLuhan brilliantly transforms the Greek myth of Narcissus into a parable for our ever more hallucinatory, hypnotic, and narcotic modern lives. His analysis shows that assuming the Internet's promise of efficiency, collaboration and "openness" will solve all of our problems in the end is like skipping through a minefield, or volunteering for a prison camp. We aren't dealing with other people online, but with our numb, self-destructive replicants.

Narcissus was a handsome but conceited man who spurned the love of the nymph Echo. Despite her repeated attempts to win his heart, he failed to notice her. One day in the woods, as Echo trailed from a short distance away, Narcissus bent down to drink at a pool of water. Upon the glassy water's surface, he witnessed the most beautiful face he had ever seen. The image smiling back at him from the water transfixed him. Each gesture and expression made by Narcissus was matched by the face he saw in the water. Hypnotized and unable to tear himself away, he forgot to eat or drink and eventually he died there by the water as Echo helplessly looked on. In some versions of the myth, Narcissus committed suicide.

We commonly think of Narcissus as the man who fell in love with himself, but McLuhan points out that this misreads the story. It is not a tale of love or self-obsession, but the dulling of senses that occurs the further we extend our nervous system through media. "Narcissus is from the Greek word *narcosis*, or numbness," McLuhan writes. "The youth Narcissus mistook his own reflection in the water for another person. This extension of himself by mirror numbed his perceptions until he became the servomechanism of his own extended or repeated image…. He was numb. He had adapted to his extension of himself and had become a closed system…. Men at once become fascinated by any extension of themselves in any material other than themselves."

Such fascination is commonly seen in the popularity of social networking services like Facebook, where some of us devote more time and energy to maintaining our "profile" than we do to maintain the health of our real lives. If we aren't careful, online avatars or an online "presence" end up demanding care and consideration at the expense of our immediate needs and health. According to McLuhan, any such extension of ourselves leads to stress and irritation for our nervous systems. The further we extend our senses, the more acute this irritation becomes. In a quest to maintain equilibrium, the body's only recourse is to dull our own sense of self, as Narcissus did. "We have to numb our central nervous system when it is extended and exposed, or we will die. Thus the age of anxiety and of electric media is also the age of the unconscious and of apathy."

The consequences to Narcissus seem like a literary exaggeration, until we remember the apathetic spirit of LULZ, KYS or passively watching as another person commits suicide. But can the extension of ourselves through digital technology really become so self-destructive, as McLuhan's reading of the myth suggests? Can we become so numb that we forget to guard against starvation or death?

The most entertaining way we use computers to become "the servomechanism of (our) own extended or repeated image" is certainly through video games, and nowhere in the world are more video games played online than in South Korea, which contained 95% of the world's broadband Internet capability as of 2011. The cities of South Korea are packed with Internet parlors where citizens binge on multi-player online games. Gaming is so popular in the country, it rises to the level of professional sport, with some gamers making upwards of $100,000 from gaming tournament winnings. Given such a national obsession, it shouldn't be surprising that South Korea also faces epidemic levels of Internet addiction. From 2009 to 2010, three tragic cases of such addiction underscored the unseen dangers of a too-willing embrace of technology, again bringing the myth of Narcissus to life.

One day in an Internet parlor, a man collapsed at his chair and an ambulance was immediately called. He had been playing a video game for five straight days and had forgotten to sufficiently eat, drink, or sleep. His physical body had become subsumed to his screen one.

Upon being taken to the hospital, the young man died of multiple organ failure.[5]

In another case, a mother was having trouble with her 22-year-old son, whom she feared had developed a severe addiction to online games. She tried to curtail his habit, repeatedly confronting him, but she had no luck in changing his behavior. After one such exchange, the mother took a nap. The young man entered her bedroom and stabbed her to death. Immediately after the killing, the son reportedly remained in the apartment for a few hours, watching television. Later, he went to a local Internet parlor, paying for the computer time with his murdered mother's credit card.

Perhaps the most horrific example of digital narcosis occurred in 2010, involving a 45-year-old man and his girlfriend, a 21-year-old. The couple was expecting their first child, but simultaneously struggled with a gaming addiction. The couple had become obsessed with an online game, in which, fittingly, the goal was to successfully raise a digital child. When their infant was born, normally the most important event in an adult's life, their obsession with the game went on, in a bizarre fashion. The couple began leaving their newborn alone in their apartment for hours at a time, while they tended to their *digital* child at a local Internet cafe. One day, they came home to find their three-month-old, motionless. The infant had died from malnutrition.[6]

These examples from South Korea are extreme, and it would be irresponsible to blame them exclusively on "the Internet." Most South Koreans do not die from gaming, murder their concerned parents, or commit infanticide out of neglect. The nation suffers from unusually high suicide rates in general, which suggests a deeper national problem. Like any addiction, Internet addiction does not develop in a vacuum. Yet these extremes demonstrate that, just as all drugs carry the dangers of dependency and disassociation from the pain and joy of real life, so too does the Internet. We fundamentally forget pieces of ourselves when employing anonymity, avatars, and selective reality online and the consequences of this can be tragic and far-reaching. Certainly, such disassociation makes it that much harder to understand or resolve a controversy as tricky as digital piracy.

What good is the Internet's radical potential for communication if we lose ourselves in the medium to the degree that we are no longer communicating about reality?

If careless, we all might become servomechanisms of our digital selves, unnervingly echoed by the popular sentiment, "You can't fight technology." The more we embrace the authenticity of our digital selves, the less important our real lives feel in comparison to the images and "friends" we find on our faithful, mirror-like screens.

If connecting to the Internet also creates a disconnection from reality, it isn't surprising that online culture so often brings out the worst in us, as if our inner demons, normally tempered by the social norms of society, are suddenly freed to run wild and wreak havoc in an abstract (and thus victimless) digital world. Like Narcissus, though, we victimize ourselves in the process, along with the people we love and the real communities we are too desensitized to participate in. The Internet offers us an illusion of power and engagement with the world, while surreptitiously conditioning us to remain listlessly isolated, numb, and vulnerable to institutions of real power.

The debate over music piracy was not only born of the online world, but also largely waged within its glass, computer-screened curtain. There, the controversy over file sharing was held hostage by the peculiar biases of online communication. Wrestling with the chaos and questions of a new medium was difficult enough without the loss of self that people experienced online. This numbness teased out our most vitriolic, irresponsible, and self-destructive characteristics, making reasonable conversation nearly impossible.

The Internet presented a genuinely new and fascinating set of problems to our traditional notions of commerce, creativity and copyright. The rails we had thoughtlessly been speeding along were suddenly in need of tinkering. A change in course was required, but in which direction? Consumers, creators, distributors and investors were handed an opportunity to join forces and make the most of the historic digital revolution. Unfortunately, the incendiary nature of online communication, combined with deeply flawed attempts by the RIAA to fight piracy and good ol' fashioned human fallibility, concocted a witch's brew of confusion and anger. All sense of navigation was lost. The entire locomotive of discourse jolted off the tracks—derailed, halted and in need of repair. It didn't take long before people simply gave up hope that workable solutions awaited at the end of the rails. Perhaps they were right to believe so.

The Decade of Dysfunction

An 18-year-old heavy metal drummer named Lars Ulrich convinced his friend, James Hetfield, to start a band with him in 1981. The band they created, Metallica, spent the 1980s releasing critically acclaimed metal albums like... *And Justice For All* and *Master of Puppets*. They built a fan base by touring exhaustively and treating their fans with respect (such as allowing concertgoers to freely tape concerts). The band represented a rebellion against the major-label rock music's popular fashion: laughable glam-inspired hair metal bands like Mötley Crüe, Ratt, and Poison. Metallica eschewed the pretense of feathered hair, caked on make-up, and hot-pink spandex. Rather, they focused on substance: the music. Millions of fans rewarded the band for their integrity by buying their albums and paying to see them in concert.

An 18-year-old Lars Ulrich could not foresee his band eventually becoming the seventh biggest-selling American music act of all time, or his millions of dollars in personal income. Perhaps most shocking to the teenaged Ulrich would be that, twenty years after Metallica's genesis, he would testify before the US Senate regarding, of all things, a software company. Or that, in doing so, he would become public enemy number one to music fans around the world.

In 2000, Metallica were working in the studio on a new song for the *Mission: Impossible 2* soundtrack. They were shocked when they heard that this unfinished, unreleased new song was already being played on radio stations across the country. The early version of the song had been leaked from the studio and uploaded to an online service called Napster. When the band investigated the service, they found their entire catalogue of music, representing two decades of hard work, available for free. Over the next forty-eight hours, the band monitored Napster and found hundreds of thousands of users downloading a total of 1.4 million Metallica songs. It was a lawless free-for-all. Metallica became the first major band to raise hay over the copyright infringement occurring over Napster's networks, and in the spring of 2001, Ulrich testified before the Senate:

I do not have a problem with any artists voluntarily distributing his or her songs through any means that artist so chooses. But just like a carpenter who crafts a table gets to decide whether he wants to keep it, sell or give it away, shouldn't we have the same options? We should decide what happens to our music, not a company with no rights to our recordings, which has never invested a penny in our music or had anything to do with its creation. The choice has been taken away from us.

The argument I hear a lot, that music should be free, must then mean the musicians should work for free. Nobody else works for free, why should musicians?... Make no mistake about it, Metallica is not anti-technology. When we made our first album, most records were on vinyl. By the late '80's cassette sales accounted for over 50 percent of the market. Now the compact disc dominates. If the next format is a form of downloading from the Internet, with distribution and manufacturing savings passed on to the American consumer, then, of course, we will embrace that format.

But how can we embrace a new format and sell our music for a fair price, when somebody, with a few lines of code, no investment cost, no creative input, and no marketing expense simply gives it away? How does this square with the level playing field of the capitalist system? In Napster's brave new world, what free market economic model supports our ability to compete? The touted new paradigm that the Internet gurus tell us we must adopt sounds to me like good, old-fashioned trafficking in stolen goods.[1]

But by the time of Ulrich's testimony, many fans already had stopped listening. Three months prior to the testimony, Ulrich arrived at Napster's offices in a limousine packed with boxes that held the names of 317,377 Napster users who had illegally downloaded Metallica's works. After boldly holding a press conference in front of the company offices, Ulrich presented the names to Napster and demanded the company block the users from the service. An unrelenting narrative was born: *Greedy millionaire rock stars Metallica versus their fans; pirating music means sticking it to 'the man.'*

The good faith between artist and fan that had sustained a commercial music industry abruptly crumbled before everyone's eyes. Metallica felt disrespected and violated by Napster and saw no recourse other than to aggressively protect their life's work. But fans felt equally disrespected and violated. Music fans loved Napster and many of them genuinely believed it meant progress for the music industry, that they were participating in a positive revolution for innovation and culture. In this context, Metallica appeared to be against progress, against technology, and against their fans. The disrespect felt on all sides turned into distrust.

Ulrich could say, as he did, that "this is not about Metallica and its fans; this is about Metallica and Napster," but fans only saw an out-of-touch, whiny millionaire with a receding hairline. An animated short entitled "Napster Bad" featured a cartoon-version of Ulrich, bragging of his fantastic wealth and condemning MP3s, while a neanderthal-like parody of Metallica singer James Hetfield grunted in the background, "Money good! Napster bad!" Another animated parody circulated, called "Metalligreed." Mötley Crüe bassist Nikki Sixx joined the firing squad, saying, "Pigs get fat and hogs get slaughtered, and I think Metallica's hogs… they're fucking their fans, and I think it's fucked."[2]

Another line of thought emerged: that Metallica was following the wrong path by attacking Napster rather than finding a way to use the service to their advantage. "They should have been a little more forward-thinking when it comes to technology," said Bob Oesca, creator of the "Napster Bad" cartoon, though examples of what it meant to be "forward-thinking" were never made clear.

In 2000, the music industry was still gorging itself amidst a pre-apocalyptic cultural landscape in which MTV's Carson Daly, a personification of mass-culture's cattle-eyed blandness if there ever was one, led suburban teenagers, flush with allowance money, repeatedly to the trough of $17 Backstreet Boys and Britney Spears CDs. In 2001, some argued that the rising CD sales proved that Napster was actually *helping* the music industry and Napster went out of their way to verify their own claims—that their service helped artists promote themselves and find a larger audience for their albums. Soon, this became conventional wisdom among young music fans who used the service. Napster and P2P was a net positive for young musicians, while the rock stars who might be hurt by the service, like Metallica, didn't need the money anyway.

Chad Paulson, a 19-year-old college student, believed as much when he founded a group at Indiana University called Students Against University Censorship[3] in response to Napster being blocked from his campus's broadband network. Paulson's advocacy proved immensely valuable for the company. He amassed 23,000 signatures in defense of Napster, providing enough positive PR to keep many nervous colleges from cutting Napster's use. Three universities named in Metallica's lawsuit against Napster even restored Napster to their networks.

Young fans use technology to fight back against greedy Metallica, and win!

The media turned college student Shawn Fanning, Napster's creator, into a folk hero for the digital age. The legend of Napster was cemented in the public memory after the Ninth Circuit Court of Appeals ruled that the service was in violation of copyright infringement on a mass scale. The court ordered the company to begin blocking users from the service in the spring of 2001 and to pay $36 million in damages to the record labels. Napster was effectively dead, but another crop of P2P websites like Gnutella, Grokster, Audiogalaxy, and Limewire soon took its place. Some of these new services made it clear that no unlicensed files were being stored on a centralized server. Rather, the sites were merely providing a space in which direct uploads and downloads between consumers themselves could take place. By merely facilitating the transfer of files between individual users, the services claimed to not be liable for individual cases of copyright infringement.

The emergence of more "Napsters" put a spotlight upon the futility of Metallica's and the RIAA's actions in trying to stop its technology through the courts. Many people blamed the music industry for not having found a way to negotiate with Napster and turn it into a legal, paid service. The choice to shut Napster down, rather than work with them, served as the music industry's original sin, one that required eternal atonement. But the RIAA most certainly did *not* atone. They took their gloves off.

————————————

Some felt it was *only* a matter of time before more artists joined Metallica in speaking out against Napster and piracy in general. Jonathan Taplin, who had managed tours for Bob Dylan, predicted,

"One of the things that's gonna happen very soon is that it's not going to be the RIAA suing Napster or Gnutella, it's going to be the artists themselves. And when Ray Charles or Aretha Franklin sues, then maybe we'll have a real debate on whether this is a right use of digital technology. Just because you can create a Napster does not mean that you should."[4]

Taplin's prediction was quite incorrect. Barely any other artists risked their reputation by filing lawsuits or even whispering criticisms of file sharing. Once Metallica fell out of the picture, essentially it was only the RIAA suing Napster and fighting piracy by any means necessary.

Despite all the inescapable ugliness of litigation, many fans still respected Metallica as musicians. Their reputation may have been sullied, but they started off with significant artistic capital to spend. The RIAA, on the other hand, represented a major label system, notorious for not paying artists the royalties they deserved, using fine print to fool artists into binding long-term contracts, infamously employing the Mafia to assist in radio promotion in the '80s, and up-marking the price of CDs in the '90s even though manufacturing costs were decreasing. The narrative of a young band getting screwed by a rapacious major label executive was burned into the public consciousness. The producer Steve Albini, a celebrated record producer and figurehead of the American punk rock scene, wrote a piece called "The Problem with Music" in the early '90s which became Exhibit A for anyone who suspected the nefariousness of record labels. When a band signed a letter of intent, he wrote, "They will either eventually sign a contract that suits the label or they will be destroyed. One of my favorite bands was held hostage for the better part of two years by a slick young 'He's not like a label guy at all,' A & R rep, on the basis of such a deal memo." After working out the advances, expenses and revenues involved in a normal band's first album on a label, Albini concludes, "The band is now 1/4 of the way through its contract, has made the music industry more than 3 million dollars richer, but is in the hole $14,000 on royalties. The band members have each earned about 1/3 as much as they would working at a 7-11, but they got to ride in a tour bus for a month."[5]

Through the '80s and '90s, labels were increasingly folded into multinational conglomerates who saw music as just another opportunity for profit in their vast portfolios, rather than something sacred, the tending of which required a certain degree of reverence, humility, and long-term perspective. Experimental music legend Frank Zappa explained the problematic shift in the music industry, from his vantage point in the late '80s:

'Remember the Sixties?' You know, that era a lot of people have these glorious memories of. You know, they really weren't that great, those years. But one thing that did happen in the Sixties was some music of an unusual or experimental nature did get recorded and did get released. Now, look at who the executives were in those companies at those times. Not hip, young guys. These were cigar-chomping old guys, who looked at the product that came in and said, 'I don't know? Who knows what it is? Record it. Stick it out, if it sells… all right.' We were better off with those guys than we are now with the supposedly hip, young executives who are making the decisions of what people should see and hear in the marketplace. The young guys are more conservative and more dangerous to the art form than the old guys with the cigars ever were. And you know how these young guys got in there? The old guy with the cigar, one day he goes, 'Well, I took a chance. We went out and we sold a few million units. I don't know what it is but we gotta do more of it. I need some advice. Let's get a Hippie in here.' So, they hire a Hippie… Okay, he becomes an A&R man. From there, moving up and up and up, next thing you know he's got his feet on the desk and he's saying, 'Well, we can't take a chance on this. Because it's simply not what the kids really want… and I know.' And they've got that attitude. And the day you can get rid of that attitude and get back to, 'Who knows? Take a chance!' That entrepreneurial spirit where, even if you don't like or understand what the record is that's coming in the door, the person who's in the executive chair may not be the final arbiter of taste of the entire population.

The "hip" cultural arbiters of the Majors held the money and influence to bribe radio stations for airplay (as exposed in payola scandals), shell out millions for prime placement in store racks and weekend newspaper circulars, and pay for the million-dollar music videos necessary to pierce through the all-important barriers of MTV. Qualitatively, the Majors were also infamous for using their promotional muscle to force "bad" music down consumers' throats: disco and progressive rock in the '70s; hair metal and synth-pop in the '80s; post-Nirvana grunge and nu metal in the '90s; and—perhaps most egregious—the boy bands and teeny-bopper queens of the late '90s and early 2000s.

Whatever plague fell upon the major label houses could only be justice.

If the Majors were unloved at the start of the 2000s, they soon became loathed. In 2003, with Apple's iTunes Store presenting the first genuinely legitimate alternative to file sharing, the RIAA commenced the ugliest chapter in the piracy wars: the RIAA mass lawsuits.

From 2003 to 2008, they opened legal actions against about 35,000 consumers who had pirated songs on unlicensed peer-to-peer networks.[6] The RIAA lawyers shamelessly besieged college students, scaring them with maximum penalties of $250,000 per copyright infringement in order to cajole them into quick settlements for thousands of dollars the students didn't have. These suits erased the savings accounts of students and their parents, who most often footed the bill. The RIAA believed themselves to be making an important point: piracy was theft and the actions of online users were not anonymous. The RIAA successfully communicated these ideas, sure, but in doing so appeared heartless to the general public.

They RIAA forced a 12-year-old girl who lived in a New York City housing project, the daughter of a single mother, to publicly apologize for her downloading and pay them $2,000. They charged a single mother from Minnesota, who made $21,000 per year as a sugar mill worker, with an initial penalty of $500,000 for her daughter's downloading. When a student at MIT informed the RIAA legal team that she was too deep in debt to pay a suggested settlement of $3,750, the RIAA suggested she pay off her penalty by dropping out of school.[7]

Any music consumer who had remained on the sidelines during the Napster fiasco was no longer ambivalent toward the ethics of piracy after the mass lawsuits. The RIAA's heavyhanded tactics resulted in backlash: their legal arguments may have been sound, but any half-sentient human being saw the enacted punishments as nakedly disproportionate to the crime. The Majors lost all legitimacy as a result and, though record sales interestingly stabilized in the first three years of the lawsuits, sales fell off another cliff in the latter half of the decade. Unless you lived underneath a larger-than-average rock, a consumer could no longer enjoy the experience of being a simple, paying fan. Now they wondered, before buying a CD or downloading a song from the iTunes Store, "Is the RIAA getting my money?" In short, buying music in the 2000s became an unconditional drag.

The lawsuits were a public relations catastrophe not just for the RIAA members, but also for all record labels. Fans lazily lumped independent record labels in with the Majors and all artists in with Metallica. "Record label" nearly reached pejorative status. Independent labels like Chicago's beloved Touch and Go Records, which offered good-faith handshake contracts and 50/50 revenue splits with artists, closed after over twenty-five years in business under the weight of declining sales, as did New York's independent hip-hop label, Definitive Jux. Both labels had back catalogues of landmark works in their respective genres, but these works apparently weren't being bought in sufficient numbers to push through.

Piracy became more and more accepted within the music community, especially among the most ardent listeners who religiously followed websites like Pitchfork, Stereogum, and Gorilla vs. Bear to stay at the crest of music trends. The influence of these sites grew through the decade, but they almost never touched the issue of piracy, much less its underlying moral questions. Piracy was something young listeners assumed each one of his or her friends was doing and few spoke of it in a more serious way than to sarcastically remark about the old days "when people still paid for music," wink, wink....

Professional journalists held greater opportunity than artists or labels to search out common ground in the piracy wars, but many of them were losing their jobs as readers migrated to free online content. The few journalists who remained, and the magazine and newspaper publishers who paid them, were loath to challenge file sharing and risk being tarred-and-feathered, as Metallica was. Some were also genuinely taken in by the youthful romance associated with rebellious music pirates, like the young Swedes at The Pirate Bay. The world's most popular torrent tracker in the late 2000s, the members of the service openly taunted the Swedish Police, RIAA, and MPAA for being unable to take their site down.

"If anyone needs to be penalized for their actions, it's the record labels, not the fans," wrote *Chicago Tribune* music critic Greg Kot in his 2009 book, *Ripped*.

In the 2000s, to be a music fan was to be angry and opinionated; not only about the relative quality of bands, but about the industry itself. Music fans were right to pirate their digital music and a number of voices in law and media were more than happy to explain why.

File sharing found its first intellectual shelter under the work of law professor Lawrence Lessig, then on the faculty of Stanford University. Lessig had released two books in the early 2000s that focused on how the public domain of American books, films, and music faced an existential threat at the hands of entertainment industry lobbyists who had pressured the US Congress to extend copyright terms again and again through the end of the 20th century.

Copyright was first set into law by Great Britain, when their united Parliament passed the Statute of Anne in 1710, serving to transfer the primary right to print books from monopolistic printers to the authors themselves. The edict read:

> An Act for the Encouragement of Learning, by Vesting the Copies of Printed Books in the Authors or Purchasers of such Copies, during the Times therein mentioned.

> Whereas Printers, Booksellers, and other Persons, have of late frequently taken the Liberty of Printing, Reprinting, and Publishing, or causing to be Printed, Reprinted, and Published Books, and other Writings, without the Consent of the Authors or Proprietors of such Books and Writings, to their very great Detriment, and too often to the Ruin of them and their Families: For Preventing therefore such Practices for the future, and for the Encouragement of Learned Men to Compose and Write useful Books...

In the interest of setting this incentive for "learned men to compose and write useful books," new authors were granted a fourteen-year term to profit from the printed copies of their books, after which they could renew their right for another fourteen years (provided they were still alive to apply for the renewal). Founding father James Madison was instrumental in bringing this principle to the nascent United States of America by including the "Progress Clause" in the Constitution, under the powers of Congress: "To promote the Progress of Science and useful Arts, by securing for limited Times to Authors and Inventors the exclusive Right to their respective Writings and Discoveries."

The constitutional authority for Congress to grant authors exclusive control over the reproduction and distribution of their work was clear. The muddy portion of the Progress Clause was the part about "limited times." Original copyright terms in the United States suggested the writers of the Constitution meant "limited" to mean a relatively short span of years, but over time "limited" came to mean anything *less* than unlimited. Under this legal understanding, so repulsive to Lessig, even a 200-year term could theoretically be accepted as "limited," despite the appearance of being so very out of step with the "limited" spirit of the Constitution.

The United States Congress quickly passed its first copyright law in 1790, matching the fourteen-year term and fourteen-year extension of Great Britain, while expanding the right to the authors of maps and charts, along with books. As Lessig noted, "In the first hundred years of the Republic, the term of copyright was changed once…. In the next fifty years of the Republic, the term was changed once again." By this point, in 1909, the maximum copyright term was fifty-six years. "Then," Lessig writes in his book *Free Culture*, "beginning in 1962, Congress started a practice that has defined copyright law since. Eleven times in the last forty years, Congress has extended the terms of existing copyrights; twice in those forty years, Congress extended the terms of future copyrights." Today, the standard copyright term is lifetime of the author plus an additional seventy years—an absurdity when paired with the original maximum term of twenty-eight years. *Gone With The Wind*, published in 1936, will not enter the public domain in the US until 2031.[8] According to Lessig, these extensions were not driven by respect for the rights of authors, but by the lobbies of corporations who owned the copyrights and were loath to let them fall into the public domain and lose their intellectual "property."

Whereas Lessig's critiques of copyright extensions might have only appealed to lawyers and a smattering of general interest readers in the late '90s, his arguments gained new relevance when the legal wrangling over Napster and the RIAA lawsuits placed "copyright infringement" on the tongues of young media types all around the world. A middle-aged man with fair Scandinavian features, Lessig spoke passionately and convincingly at countless lectures around the world in a slow, soft, and almost hypnotizing cadence about the subversion of copyright's original spirit. He argued that copyright no longer benefited artists or cultural progress in the way it was intended. Rather, it was increasingly a legal weapon wielded by "Big Content" corporate lobbies like Disney, the MPAA and RIAA to exploit the copyrights of artists who had long since died and stifle new forms of creativity, in their profit-driven zeal to control ideas and culture. Lessig feared something critical was being lost in the process: the democracy of our cultural space. The cultural "commons" that the public domain represented, an opportunity for new generations to learn from and build upon the past, was shrinking with each copyright extension.

Lessig idealized "read-write" culture, in which ideas could be quickly distributed to the masses and "remixed." He equated such read-write creative processes with participation, democracy, and artistic purity. He saw such processes as the Internet's greatest potential contribution to society. "In my view," Lessig said at a TED conference in 2007, "the most significant thing to recognize in what the Internet is doing is the opportunity to revive the read-write culture," which was a substantial judgment considering the broad significance of the medium.

Lessig borrowed a piece of romance from turn-of-the-century composer John Philip Sousa, who feared that emerging audio devices like the phonograph would eliminate the human vocal chords "by a process of evolution." After the phonograph, children would no longer sit on the front porches together, "singing the songs of the day," as Sousa remembered from his childhood. For Lessig, the wholesome mental image of these singing children was analogous to what the Internet offered: the potential for cultural participation, if not a return to innocence. He disparaged "read-only" culture created by professional musicians, filmmakers, and authors (odd, since he was one), which inherently depended upon robust copyright protections for its market to function. "Never before in human history," he said, speaking of the present, "had [creative culture] been as professionalized, never before had it been as concentrated, never before had the creativity of the millions been as effectively displaced." He believed we should ignore the professionals and instead celebrate the "amateurs" of read-write culture, a "culture where people produce for the love of what they're doing, not the money."

If, as he suggested, the commercial sale of creative work was inherently less loving and authentic, then a refusal to pay for copyrighted content was really an aesthetic choice, if not a form of civil disobedience. Piracy could be construed by these statements, especially in the context of Metallica and the litigious bigwigs behind the RIAA, as a political statement for keeping art that much more "pure."

Lessig's was a thinly veiled advocacy for file sharing. In a 2008 column, he wrote, "I do not support peer-to-peer 'piracy.' In my books *Free Culture* and *Remix,* I condemn explicitly and repeatedly such uses as wrong. And in the hundreds of talks I have given on this subject, I plead with kids not to use technologies in ways that give others a justification for wrecking the Internet. But though I believe kids should not use the Internet to violate others' rights, I oppose these failed copyright wars."[9] In other words, the "copyright wars" were the primary problem, rather than the mass piracy this "war" meant to address. This matter of emphasis left Lessig appearing to be more on the side of file sharers than rights holders, a powerful development for the piracy debate.

Lessig's admission to pleading with young people to stop file sharing, not because they were violating the rights of creators, but because file sharing "give(s) others a justification for wrecking the Internet," was also striking. In the equation, the ultimate right of the Internet not to be "wrecked" is also presented as more important than addressing piracy itself. Lessig never openly advocated violating artists' rights, he merely didn't present those rights as being comparably important to those of consumers or a non-"wrecked" Internet.

Lessig felt the dangers of piracy were less than those of an insidious "permission society" in which "the past can be cultivated only if you can identify the owner and gain permission to build upon the work. The future will be controlled by this dead (and often unfindable) hand of the past."[10] It was usually nefarious corporations presented as holding these perpetually extended copyrights, not working artists of today struggling to build a career, or artists who were happy to offer their permission so long as the derivative work didn't offend them. Infringement (and by extension, piracy) was again presented as the lesser of two evils.

Lessig understood that the legal rights of creators were being violated by copyright infringement, but he recoiled at the RIAA mass lawsuits against my generation, which he labeled "our kids." Lessig absolved the younger generation (so-called digital natives) of any responsibility for their actions, explaining that "remixing" was merely how "[kids] understand access to this culture." The youth didn't understand the purpose of copyright or the rights of creators, nor could they be bothered to care, because they had grown up with peer-to-peer technology. "They are not like us," Lessig sermonized to his audience of hopeless TED Conference elders. Copyright infringement and piracy was like breathing to this younger generation. They could never be expected to learn about the spirit of copyright and alter their behavior as a result. Piracy might not have been justified, but the sort of copyright enforcement being pursued by the RIAA was futile.

So what were Lessig's solutions?

After coming out on the losing end of *Eldred v. Ashcroft*, a Supreme Court case in which he argued that the lifetime-plus-seventy years copyright term was unconstitutional, Lessig concluded that copyright terms could only be reduced through legislation. He suggested a new minimum copyright term of fifty years, with a requirement for rights holders to file for the maximum term of lifetime-plus-seventy years if they so desired an extension. But since the US Congress was so deep in the pockets of the entertainment industry, Lessig openly conceded that sensible copyright reform was probably impossible. Despite this lack of faith in Congress, he offered another idea that would require legislation to effectively legalize file sharing.

He claimed that up to 70 percent of "kids" had engaged in piracy, and that protecting the rights of creators was not worth "criminalizing a generation."[11] Lessig offered his remedy in *US News and World Report*:

> [Solutions] include a voluntary collective license, allowing individuals to file share for a low, fixed rate; a more expansive "noncommercial use levy" that would be imposed on commercial entities benefiting from peer-to-peer file sharing, to help compensate artists; or most expansive of all, that

copyright give up regulating the distribution of copies and instead compensate artists based upon the estimated frequency by which their works are consumed. These and a host of other ideas all raise different advantages and disadvantages—but are better than criminalizing a generation.

The main problem in Lessig's solution of decriminalization, aside from subliminally communicating to file sharers (again) that piracy was excusable, was that it was unrealistic. The solution was dependent upon massive government regulation of the Internet, hefty coordination by Internet Service Providers (who benefitted from the demand created by piracy and had shown little to no interest in policing copyright infringement up to to that point) and the existence of concerted political pressure to enact such changes in the first place. In a counterpoint to Lessig, Patrick Ross, Executive Director of the Copyright Alliance, lambasted such proposals as foolish:

> They call for a licensing scheme that would allow unfettered file-sharing while we pay an imposed flat tax, regardless of how much we upload or download creative works. Those taxes would then be collected and distributed to rights holders by a third party. Nothing could be more ill-conceived than this all-powerful über-distributor. Could this organization have the omniscience needed to track every digitized work when they continue to replicate every millisecond? Could every public and private network be monitored? Could our privacy rights be protected from this Big Brother? And could a fixed and finite amount of taxes be distributed fairly among millions of rights holders? The answer to all of those questions is clearly no.[12]

Ideas for "decriminalizing" file sharing, treating digital music more like a utility that everyone pays for and has access to, had been around since the early days of Napster. Yet, for all the well-intentioned theorizing, only the tiny Isle of Man actually announced plans to experiment with such a "flat tax" in 2009. The plan went nowhere (and was still waiting to be implemented as of 2012).

Not all of Lessig's solutions were so unrealistic, but they did little to resolve the tension between rights holders and consumers who thought themselves entitled to the convenience of "free." The professor was instrumental in leading Creative Commons, a visionary non-profit that provides artists with a variety of non-commercial legal licenses for their works. With Creative Commons, some of Lessig's fears of an insidious "permissions society" appeared to find remedy. Artists finally had agency in rejecting the obscene terms and stringent controls of copyright, allowing their fans to freely "remix" a widening array of creative works protected by Creative Commons licenses. This delivered on some ideals of the Internet, such as transparency and expanded choice, but ultimately offered little to ease the tension between information that "wanted" to be both free and paid for.

Despite his criticisms of the entertainment industries callous extension of copyright terms and wrongheaded enforcement policies, Lawrence Lessig recognized the importance of copyright and digital piracy's potential harms to some creators. Others, like author and activist Cory Doctorow, didn't quite see a problem. Whereas Lawrence Lessig seemed genuinely animated by an ideal of cultural participation, Cory Doctorow—a science fiction author, editor of the gadget-culture blog BoingBoing, and advocate for a "free" and open Internet—was considerably more bleak.

Doctorow embraced Internet culture in both style and substance. He kept his head shaved into an angular buzz cut and adorned his face with thick, black-framed glasses. He mismatched sport coats with t-shirts and hoodies, and regularly appeared at public speaking engagements with a pair of white iPod buds hanging down from his neck. His was a proudly geeky fashion sense, instantly familiar to his kinship of hackers and programmers. The iPod buds functioned much like an American politician's ever-present flag pin. Whereas the flag pin messaged "patriotism," the iPod buds subliminally told his audiences, "I am connected. I am on the side of gadgets."

Computers were inherently designed to make copies, he said, and as computers advanced, so would the ease with which consumers would make unlicensed copies of creative works and redistribute them. He rendered all content and digital culture into objectified "bits." Bits were constantly being copied in the digital age whether we liked it or not, he said. In such a reality, the enforcement of copyright, which regulated each copy of a creator's work, was not only impossible (and therefore irrelevant) but it meant holding the Internet back from its true potential. Restricting that potential would ultimately cripple artists' capabilities to speak and create freely. Hence, Doctorow interpreted any perceived limits placed on this potential for "openness" as inherent censorship, which he believed to be a greater harm to creativity than artists' inability to be compensated for their digitized works.

Trying to regulate digital technology's "true" nature was akin to regulating gravity: a fool's errand. He quoted Bruce Schneier, a digital security expect, as saying that "Making bits that are harder to copy is like making water that's less wet."[13] Doctorow explained in *The Guardian* in 2010, "As a practical matter, we live in the 21st century and anything anybody wants to copy they will be able to copy. If you are building a business model that says that people can only copy things with your permission, your business is going to fail because whether or not you like it, people will be able to copy your product without your permission."[14] And if they could copy, they most certainly would. No one would *think* of paying for bits. Why would they?

If computers made bits easier to copy and distribute, we should trust enough in technology to believe we will be rewarded in the long run, even if the immediate interests of creators are trampled in the process. But this was not a matter of right or wrong. The changes to society brought forth by digitization, like widespread piracy, *were going to happen whether we liked it or not* because *you can't fight technology*. In an interview with the *New York Times* in 2002, David Bowie (a surprising messenger) summed up this deterministic attitude, which would serve as the basis of many consumers' assumptions about the future of digital content:

The absolute transformation of everything that we ever thought about music is going to take place within ten years, and nothing is going to be able to stop it. I see absolutely no point in pretending that it's not going to happen. I'm fully confident that copyright, for instance, will no longer exist in ten years, and authorship and intellectual property is in for such a bashing. Music itself is going to be like running water or electricity…. It's terribly exciting. But on the other hand it

doesn't matter if you think it's exciting or not; it's what's going
to happen....

Bowie's interjection that this unknown future was "terribly exciting"
captures the sense of enthusiasm many held for the digital revolution
throughout the 2000s, wondering just how far computers could take
us. How much could we change? By embracing technology, how
advanced might we become as a human race?

Kevin Kelly, the co-founder and former executive editor of
Wired magazine and a leading figure in Silicon Valley, articulated the
overtly religious tendencies of techno-utopianism as early as 1994,
when he wrote in *Harper's*, "A recurring vision swirls in the shared
mind of the Net, a vision that nearly every member glimpses, if
only momentarily: of wiring human and artificial minds into one
planetary soul." For this strain of techno-utopianism, the debate over
copyright served as a critical turf war for Kelly's "planetary soul."
Any regulation or boundary placed on the Internet was treated as a
threat to this emergent utopia. The right of the Net to be free and
open to whatever innovation came its way mattered far, far more
than the preserving the business models of a few entertainment
companies. Prognosticators like Kevin Kelly or Ray Kurzweil—
who prophesied that a coming "singularity" would lead humans
to unite with technology, "transcend" our biology and conquer
death—painted visions of utopian ends that any contemporary
means justified, no matter how harmful they might sound to our
ignorant, analog ears.

In his 2010 manifesto, *You Are Not a Gadget*, Silicon Valley programmer
Jaron Lanier noted, "The open culture crowd believes that human
behavior can only be modified through involuntary means....If flawless
behavior restraints are the only potential influences on behavior in a
case such as this, we might as well not ask anyone to ever pay for music
or journalism again."[15] That is precisely how Cory Doctorow suggested
content companies treat the Internet: never expect consumers to pay
for *any* of it (except access, of course). This may have been disregarded
as a political scare tactic, employed by digital utopians to protect "their"
Internet from the creeping debasement of money and copyright, if it

weren't also true that newspapers and record labels that tried to sell content online (Doctorow's "bits") at the time were failing miserably. In the midst of the Great Recession, media observers wondered if this was a temporary downturn for creative industries, or whether the techno-utopians were correct and the idea of paying for content truly was going the way of the horse-and-buggy, that there was no use in "fighting" technology.

"This is why I give away digital copies of my books," Doctorow explained, "and make money on the printed editions: I'm not going to stop people from copying the electronic editions, so I might as well treat them as an enticement to buy the printed objects."[16] Doctorow self-righteously promoted this fact—that electronic versions of his books were offered for free through a license from Creative Commons—and sales of his physical books had skyrocketed as a result. He couldn't prove the correlation equaled causation, but it was an enticingly counterintuitive idea that seemed as viable as anything else in the late 2000s, when creative industries were desperately searching for answers. Certainly, any solution seemed better than validating the underlying copyright-based worldview arguments of litigious rights holders like the RIAA.

So perhaps Doctorow was correct and—whether it was harmful to artists or not—copyright was simply incompatible with a digital age, was not worth protecting when "wiring human and artificial minds into one planetary soul" sounded like such a more exciting and worthy project. History appeared to be proving Doctorow right. One of his Young Adult science fiction novels, *Little Brother*, had made it to the *New York Times* bestseller list and the media showered him and his new business model with attention.

Armed with techno-utopian assumptions, a file sharer had a new way to understand their choice to not pay for their digital content: they were only doing what the computers "wanted." File sharing meant welcoming in the future with open arms and this sentiment absolved them of guilt from any lurking doubts that, just maybe, artists still deserved some compensation for their digitally reproduced works. But if such a sense of responsibility rose to the surface, Cory Doctorow had a ready answer for the doubting techno-utopian: artists don't deserve to be paid anyway.

"Copyright is not an ethical proposition," he said. "It is a utilitarian one."[17] As long as it appeared as though creative diversity was being served for the public interest, it didn't much matter whether copyright was being infringed upon or whether artists were being directly paid for their creative work. The technology and practical results were important, not the creators themselves. The rights of creators became increasingly invisible in the piracy debate toward the end of the decade. Advocates of creators' rights sounded too similar to the pleas of Lars Ulrich before Congress or the legal arguments filed by the RIAA—entities that still haunted the debate. Trying to ignore these voices from the past, the piracy discourse looked further ahead for solutions.

New media experts made the case that piracy was not a rights violation… it was an opportunity! "The greatest threat to artists isn't piracy, it's obscurity," Doctorow claimed, paraphrasing new media theorist Tim O'Reilly. New Media minds focused on how creators could use the "free" and "open" Internet to gain attention, and how that attention might be leveraged to make even more money than they used to receive by selling their works.

Wired magazine editor-in-chief Chris Anderson became a bestselling sage of the business and marketing communities with his 2006 book, *The Long Tail*, in which he prophesied that the infinite "shelf space" allowed by online commerce meant that more products could be marketed to consumers than ever before. The future of the music industry, he argued, would not be found in the mega-hits of yore, but in the digital "long tail," where an infinite supply of music meant expanded niche markets for previously ignored musicians (or content aggregators) to exploit. As Anderson explained, "Disney and Metallica may be doing all they can to embrace and extend copyright, but there are plenty of other (maybe even more) artists and producers who see free peer-to-peer ('P2P') distribution as low-cost marketing. Musicians can turn that into an audience for their live shows, indie filmmakers treat it as a viral resume, and academics treat free downloads of their papers as a way to increase their impact and audience."[18]

In 2009, Anderson continued to sing the praises of digitization in another book, *Free: The Future of a Radical Price*. Borrowing Doctorow's logic, he argued that the ever-decreasing transmission and production expenses associated with bits meant their marginal costs would soon reach zero. Therefore, digital content could literally be given away for free at no cost to the producer and that free content could be "leveraged" in order to convince consumers to pay for "premium" content, services, or associated scarce goods. He called this model "Freemium" and spent the book convincing his audience of business professionals that it was their digital destiny. "Every industry that becomes digital, eventually becomes free," he flatly declared.

"The web has become the land of the free, not because of ideology but because of economics," Anderson argued.[19] Because creative works could be so easily, cheaply and infinitely copied by computers, creative content was no longer operating upon the logic of scarcity that normally interacts with demand to set costs. Piracy was merely a sign that we were entering a new paradigm of "post-scarcity" economics, which meant that post-scarcity products like digital content were destined to reach a price point of zero. "Piracy is like the force of gravity. If you're holding something off the ground, sooner or later gravity is going to win and it will fall. For digital products it's the same thing—copyright protection schemes, coded into either law or software, are simply holding up a price against the force of gravity. Sooner or later, it will fall…. This is not to condone or encourage piracy, only to say that it is more like a natural force than a social behavior that can be trained or legislated away…. Economics has little place for morality for the same reason that evolution is unsentimental about extinction—it describes what happens, not what *should* happen."[20]

By evoking gravity, nature, and evolution Anderson placed the future of digital piracy outside the bounds of human influence, much as Cory Doctorow did. Anderson also borrowed some of Lessig's rhetoric in noting the emergence of "Generation Free"—a generation of teenagers that would never, ever pay for digital content—making any debate over creators' rights moot. These digital natives had "come of age in a world of Free" and "somehow understand near-zero marginal costs from birth."[21]

So, the question followed, how was one supposed to compete with "free"? "Simply offer something better or at least different from the free version," was Anderson's answer. The job of creators was to "add value" to their products to somehow induce people to pay for them. The burden of responsibility was on artists' shoulders to "evolve," not on the consumers' to respect copyright, which was, after all, quickly becoming irrelevant.

Mike Masnick, who ran the blog Techdirt, aligned himself with the thinking of Anderson. Masnick treated record labels and efforts to enforce copyright law with disregard or derision. "Perhaps, instead of suing the innovations that would help move [the recording industry] into a modern digital era, it should have been looking for ways to embrace them," he characteristically wrote in 2012.[22] Masnick believed that legal challenges that had taken down P2P sites like Napster and Grokster accomplished nothing. Where others saw a threat to artists in digital piracy, he saw opportunity.

Masnick offered an easy solution for artists who were confused as to how to negotiate the new realities of digital commerce. He provided an equation that he said solved the problem of artists making money: Connect with Fans + Reason to Buy (CwF + RtB). Ostensibly, this equated to cold hard cash for creators. Masnick suggested that creators "stop worrying and learn to embrace the business models that are already helping musicians make plenty of money and use file sharing to their advantage, even in the absence of licensing or copyright enforcement.... Let's let the magic of the market continue to work. New technologies are making it easier than ever for musicians to create, distribute and promote music—and also to make money doing so. In the past, the music business was a 'lottery,' where only a very small number made any money at all. With these models, more musicians than ever before are making money today, and they're not doing it by worrying about copyright or licensing."[23]

He encouraged artists to "stop worrying" and to use social media and blogs to directly "connect with fans" and then give them some product or experience that added enough "value" to get consumers to pony up. This could involve selling merchandise, concert tickets, artist face-time, or even the right to contribute to an artist's recording.

Selling merchandise and concert tickets weren't new concepts in any way, but the fan-direct "Crowdfunding" of services like Kickstarter was a new model altogether, at least by initial appearances. Masnick cited the musician Amanda Palmer, who made thousands of dollars one night on Twitter in 2009, when she auctioned off random items in her apartment to fans, and then took in over one million dollars in donations with a Kickstarter campaign in 2012. A session drummer named Josh Freese offered fans paid-for experiences: anything from a dinner at Sizzler, to a trip with Freese to Disneyland, to the artist actually serving as a fan's personal assistant. According to Masnick, "by connecting with fans, and giving them something of scarce value, Freese was able to create a business model that worked." Jill Sobule, a major label one-hit wonder in the '90s, followed a similar route in order to fund one of her albums. She even allowed a fan, who shelled out $10,000, to sing back-up vocals on one of her songs.[24]

Many began to ask whether a record label was even necessary in the digital age. Why bother with the legal wormhole of a record contract if artists could go directly to their fans? A few famous musicians asked themselves the same question.

After a long period of stylistic evolution and critically adored albums, Radiohead was both the biggest and most well-respected rock band in the world in 2007. So it shocked the music industry when they decided against re-signing with their label, EMI, and chose to release a new album themselves. What's more, they obliterated convention when they placed the album, *In Rainbows*, for digital sale on their website and allowed fans to pay whatever they wanted, even zero. In the context of the piracy wars, Radiohead seemed to be asking their fans the revolutionary question, "What is digital music really worth to you?" After two months of the pay-what-you-want download, in which the average fan paid about $6, the band took the pay-what-you-want option off of their website and replaced it with a deluxe edition of the album including both a vinyl and CD version for $80. In January 2008, they finally released the CD version of the album to stores through TBD Records and a major label distributor. The album's staggered, unprecedented rollout was a marketing coup and the album reached number one in both the US and United Kingdom despite the early digital release. The vinyl version of the album was the number one selling vinyl record of 2008. As the industry struggled with what to do about piracy, Radiohead's model looked like a certifiable solution and they were hailed as visionaries, finally breaking the chains of the old record label model.

Trent Reznor sold millions of albums with his moody, industrial rock group Nine Inch Nails from the '90s into the 2000s, but when his major label contract expired, he also decided to go it alone. He released *Ghosts I-IV,* a collection of thirty-six instrumental songs, himself. Reznor offered an array of purchase options for consumers on the band's website. A digital download of the album cost five dollars, while a limited edition deluxe version (including vinyl and CD versions along with artwork) was priced at $300. Other pricing options split the difference between those extremes.[25] Within only a week, Reznor reported $1.6 million in gross sales. His post-label experiment appeared to be a success, providing further evidence that the record label really *was* an antiquated institution.

In the context of these new models, music fans received a flurry of messages from major artists that major labels were the "bad guys" and fans shouldn't worry too much about supporting them because they were dying anyway. Reznor called record labels "thieves" and suggested there was little reason to pay for physical albums when practically none of the money went to the artist.[26] Amanda Palmer announced at the MIDEM music conference in 2010 that "the traditional industry, the way things have run—obviously—records, labels…. It's just dead. I mean, if it's not completely dead it's heaving its dying breath as we speak."[27] When asked what advice he would give to young musicians in 2010, Radiohead singer Thom Yorke advised young artists to avoid labels altogether: "Don't tie yourself to the sinking ship because, believe me, it's sinking."[28]

A DIY, or Do-It-Yourself, business model—the "good" to the major labels' "bad"—suddenly appeared possible thanks to the examples of Radiohead, Trent Reznor, Amanda Palmer, and myriad options offered by digital commerce. The website Kickstarter, which launched in 2009, was assisting thousands of artists in taking advantage of crowdfunding. The website took five percent of all raised funds (only if the funding goal was met) while providing any artist with a free medium to set up their own donation space. Funding drives were created by countless bands for studio time, to purchase equipment, or to help fund a band's tour if they lacked support from a label. Another site called Bandcamp allowed artists to easily set up their own online digital store, where they could sell high quality digital files and merchandise directly to consumers, setting whatever price the artist deemed fair. Similar to Kickstarter, Bandcamp was a free service but they took a percentage of all sales. Tunecore, an online digital distributor, provided distribution to iTunes and other digital stores for around $50 a year. An artist could conceivably handle their own publicity through social media and then arrange these online services in such a way that duplicated much of what a record label would normally offer.

Could artists really build their own careers without the support of a label? As for crowdfunding sites like Kickstarter, "fan financing of music seem[ed] best suited to exceedingly small projects," as reported by the *New York Times*. "Support that is enough for full-time pursuit of music is still nowhere in sight."[29] The purely Web 2.0, new media success stories were hard to come by. Amanda Palmer's success raising over one million dollars on Kickstarter was a feel-good story of a career artist reaching a heartening climax of fan support, but most working musicians were still signing with independent and major record labels. Jill Sobule or Josh Freese failed to emerge as the vanguard of the "new normal" in music. Many people assumed the pay-what-you-want model of Radiohead and the similar strategy by Trent Reznor were only the beginning, but no other artists reached close to their scale of success (few artists have their considerable resources to engineer their own release). In fact, even Radiohead abandoned the pay-what-you want model when they released their following album in 2011, *King of Limbs*, and charged $9 for the MP3 version, $14 for the higher quality WAV file.

As Jaron Lanier recognized in his book *You Are Not a Gadget*, when examining such CwF+RtB solutions for artists in a post-copyright era, "The tiny number of success stories is worrisome. The history of the web is filled with novelty-driven success stories that can never be repeated." Also interesting was that all of the artists mentioned above spent time on, or worked with artists who were on major labels, where they built reputation and audiences off of record sales-funded publicity. How much of these DIY artists' successes were due to the marketing and promotional budgets of the same record labels that now appeared to be dying?

As from the beginning of the piracy debate in 2000, arguments and predictions swirled and circulated. But could anyone claim the keys to unlocking the piracy problem? The music subscription service Spotify was hailed as a potential savior for the music business for years. But when it finally arrived on US shores, tiny artist payouts and disappointing growth in paid subscribers reminded everyone that solutions to the existential crisis of piracy weren't as obvious as New Media thinkers—who came more from marketing or technology backgrounds rather than artistic ones—made them out to be.

Touring revenues were on the rise as record sales fell, but could we be so sure that those revenues were scaling down to the independent and emerging artists who were most in need of some kind of financial support to maintain their careers? The UK singer Imogen Heap poked holes in the idea that file sharing was acceptable because artists were making up for the lost money on the road when she took to her Twitter account in 2010 to write, "This may be the last tour for awhile. Ugh. Not easy keeping afloat in this climate!... So expensive to tour! Just had a rather depressing meeting with tour manager. Record sales low (across the industry) really impacting me.... Sad truth is touring US especially such a monopoly. Audience end up paying double ticket price to the venue.... Huge mark up."[30] As the new media crowd defensively held up increased touring revenues as evidence that The Long Tail, Freemium and CwF+RtB were valid business models that made up for losses to digital piracy, few people were considering how much of those increased revenues were actually making it into band's pocket, especially for smaller acts with less negotiating power.

"That's the brutal reality of touring today," wrote Charles Arthur of *The Guardian*. "Many of the larger venues are owned by the same company, which can set the ticket prices to the fans while also setting how much the artist receives.... Heap, who in effect has to support herself through record sales to fund the tours, and vice-versa (because she doesn't have major label backing), therefore gets squeezed. If an artist like Heap—adored by her fans, making copious use of social media such as Twitter, Flickr and MySpace—can't make it work in the modern world despite touring like a Trojan, and having devoted fans, but without selling truckloads of CDs or getting major label investment, might that really mean that the big labels—so reviled in so many corners—actually are needed?"

Perhaps artists couldn't do much of anything on a sustainable scale alone, and they needed the support and infrastructure of a label, or an organization that closely resembles one. Will Page, chief economist for the UK performance rights society PRS for Music, addressed this issue in his analysis of the 2009 UK music industry. Of the rise in UK concert revenues, he wrote, "the artists generating these big numbers can be characterized as heritage acts." In other words, acts that benefitted from the consumer-patronized "old model" of record label support. The report went on:

> This growing inequality between heritage acts and the rest of the pack mirrors a separate trend identified in digital music, where more choice led to a widening gap between the hits and niches.... A "digital Britain" faces a problem with the investment in creative industries. Sure, recorded is down and

live is up—but it's recorded music which makes the primary investment in new talent, and given the damage already done to investment calculations by piracy, therein lies a "conveyer belt" style question: who's going to invest in the career development of artists to create the heritage acts of tomorrow?

At the end of the day, were crowdfunding or DIY really anything but a less efficient version of the record label system? In both cases, large blocks of fans pay small amounts of money, and that money was going into paying back a royalty advance and funding promotion, marketing, recording costs, and tour support. What was the difference between crowdfunding and labels, beyond the superficial stamp of Web 2.0 and circumvention of reckoning with the baggage of Napster and the RIAA?

Well, there was a difference. That difference was the fact that keeping the discussion focused on Web 2.0 models ensured that respecting creators' rights and paying for digital music was off the table of acceptable options. And this wasn't in order to build a better culture or to support artists, it was so that the likes of Chris Anderson and Mike Masnick could maintain their own brands as people who really *got* technology and understood where it was taking us, and where it was taking *your* business. You too, my little marketing executive or boutique PR agency, could benefit from understanding the *tremendous innovation* happening in the *technology sector* and learn how to increase profit margins by *connecting* with customers and *adding value* to products…

Those who presented a false choice between "innovation" and respecting copyright marketed themselves as media visionaries, choosing to throw artists and their legal rights under the bus for their own self-promotional benefit. Ironically, the hardcover edition of Chris Anderson's *Free* was priced at around $27 and, under his helm, *Wired* was one of the first magazines to sell digital editions for the iPad (under copyright). When Mike Masnick revealed his CwF+RtB formula, *Billboard* Magazine's Antony Bruno bluntly reckoned with the corrosive and dishonest element of such agenda-driven new media sage-ism:

> Masnick's formula is designed as a rationale for eliminating copyright protections and licensing laws…. It's also a nice self-promotional tool. Too many journalists and bloggers create and promote business theories as way of making money off

of speaking fees or the eventual book (Masnick will speak at your company event for a mere $20,000). Now I can't fault a reporter for trying to make a buck in these trying media times, but some become so personally invested in the viability of their theories that they are no longer able to take an objective viewpoint on their reporting. Masnick is doing the same here, making what he writes more about proving himself and his theory right than about exploring the nuances of the marketplace. It's just an easier sell.[31]

In fact, Masnick even decided to "experiment" with CwF+RtB in 2009, offering a number of merchandise or experiential packages for sale on Techdirt. Above the list of packages, which ranged in price from $5 to $100,000, the instructions read, "If we've connected with you, then check out the packages below and hopefully one of them gives you a reason to buy. Then, by buying, you'll be helping us prove that this model works."[32]

Bruno was the exception in his open criticism of such figures. Any model seemed worth consideration in an age of turbulence. For the most part, musicians remained in the lurch. If they complained about the unfairness of piracy, they were called whiners and accused of not "understanding technology" or doing a good enough job of "connecting with their fans." Once more, consumers were left off the hook for their actions, but the problematic reality of digital piracy would not just disappear. Michael Gira, the leader of the bands Swans and Angels of Light, founder of Young God Records and a luminary of New York City's so-called no-wave music scene of the 1980s, was brutally honest in 2010 when journalist Jen Long asked him how he was dealing with the emergence of digital piracy:

> I don't care about major labels, they can die, although they do release a lot of good music, but the whole complaining about the Internet... is valid. I'll give you an example... of why I hate people who steal music which is what it is when you download something illegally, you're stealing from me, from the artist, someone who works. One thing I just did to raise money to be able to pay to record this album was I made a thousand copies of a handmade CD/DVD double thing where I made a woodblock print and I printed a thousand copies of these and then I went over each one of these copies

with a different color felt pen and marker four times, that's times a thousand I did that, signed them all, packed them all up, shipped them out. I worked hundreds of hours making these. Hundreds. Like literally, weeks of repetitive, boring, stressful work trying to get this done. And people through the website bought these in order to help fund the Swans album. So I did all that work and then I just now paid all the money I made from that and plus more from my savings to record this album. Now I'm gonna put this album out there after all that work and all that investment of time and energy and my whole life's influence and all the experience I've gained, I've put into this album. I put everything, heart and soul into it. Now I'm going to put it out there and people are going to steal it. So how would you feel if you were me?[33]

There were other interesting developments taking place in the music industry as the piracy wars played out.

Aided by an increase in online exposure though music blogs like Pitchfork and Stereogum, independent artists were receiving offers for corporate sponsorships and commercial licensing. More and more musicians were taking such offers. In an era of reduced album sales, licensing a song for a commercial or television show became one of the best ways for musicians to earn a decent check and gain significant exposure from their recordings. Traditionally considered by many to be "selling out," hearing bands like Grizzly Bear, Modest Mouse, Smith Westerns, Vampire Weekend, or The Black Angels serve as the backing track for car, clothing, or even state lottery ads became commonplace by the end of the millennium's first decade. The notion that there was anything wrong with such branding of music harkened back to an old and lost world when music fans, well, still paid for music.

Record sales had shrunk by more than half since that millennial high-water mark. So major labels also began pursuing "360 Deals," in which the label paid bigger advances and offered more support, but also took a cut of touring revenues and merchandise sales. Major artists like Madonna and Robbie Williams signed on to such models, though the independent community was somewhat skeptical.

Every revolution requires their Jacobins, the well-intentioned purists who gave in fully to ideological purity, offering world history the Guillotine and Reign of Terror of the French Revolution. For piracy, the Jacobins first arrived in the form of The Pirate Bay, a small group of anarchistic young Swedish hackers who ran a torrent tracking service of the same name. The Pirate Bay filled the revolutionary shoes of Napster and facilitated the sharing of millions of media files each day between their global network of users, or "pirates." The Pirate Bay weren't necessarily for or against anything—other than upholding their own freedom to download all the music, pornography and movies the world could offer. That freedom was presented in the rhetoric of individual rights, "the freedom of the Internet," "freedom of speech" or the "right to privacy." They viewed rights holders as enemies of freedom and copyright as nothing but a tool for censorship.

The Pirate Bay might have just been another tracker service for torrent files, except for a couple of factors.

First of all, they were extraordinarily media savvy. Their name and its appropriation of the title "pirate" became a rallying cry for file-sharing advocates around the world, and the site's founders weren't shy about appearing on television or participating in films to spread their message, which, stripped of its lofty rhetoric, was essentially, "Fuck You."

The adolescent "Fuck You" message originated from the second reason for The Pirate Bay's popularity. Like Shawn Fanning, they achieved a certain folk-hero status when the Swedish police raided their servers and shut the site down in 2006. As a testament to the site's influence upon content use, when the site shut down about 35 percent of all European Internet traffic reportedly vanished. As a sign of their power, in just three days the site was back up again. They became heroes for "pirates" everywhere and soon a Swedish political party, The Pirate Party, began to grow in popularity and spread around the world. The party platform was the legalization of file-sharing, enveloped in their usual rhetoric about freedom of speech, privacy, and the freedom of the Internet.

"You could argue that this is stealing," one Pirate Party leader told the BBC in 2009. "The point is, it doesn't matter."

Yes, they were a bit nihilistic as well. In another interview by the BBC, also in 2009, Pirate Bay spokesman Peter Sunde was forthcoming in the group's mentality:

I think it's okay to copy. [Entertainment companies] get their money from so many places that the sales is just one small part. Take the latest James Bond movie. What car was it? Oh, it's a BMW. His phone is a Sony Ericsson. I don't think that's a coincidence. I think they got a load of money for having those products in the movie…. I don't care. That's the big thing, I don't care. If I want it, I take it, 'cause I can. It might be immoral to some people but I think it's up to me to decide…. I do pay for [music] by listening to music, by bringing the music to my friends, they bring it to their friends and they go to concerts, I go to concerts. The actual product doesn't have to cost anything in order to make money. Nobody is crying that people who used to go around selling ice to people do not have a job anymore because of the fridge. It would be stupid but it is the same thing.

Of course, it was not "the same thing." When people stopped selling ice door-to-door, it was because people no longer wanted or needed someone else to make their ice. Demand evaporated and the market failed. On the other hand, Peter Sunde and his brethren clearly wanted, were even addicted to, the films and music that creators, labels, and film studios were still necessary for the creation of. So his argument was illogical because….

Then again, what point is there in arguing with the logic of someone who is honest enough to reveal the raging Id behind some advocates of unlicensed file sharing, by admitting, "I don't care. If I want it, I take it, 'cause I can." Now, that was honesty, which called into question how much copyright law, economics or failures to innovate really had to do with file-sharing or the motives of those (like The Pirate Bay or Megaupload) who facilitated it on a mass scale.

Despite such empty, adolescent statements (or perhaps because of them), The Pirate Bay traffic swelled after their servers were raided, to 2.7 million registered users and 12 million anonymous ones. The writer and author Stephen Fry publicly advocated for the group, whom he considered to be honorable revolutionaries. Search Google Images for "Cory Doctorow" and you will likely find a black and white picture of him wearing a Pirate Bay t-shirt, accessorized by his gimmicky iPod buds. What a fitting end to the Decade of Dysfunction; that understanding of the basic issues surrounding piracy would become so garbled by an incoherent discourse that the poster boys for empty protest at The Pirate Bay would appear to intelligent individuals, like Doctorow and Fry, as a cause worth endorsing.

In a documentary about The Pirate Bay, *Steal This Film*, made by an associated group, Peter Sunde says, "Making money is not the point with culture and media, making *something* is the point with media." From the wisdom of his earlier quote, we certainly shouldn't have expected Peter to see a connection between the two, but in any case, what new created works was he or The Pirate Bay facilitating? Did The Pirate Bay brain trust really believe that by helping people illegally download *Harold and Kumar* movies and Robbie Williams albums for free that they were contributing to society? Somehow, someway, the idea perpetuated within their subculture that they were turning consumers into creators, and the *one thing* the MPAA and RIAA would never allow was… *gasp*… people "making stuff," and that was the real reason The Pirate Bay was so hated, rather than the mass violation of legal rights facilitated on their networks.

In *Steal This Film*, one of the interviewees represents a group called Pirate Cinema. He is a skinny, pale fellow in his late twenties with bugged out eyes and a vaguely German accent. He is, essentially, a brooding villain from a Harrison Ford action movie—smoking a cigarette, making sure that he is taken for a serious fellow. In his words, we achieve a glimpse of where the logic of unchecked piracy leaves us, entirely unable to deal with the world as it is and ready to accept any notion that will only validate our opportunistic beliefs.

> The panic of the movie industry and the music industry is that people could actually start to produce. And that file-sharing networks, file-sharing technology, allows them to produce…. People have lamented much the "Death of the author." What we're witnessing is far beyond. It's becoming producer of former consumers. And that suggests a new economic model for society.

Piracy fooled some people into believing that a new model of exchange was actually being developed. When I engaged in my first online spats on this issue, one of my challengers nonchalantly said in the middle of his argument, "Well, under our *current* economic system…" as if that system were about to change and so could be dismissed for the purposes of the topic at hand. And so the potential for hallucination, hypnosis and narcosis offered by the Internet seemed to manifest itself in The Pirate Bay and its followers, who saw no reason to question their own actions or even to defend them. Like Narcissus, soon nothing mattered but their ability to gratify themselves without compromise. The Decade of Dysfunction concluded with masses of young consumers fleeing self-righteously to their own utopias in blissful ignorance, willfully blind to the cultural self-destruction that awaited.

ONWARD, DOWNWARD

By 2011, the existential crisis of the digital age—to pay or not to pay—remained unresolved as ever. A decade of dedicated handwringing on the part of the music industry and its observers, beginning with the Napster controversy, ended not in progress for creative culture, but in the trendy nihilism of The Pirate Bay and a cottage industry of New Media prognosticators who had little stake in the outcome for artists or creative industries.

Meanwhile, record sales continued their terminal slide. In the first five weeks of 2011, three different albums broke the US record for the lowest-selling album to place at Number One since SoundScan started tabulating the figures in 1991.[1] Crossover country-pop princess Taylor Swift and the rock band Cake, a relic of '90s alternative radio, each held the dubious distinction until singer-songwriter Amos Lee unseated them, achieving pinnacle status in the United States after selling just 40,000 total units in one week. Compared to ten years earlier, when Number One albums moved close to one million units on a semi-regular basis, the collapse of the record industry was ever more real.

An unending parlor game commenced: when would the record industry finally bottom out? *Would* it ever? Overall record sales hadn't increased since 2004, in the middle, as it so happened, of the RIAA mass lawsuits. By early 2011, the recording industry wasn't just in a down period—it appeared to be dying a slow, heaving death in front of our eyes at the hands of rampant digital piracy and all the confusion it spawned.

The global entertainment industry, however, still accounted for tens of billions of dollars each year in sales and had the long tradition of copyright law on their side. In the United Kingdom, France, Spain, Australia and New Zealand legislation intended to stem the tide of digital piracy was debated or passed into law. "Graduated response" or "three strikes" schemes were implemented, in which those users caught file sharing would be warned at first, then punished with fines, bandwidth throttling (in which the amount of data a consumer can transfer is limited), or temporary suspensions of user Internet access. Courts in Ireland, Belgium, Italy and the Netherlands began ordering Internet Service Providers to block access to services like The Pirate Bay. Only a few independent film companies were still pursuing litigation against individual downloaders and major entertainment companies seemed to understand the hopelessness of that strategy. They turned instead to attacking the problem through the courts and through legislation that focused on the major facilitators of piracy, like Internet Service Providers, search engines, public cloud storage companies like Megaupload and torrent trackers like The Pirate Bay. These measures were balanced with graduated response policies for consumers that would hopefully push them toward licensed services like Spotify, Pandora, Netflix, Hulu or iTunes. In 2011, this strategy came to the United States in the form of the Protect IP Act in the Senate and its companion bill in the House of Representatives, the Stop Online Piracy Act (SOPA).

SOPA was the first piece of legislation scheduled to come to a vote, so it garnered the lion's share of attention. The United States had been seizing hundreds of domains of domestic websites, found to be dedicated to copyright infringement, for years through the Immigration and Custom's Enforcement (ICE) wing of the Department of Homeland Security. One music blog, djaz1.com, was apparently seized in error in 2011 resulting in a serious black eye for the agency, but the illegality of the hundreds of other sites closed down by the agency was never questioned. Sean Lovelady of the California-based IMAGiNE Group was convicted of willful distribution of copyrighted movies in 2012 by the ICE. Lovelady plead guilty and faced up to five years in prison and a fine of $250,000.[2]

The ICE enforcement measures, mixed with P2P service Limewire being convicted of copyright infringement by a New York District Court in 2010, after four years of legal wrangling, provided a stark disincentive for any company playing fast and loose with copyright law in the United States. But the ICE had no authority to prevent US consumers from using offshore P2P services like Sweden-based Pirate Bay or any number of other services based around the world. Enter, SOPA.

SOPA sought to restrict the United States market from overseas websites that violated United States copyright law. If either the

Attorney General's office or a private rights holder believed a foreign site was, to quote the legislation itself, "dedicated to theft of US property;" was "used by users within the United States;" and was "primarily designed or operated for the purpose of, has only limited purpose or use other than, or is marketed by its operator or another acting in concert with that operator primarily for use in" copyright infringement, "detailed" evidence would be brought before a Federal judge.[3] If the Judge were to find the evidence to be sufficient, the court would serve an injunction to block access to the site while the defendants had five days to provide counter claims, in accordance with the Federal Rules of Civil Procedure. If a defendant could not provide sufficient evidence that they were innocent, Internet Service Providers under US jurisdiction would be ordered to block access to the website through the Domain Name System (DNS); websites and search engines would be required to make "reasonable" measures to filter hyperlinks that led to the offending domain; advertising networks and payment processors would also be ordered to terminate their commercial associations with said sites. If any of the above parties could provide evidence that they were unable to comply with the court order, they would be under no obligation to do so. However, a website, ISP or payment processor that was found to be willfully ignoring or circumventing the court order would be liable. Otherwise, the court order would have been meaningless.

SOPA was a broad and biting piece of legislation that attempted to root out the "worst of the worst" violators of copyright, as the bill's champions from the entertainment industry and labor unions claimed. The Digital Millennium Copyright Act (DMCA), which placed the burden on rights holders to file complaints of infringing content or links, offered the "third parties" who had infringing content on their networks "safe harbor" from liability, so long as they complied with takedown requests and didn't "knowingly" host or distribute infringing content on their networks. The problem with the DMCA was that, if an infringing link was taken down, a new link could appear on a public storage service almost immediately, rendering the process pointless for many rights holders, especially independent ones who didn't have the time to file complaints for hours each day. US-based sites that were found "dedicated" to infringement were already liable under United States law. Their domains could be (and were) seized by the ICE and they could be sued for knowing infringement by rights holders in civil court. In other words, third parties based in the United States, like Twitter or YouTube, would be under no greater legal liability under SOPA. Third parties were already liable for "knowingly" ignoring the infringing links on their sites.

If a foreign site was ruled by a Judge to be "dedicated" to infringement, the burden would now be mostly placed upon payment processors and ISPs. Internet Service Providers had long been vilified by the entertainment industry for profiting off of the consumer demand created by digital piracy and holding up any efforts at enforcement. But ISPs became more cooperative, as companies like Comcast and Time Warner also owned media companies that relied upon digital enforcement, and tacitly supported SOPA.

But from the technology sector, there were early signs that the legislation was seen as an existential threat. As early as May 18th in 2011, Google CEO Eric Schmidt warned that SOPA measures were classic cases of government censorship. As reported by *The Guardian*, he said, "If there is a law that requires [Domain Name Systems] to do x, and it's passed by both houses of Congress and signed by the President of the United States, and we disagree with it, then we would still fight it…. I would be very, very careful if I were a government about arbitrarily [implementing] simple solutions to complex problems. So, 'let's whack off the DNS.' Okay, that seems like an appealing solution but it sets a very bad precedent because now another country will say 'I don't like free speech so I'll whack off all those DNSs' – that country would be China."[4]

SOPA arguably went too far to combat infringement. The legislation could have focused entirely on cutting off payments and advertising to offending foreign sites, leaving out the site-blocking mechanisms for a later piece of legislation if still needed. The Private Right of Action, which allowed private rights holders the ability to trigger the mechanisms of SOPA, was similarly unnecessary and gave credence to criticisms that the bill was overly broad and a ticket to the RIAA to take down whatever site they saw fit. Both the *Wall Street Journal* and the *New York Times* published editorials supporting the aims of SOPA but calling for the legislation's language to be tightened.

However, most criticism of SOPA flew badly off the rails, offering paranoid predictions that had little basis in truth. No one disagreed with the law's intention, which was to stifle foreign sites "dedicated" to infringement and enabling mass piracy, and many critics vocally agreed with the intentions. Rather, they leveled a series of unfair and misleading critiques. SOPA was a "censorship" bill which would equate the United States with states like China and Iran who do not respect freedom of expression. By seeking to shut down websites, any website, SOPA was called an attack on legitimate speech. Because the measures went into effect quickly, the law violated Due Process. The bill was written by lobbyists for the entertainment industry and served to preserve corporate profits, while supposedly destroying the P2P infrastructure that new artists relied on. SOPA's measures were draconian and worried Internet users were told that Tumblr, YouTube or Facebook could potentially be taken down for having even a single infringing link on their network. Consumers who uploaded even a single infringing link could be punished with up to five years of jail time. And SOPA wouldn't even solve the problem, because the blocked websites could still be accessed by just typing in the underlying IP address (similar to a website's telephone number) rather than the domain name.

Websites like FreeBieber.org, AmericanCensorship.org and IWorkForTheInternet.org encouraged users to fight SOPA and other attempts at destroying the "open" Internet through copyright enforcement. These sites provided readymade petitions to sign and letters to be sent to local politicians. A slick online video on the dangers of SOPA's Senate companion bill became an introduction to the issue for many. In the video, a young male voice warned of the bill:

> Lots of trailblazing websites could look like piracy havens to the wrong judge... wherever people express themselves, make art, broadcast news or organize protests, there's plenty of tv clips, movie footage and copyrighted music mixed in...This is the Internet we're talking about. It's a vital, vibrant medium. And our government is tampering with its basic structure so people will, maybe, buy more Hollywood movies. But Hollywood movies don't get grassroots candidates elected, don't over-throw corrupt regimes, and the entire entertainment industry doesn't even contribute that much to our economy. The Internet does all these and more...[The entertainment industry] has a history of stretching and abusing their powers. They tried to take a baby video off YouTube just for the music playing in

the background…The question is, how far will they take all this. The answer at this point is obvious: as far as we'll let them.

The end of the video provided a link to FightForTheFuture.org, which also provided easy ways for concerned Internet users to get involved. Fight For The Future led Amercian Censorship Day on November 16th 2011, and rallied websites to place fake banners across their home pages, illustrating the censorship that was to come thanks to SOPA. The day led to the first surge in greater awareness for the supposed evils of the legislature. On December 22nd, a user on the Internet forum Reddit said that he was taking dozens of his own domains off of the web hosting service GoDaddy, on account of their support for SOPA. By the following day, a new website called GoDaddyBoycott.org was live and helping facilitate the boycott. It only took another few days before GoDaddy publicly switched its position on the legislation.

Just before the New Year of 2012, talk began circulating on tech blogs of the idea for a wider protest of SOPA. Cnet reported that some in the tech industry were considering a "nuclear option." "When the pages of Google.com, Amazon.com, Facebook.com, and their allies simultaneously turn black with anti-censorship warnings that ask users to contact politicians about a vote in the US Congress the next day on SOPA, you'll know they're finally serious," wrote Declan McCullagh.[5] Markham Erickson, leader of the NetCoalition, a trade association for the tech industry, said of the blackout, "There have been some discussions about that. It has never happened before."

On January 10th, Reddit officially announced that it was going forward with a blackout of its own site on January 18th, the day of a SOPA-inspired hearing at the US House of Representatives where Reddit co-founder Alexis Ohanian was scheduled to testify.[6] As a few other websites announced their own participation in the boycott, the attention, phone calls and letters being sent to politicians through websites like SopaStrike.com were already having an effect. Over the weekend, SOPA was stripped of its site-blocking provisions, the very provisions that garnered attacks of "Censorship." The hearing on January 18th, which was the basis of the protests' timing, was canceled. But the blackout went on with participation of Google, WordPress and Wikipedia. Millions heard of SOPA for the first time, learning that the bill could close down their favorite social networking sites or send them to jail for a single infringing link. The protest caused dozens of politicians to pull their support for SOPA and the bill died, along with PIPA.

On the popular technology blog TechCrunch, David Binetti gloated over the victory in an opinion piece:

> You've got to feel sorry for the SOPA guys. They did all the right things. They got legislation introduced that would pro-tect their industry from inconvenient threats—like that pesky Internet... Not a single anti-SOPA lobbyist was hired for yesterday's protest... A well-organized, well-funded, well-connected, well-experienced lobbying effort on Capitol Hill was outflanked by an ad-hoc group of rank amateurs, most of whom were operating independent of one another and on their spare time. Regardless of where you stand on the issue—and effective copyright enforcement is an important issue—this is very good news for the future of civic engagement.[7]

This above quote is interesting because it gestures toward the importance of copyright enforcement, while treating the defeat of legislation that attempted to address that very thing as a triumph, solely on account of its grassroots appearance. The bill's defeat was automatically a good thing because, supposedly, one side had lobbyists, money and organization while the other side was just a rag tag group of tireless idealists, operating out of passion and love. The substance of the legislation and the ultimate question—well, what *should* we do about sites like The Pirate Bay?—was forgotten in the fog of war.

The day after the blackout, David Pogue, technology columnist for the *New York Times*, expressed his misgivings.[8] In his article, titled "Put Down the Pitchforks on SOPA," Pogue recognized the remarkable power of the protests, but didn't flinch in the face of its flaws. "Of the millions joining in outraged protests," he wrote, "I'll bet that only a few have actually read the proposed bills. Everyone else is, no doubt, swept away by the Web sites' shock language. These bills, say the opponents, will allow Hollywood to censor free speech, kill innovation, and 'fatally damage the free and open Internet,' as Wikipedia put it. Light the torches! Grab the pitchforks!" Pogue noted that the SOPA criticism was disjointed. Some argued for the goal of the bill, but criticized the methods. "But there is another group of people with a different agenda. They don't even agree with the purpose of the bills. They don't want their free movies taken away. A good number of them believe that free music and movies are their natural-born rights. They don't want the big evil government taking away their free fun."

"It was a sloppy success," Pogue concluded. "The scare language used by some of the Web sites was just as flawed as the Congressional language that they opposed."

Were the SOPA protests, leading up to the blackout on January 18th, conducted in good faith? The popular propaganda relied upon slippery slope arguments that assumed total villainy on the part of rights holders—who would viciously abuse the law to censor any website they saw fit—and total ineptitude on the part of the Federal Judges, who would decide whether or not enough evidence existed that a foreign site was "dedicated" to infringement. Such critiques preyed upon a paranoid attitude toward institutions, the rule of law and the entertainment industry. In the SOPA blackout, the chickens of the Decade of Dysfunction all at once came home to roost. Years of haphazard debates, misunderstanding of the issues and demonization of rights holders had left a population of Internet users who were vulnerable to propaganda from a technology industry that was (in the form of search engines and social media) facilitating what felt like their lives. As is the modus operandi of any propagandist, the ends of killing SOPA justified the means of misleading the public and preying on their distrust of the entertainment industry. SOPA was conflated into being an attack on the Internet itself, rather than an attempt to regulate online business practices that arguably were violating the legally held rights and incentivizing the illegal exploitation of United States citizens and business. And in the end, a law that very well may have had a positive impact upon the problem of piracy was turned into another warning to creators not to advocate for their own rights as citizens. Solutions to the piracy wars seemed to retreat evermore.

SOPA was presented as purely functioning to protect big media "gatekeepers" and their antiquated business models, but was this the whole story or just another piece of useful propaganda?

In August of 2011, Google was forced to pay a $500 million penalty for violating Federal law after admitting to knowingly assisting Canadian pharmacies who were using AdWords, Google's online advertising service, to attract illegal prescription drug sales to US customers. Google was warned about the practice in 2003 but continued it all the way until 2009 when they realized they were under criminal investigation. In other words, they knowingly broke the law until they were caught. Another Google advertising service, AdSense, is commonly used on the same "rogue sites" that SOPA would have targeted.

During the SOPA brouhaha, an independent filmmaker named Ellen Seidler write a blog post detailing her efforts to use the mechanisms of the DMCA to protect her own work from being unlawfully distributed online. Seidler noted that Katherine Oyama, a representative from Google, one of the staunchest opponents of SOPA, had told the *New York Times* that "Google also ejected companies from its advertising system when notified of illegal activities." Seidler took significant issue with the statement:[9]

> Over the past year and a half I've repeatedly sent DMCA notices to Google reporting pirate sites featuring AdSense advertising (and links to our film). While most of the links I reported were eventually removed, most infuriating was the fact that the pirate sites didn't skip a beat and continued to display Google ads aside their myriad pirated movie offerings. As far as I could tell… these AdSense accounts were rarely, if ever, disabled by Google. To add insult to injury, in most cases I usually discovered fresh links to our film posted on those very same sites a day or two later. AdSense accounts were never disabled despite clear evidence the reported site was in the business of pirating movies… Google makes a practice of sending DMCA notices to the Chilling Effects website, in a veiled effort to dissuade (intimidate) rights holders from exercising their rights under the law.

In the case of Seidler, Google was clearly profiting off of the existence of SOPA's so-called "rogue sites" and doing a lousy job of complying with the law. The result was an independent filmmaker watching helplessly as huge corporations and distributing websites profited off of her work, and that of her creative brethren. Why did remedying such instances conflict with an "open" Internet? Did "openness" excuse exploitation? Was it fair to label the government protecting Seidler's legal rights as a US citizen "censorship"? Did the foreign websites illegally distributing Seidler's work deserve protection on account of free speech concerns?

Such questions, which got to the heart of the digital piracy problem, were consistently ignored by SOPA critics during the debate. Ellen Seidler and the independent artists like her may as well have not even existed. Believing in the myth that only huge entertainment corporations benefitted from copyright enforcement meant ignoring independent artists and their own views on piracy. A consumer wasn't going to feel guilty violating the rights of a big corporation or Metallica, but what about Seidler and the millions like her who had sacrificed for their art and were just looking for basic fairness from the marketplace? Were we to ignore their condition based solely on the vague notion that "you can't fight technology," that any attempt to regulate digital commerce was hopeless?

In a 2010 article on digital piracy, *The Atlantic* reported, "Computational neuroscientist Anders Sandberg recently noted that although we have strong instinctive feelings about ownership, intellectual property doesn't always fit into that framework. The harm done by individual acts of piracy is too small and too abstract. 'The nature of intellectual property,' he wrote, 'makes it hard to maintain the social and empathic constraints that keep us from taking each other's things.'"[10]

For me, it was those very same social and empathic constraints that were reawakened in Brooklyn, when I realized that the famous musicians I knew needed and deserved my respect and support. Immediately, the assumptions I held on digital piracy developed ugly cracks in their armor. The myth that enforcing digital copyright only had to do with big nasty corporations and whining rich artists kept our collective empathy in check for years on this issue, helped along by the fact that people like to have things for free if given the choice. In an attempt to re-contextualize the issue of digital piracy, or at least begin that process, I set out from 2009 through 2011 to speak with various musicians, representatives from record labels, record store employees, promoters—all from the independent music scene or having risen from it. Most of the interviewees had zero connection to the RIAA and, if they did, the connection was incidental at best. Perhaps these voices from the independent community could enlighten us on the realities of digital piracy and help us begin again on our journey for greater wisdom and, ultimately, solutions.

The Decade of Dysfunction thrust us further and further into the dense thickets until we were surrounded. Unable to see a way out, we accepted our hopeless entrapment as plain reality. Though unsatisfying, we had no choice but to accept it.

But streaks of blue still shone, barely, through the tangled wood. Something appealing was out there: clarity. It would take time, work and patience to cut a new path to that place of understanding. Despite the effort, the fleeting streaks of blue called forth with the promise of illumination. Perhaps a new world of beauty was waiting out there.

It is time to blaze a new path.

PART 2

Ground Clearing

THE WORLD WE ALL DESERVE

If the Decade of Dysfunction began with musicians' piracy concerns being discredited due to an imperfect messenger in Lars Ulrich, it made sense to look for a complement in the independent industry; a musician who couldn't so easily be dismissed as a greedy millionaire. I found my first such complement in Andy Falkous.

In 2009, Falkous and his Welsh post-punk band Future of the Left labored through over six months of songwriting and recording until they completed a new album, set for release on beloved UK record label 4AD. The band, which included bassist Kelson Fuller and drummer Jack Egglestone, named the album *Future Travels With Myself And Others*. In the midst of these final stages, Falkous received a call from 4AD (part of the Beggars Group label group). The album had leaked, the label representative told him. Weeks before its scheduled release, music blogs had blithely posted links to free album downloads. Any fan who knew of the leak could obtain an unlicensed digital copy within one or two minutes of entering "Future of the Left leak" as a search engine query.

Falkous was irate, disillusioned, frustrated. After a few days, he took to the band's MySpace account (at the time the dominant social networking tool for musicians) to tell his fans—and Internet users at large—exactly what was running through his mind:

> It's difficult to express exactly what I felt when I found out, last wednesday, that the album had made it's way onto the Internet. 22nd april—approximately eight and a half weeks before release and only three since the fucking thing was mastered and whilst members of the band don't have shiny little embossed copies there is a promotional cd of the record on sale at ebay for twenty five quid.
>
> I drank a bottle of Jamesons and began to lecture the cat on copyright control. To her credit, she simply fell asleep as Law and Order went about its business in the background.

Myself, Kelson and a couple of the guys at Beggars spent 72 hours or so pissing around, sending angry emails to proud bloggers (and oh, the fucking pride of the feckless thief) and, amongst others, a Russian website that was already charging people for the songs. Motherfuckers. I guess that since the bottom has fallen out of the arms trade, any collection of notes, however obscure, is a legitimate income source.

So, anyway, the fucking thing has leaked despite our desperate delaying tactics and you may have listened to it / be downloading it this second / have taken the position that you'd rather wait for the actual release—regardless, it feels that getting annoyed about downloading in this valueless modern age is like taking issue with water for being wet or night for gradually turning into day because ultimately the entitlement that most people feel for free music completely overshadows any moral or legal issues and conflicts that may arise in the hearts and minds of better people, people who understand that actions, on both an individual and group level, have consequences far beyond that moment of instant gratification.

There's so much to say with so little effect on this issue, so many well-intentioned but wasted words devoted to it... but anyway, thank you for downloading in barely a minute something that we poured a year of our lives into, attempting (successfully, I believe) with a great and furious pride to better our previous low-selling (and leaked three months early) album, a record which flew under the radar for many reasons but mostly because most of the goodwill poured on it happened and had dwindled several months before it was available to buy.

Yes, buy. Such a dirty fucking word. Currency exchanged for goods and services. Food, Clothing, Butt-plugs and fucking H2O. How far, I wonder does this entitlement for free music go? My guitars, should they be free? Petrol to get us to shows? Perhaps I should come to an arrangement with my landlord, through the musician-rent-waiver programme...

Anyway - please be careful, or we'll get the world we all deserve. Hobby bands who can tour once every few years if they're lucky, and the superstars, freed from such inconvenient baggage as integrity and conscience, running the corporate sponsored marathon of £80-a-ticket arena tours and television adverts 'til their loveless hearts explode in an orgy of oppressive branding and self-regard. Some of us, in all honestly, just want to make the music we love and play it around the world without living in poverty...

Do consult your surroundings before proceeding.

Falco

A few months after the leak and subsequent attention, Andy sat on a couch backstage at the Music Hall of Williamsburg in Brooklyn. With jet-black hair, thick sideburns, and dressed in a black leather jacket, he certainly looked the part of rock star. Eyes full of suspicion, he glared out from his seat, methodically replacing the strings on his guitar before their headlining show, to take place upon the stage downstairs. Kelson and Jack sat in nearby folding chairs, next to a table covered in unopened bottles of mineral water and Coca-Cola. Kelson, sandy-haired and burly, with a full beard and shaggy hair, interjected as Falkous discussed his blog post and its aftermath. Despite his effort at maintaining composure, the sardonic musician occasionally seethed while he shared generally pessimistic views on the issue of piracy and the inability of file sharers to see the consequences to their actions.

As for the many people who are apologists for downloading—I think it's important to label them as apologists because that's in effect what they are—you're talking about music in general being devalued, you're not just talking about recorded product. I was standing in a bar in Cardiff, and some man was going to see his favorite band a couple of nights later—some inconsequential band-in-skinny-jeans-bunch-of-cunts. The guy said to me, "I can't believe it, man, I have to spend twelve quid to see those bastards." So what's that, seventeen... eighteen dollars? Then, he turned around and spent twenty-four pounds on drinks. So, there you go. There's the value. People can talk all they want about how bands are going to be getting this mythical amount of money back from live shows. That is not my direct experience.

Personally, I've downloaded two things in my life that weren't yet available—television shows that I've later gone out and purchased. I've never downloaded music because I prefer my music to sound like music, compared to a tinny-sounding MP3 version of music. When somebody rips a couple of MP3s off our album and listens to them on their computer speakers and then says they don't like our album, guess what? They haven't fucking listened to our album and fuck 'em! That's like rubbing their underwear on my face and me saying they've got a small dick—it makes absolutely no sense whatsoever.

The obvious thing is, people can get stuff for free—they want it for free. If those people then piss common sense into the metaphorical semi-darkness and get on with their free stuff and don't try to morally justify their actions, then I wouldn't go so far as to say there isn't a problem, but there almost isn't a debate. If you can get free shit, a lot of people are going to get it. I've heard a lot of people say, "Well I'm a Marxist and I think everyone should get their music for free." I'm like, "Do you understand what a Marxist is? Do you understand the words you are using? Do you understand that people should be rewarded for their labor—to a fair and equitable amount?" I mean, people will bandy about terms without even the faintest fucking idea of what they indicate or once meant. This is the problem.

A guy said to me, "Man you're just a Luddite!" Or they'll say, "You gotta adapt with the times man, it's all emerging!"

So, you're telling me that I spent years learning an instrument, writing songs and putting my heart and soul into this music to become a fucking t-shirt salesman? Because that is so contrary to the "all music is made for free" crowd's stated goal. "Free music" pushes bands that are genuinely in it for the love of music—and there are more bands like that than one would think—towards a more explicit commercial understanding of their music. And I'm not just talking about careerist bands, I'm talking about any band that wants to tour.

In the States you get, what, eleven days vacation... two weeks? You can't tour but a couple of hours away from your hometown. If you want to be a real band and play in other countries—the live experience obviously being crucial to rock n' roll—you need to approach it in a relatively full-time way. I don't have a mythical, magical part-time job that I can just return to and earn money on a casual basis when I'm not touring. It doesn't exist. So, if there are zero royalties, advances or tour support from the label's ability to sell records, what happens? How are you supposed to make up for that vaporized income?

In principle, I'm against bands lending their music to advertisements, but if somebody offered us $100,000 tomorrow—even a slightly objectionable company—I'd be an absolute fucking fool not to take that money. Ten years ago, being in a band, I would have been in a much stronger position to say no. Today, it's not even a question. And that money certainly isn't going to go into fucking heaters for my swimming pool, it's going into paying my rent and my credit card bill. This is a question of survival for a lot of bands, as opposed to making money. It's not like I have savings bonds or anything.

I've heard the patronage argument. Patronage just doesn't even apply when it comes to being a rock band. Michelangelo was never forced to take the Sistene Chapel on a sixty-day tour of America. It requires a constant influx of funds to keep the whole machine running, even a sputtering little machine like ours. Anybody over the age of six who offers the patronage argument deserves to be punched in the face. Anyone who first accuses you of being "out of date," and then brings up patronage deserves to be informed about the looming threat of the Spanish Armada off the British coast. Because they are fucking imbeciles.

To be clear, I am totally against the record company lawsuits or threats to cut off people's Internet. My issue lies more with the uploaders than the downloaders, but there has to be some acceptance of responsibility on the part of downloaders.

Some man said to me, "What's the difference if I pay? You'll only get a dollar or two from that anyway." My response was, "You should probably get it for free then and, when you see me in the street, kick me in the fucking shins as well." It's besides the point how much money we are getting at the end of the day. All right, the record industry model is archaic and it's begun to change, but it is really only the bands who have massive power through major label marketing, only bands like Radiohead or Nine Inch Nails, who've been able to use the changes to their advantage. Hardly any other bands have that advantage of profile.

A label representative from 4AD stepped into the room, wordlessly handed each member of the band a ten-dollar bill, then walked out. Falkous deflated a bit into his seat, embarrassed, while Kelson perked up, leaning against the table on the other side of the room.

Falkous: *That ten dollars is my food for the night.*

Kelson: *The thing is, when the regular public—the regular music fans—sees his or her favorite rock band, it's very dreamy. They don't see them as working people. When they see them on stage it seems like, "Oh, they've made it. They've obviously got it well money wise," which in eighty-five percent of cases is not true. You know, having a music career is a struggling, hard thing. Some fans see it as luck. They come and see us live and see us jumping around, which is our equivalent of a sports team's highlight reel.*

Falkous: *The live show is like the montage of all the great moments. You don't see the hard work. You don't see all the disappointments. Sitting in vans, listening to other men snore.*

Kelson: *It is the transfer of money between bank accounts that are all overdrawn. Regular, everyday bullshit. I don't want to moan and complain about it, but that is the reality.*

Falkous: *The other day, I haggled with somebody for a packet of M&Ms 'cause I didn't have enough money.*

Kelson: *Not really "rock n' roll," is it? The frustrating thing is that when you then confront people with the consequences of "free music" and start talking about punishments for piracy, that drives people in the other direction where they get so defensive, they can't even talk about this in a reasonable way.*

Falkous: *I think the beginning of downloading being expressed by such wildly disparate poles as Metallica on one end—where you couldn't have gotten a more corporate-branded entity—and Napster on the other—which was characterized as this college kid alone in his bedroom, just trying to help people.... That still polarizes the debate to a ridiculous degree, so the real issues aren't even looked at anymore.*

Kelson: *Because "free music" is made out to seem like it's you versus "the man."*

Falkous: *I mean, theft is theft. Personally, I could give a fuck about Metallica's bank account. It doesn't change whether it's right or wrong.*

Kelson: *In my mind, what we have gotten is a case of the technology controlling the people, rather than the people controlling the technology.*

The Laziest Rebellion

As we have seen, the RIAA gave file-sharing fans an easy out. If confronted with their basic responsibilities to compensate artists or labels for their products, a fan could simply say, "I refuse to support RIAA lawyers with my money. Artists don't get any money from record sales anyway." A rational response to the RIAA transgressions might have included a renewed call to support independent labels (who are not members of the RIAA) or look for ways to secure better royalty rates for musicians. Rather, the digital pirates of the Decade of Dysfunction painted the entire record industry with the same clumsy brush. An independent label, no matter how small or progressive, was irrationally associated with the major labels. This kneejerk association on the part of consumers evidenced an undercurrent of entitlement in need of a protective facade.

Sufjan Stevens garnered wide acclaim and a devoted audience with the release of his first two LPs, *Michigan* and *Illinoise*, along with a slew of other EPs and concept albums in the 2000s. Sufjan pursued his version of DIY by releasing his own albums on Asthmatic Kitty, a record label he started along with friends and fellow musicians from his hometown Holland, Michigan. The label survived from 1999 to 2012 on the strength of Sufjan's album sales, and they built a roster of quirky, experimental artists along the way. Asthmatic Kitty saw themselves as the good guys in the industry, trying to do right by their fans and artists in service to good music. It was in this spirit of respect that one member of Asthmatic Kitty, John Beeler, wrote an email to some of the label's customers in 2011 after he learned that Sufjan's new album, *Age of Adz*, had been chosen for a promotion on Amazon's MP3 store, in which Amazon priced the digital album at just $3.99 for its first week of release. Amazon would fully compensate Sufjan and label just the same, using it as a loss leader to draw in customers to their digital music store.

When they were informed about the $3.99 promotion, Asthmatic Kitty employee John Beeler was flattered, and felt it would likely increase sales. But he was also worried. Some of the label's customers had pre-ordered the digital version of *Age of Adz* at a higher price through Bandcamp, the artist-direct service Asthmatic Kitty used for their digital sales. Beeler wanted to make sure Sufjan's fans understood that the label wasn't trying to screw them over, that they had nothing to do with setting the $3.99 promotional price. In the spirit of transparency, he sent a letter to all the fans who had pre-ordered Sufjan Stevens albums in the past, taking the opportunity to also make clear the label's feelings on pricing in general:

> …We have mixed feelings about discounted pricing. Like we said, we love getting good music into the hands of good people, and when a price is low, more people buy. A low price will introduce a lot of people to Sufjan's music and to this wonderful album. For that, we're grateful.
>
> But we also feel like the work that our artists produce is worth more than a cost of a latte. We value the skill, love, and time they've put into making their records. And we feel that our work too, in promotion and distribution, is also valuable and worthwhile.
>
> That's why we personally feel that physical products like EPs should sell for around $7 and full-length CDs for around $10-12. We think digital EPs should sell for around $5 and full-length digital albums for something like $8…

This letter was courageous for its honesty in discussing price and explicitly communicating to consumers that, though it should have been obvious, the label believed good music was worth paying for. John Beeler and his colleagues took pains in the letter to explain that they were a small operation working in good faith, "while the Internet swirls with bittorrents and rapidshares and full-album-mp3-blogs and heavily discounted pricing. So this is us, out here on the raggedy edge. And honestly, we like it here…. There are lots of us out there, doing what we do because we love to do it and hoping somebody pays us long enough to keep doing it a little while longer."

Techdirt's Mike Masnick responded in a blog post by vaguely suggesting that the label should focus on adding "value" to their products rather than speak up on the issue. He wrote, "The whole email does feel a little off. The simple fact is, if people want the music… they can find it somewhere for free. Amazon's prices are meaningless when it comes to the 'value' of the music. Price and value are not the same thing. Rather than complaining about the price that Amazon sets on the album, why not give people additional reasons to pay directly at Bandcamp—such as providing valuable extras if they do. Or discounts on other merchandise. There are all sorts of positive ways to get people to find it worthwhile to spend money without making them feel guilty and bad for paying a price that is legitimately offered by a retailer."[1]

Beeler spoke of the letter and the reactions it inspired from the basement of his family home in Indiana.

In all honesty, we're not even too attached to those pricing numbers. I think Sufjan himself has said he's okay with $5 albums. Get lower than that and it gets hard to spread the money around for the artist and label. Those numbers just represent what we think is fair right now.

Unfortunately, the letter instantaneously became misrepresented online. I wish we had worded it a little differently, but we weren't writing to the whole Internet, we were only emailing people who had already paid for previous Sufjan albums. We initially received about forty emails back and only one of those emails was negative, only because that person thought it was spam. Everyone else seemed to appreciate the letter.

We felt genuinely bad about what had happened with Amazon. Seemed like it was ripping people off to have Amazon undercut the price after fans had gone through the trouble of pre-ordering it for a higher price… so it made sense to clear the air. Then, the email was passed around and picked up by music blogs as being a letter to the entire industry, which would have been a pretty pretentious thing for us to do. Interestingly, people in the industry— managers who represent huge artists, booking agents, musicians—privately told us, "Right on!"

The controversy died down pretty fast. I don't think it changed anything in the short-term, but over time I hope it helped a little to move conversation forward in the industry.

The most shocking thing about reactions to the letter on blogs was how quickly people lumped us in with the major labels. People wrote us saying,

"Who are you motherfuckers asking me for more money?" The first headline we saw about the letter was from a mid-sized European blog—the UK equivalent of Stereogum. They said something to the effect of, "Sufjan Stevens Will Eat Your Baby If You Buy From Amazon." In part, us not being aware of how people might misconstrue the letter was us not being savvy. Nothing in the letter suggested that Sufjan wrote it, but people just assumed.

Techdirt wrote about it and their post had at least fifty comments and all of them were negative. Again, that shocked us. Techdirt had done something on us before, which was very complimentary… I guess they liked something we had said about the industry. But after our letter, they flipped their opinion on us completely.

We are a small business—a maximum ten person staff, and that's only during the holiday season. Last year, the label lost money until Sufjan put out a record. So, having worked for this label for years, it was disconcerting to be slapped with the major label rap sheet. Take Sufjan—he could be making more on tour than he is, but he doesn't believe in just taking fans for everything they're worth. He believes in giving back. Just about everyone who works for Asthmatic Kitty technically works part-time, but puts in full-time hours and we all have other jobs and families on top of that. The idea that we were whiney guys trying to price-gouge fans was just ridiculous. We work twelve-hour days. All of our artists work really hard. Sufjan—who is actually able to make a living—he is working as hard as anyone. So that reaction was insulting, really. Guys who do happen to work at the big labels—they work twelve-hour days, too.

I realized there was a near total lack of understanding out there of music as a product. Some fans have no concept of intellectual property. I assumed that people had figured that stuff out by now, but I guess not. It struck me as funny that, probably, a lot of this sentiment is coming from IT people whose paychecks come from writing code. I wonder what they would say if their work became so easily copied?

It is hard to bitch about Amazon pricing an album at under $4 when a consumer can type, "Sufjan mediafire" and get the album for free in a matter of seconds. In the real world there's not a magical machine where you push a big flashing button and free cigarettes come flying out, but the Internet is effectively a magical machine for music. As a label, we are living in a real world where we have to deal with the cost of distribution, studio time, promotion… But the consumer is standing there at that magical machine.

I know that the major labels have not done much to elicit good faith with consumers and unfortunately that has colored the image of all labels in the minds of some fans. What the RIAA did with the mass lawsuits is a great example of how to really piss people off, so there just is not a lot of good will out there. Say "record label," and fans seem to imagine a hundred of us in suits and ties sending out cease-and-desist notices. That is the main problem, along with the sense of entitlement that comes along with the "magic machine." If piracy is a rebellion, it's the laziest rebellion anyone could ever imagine. If you're gonna rebel, fine. But don't just sit around, clicking and consuming in front of a computer screen.

We definitely need to meet fans where they are, but that doesn't mean I am their personal monkey—and neither are our artists. We want to meet our fans in the middle, but we're not gonna come walk their dog for them. That said, I do think Kickstarter is changing the environment a little bit—one of our artists used it to fund the whole vinyl side of his album. For $25 all the way up to $75, he'd send fans a handwritten note or give them a phone call. He's just a super-appreciative type of artist.

I think the music industry works best when artists feel lucky people are buying the music, and fans feel lucky that the artists are making the music for them. Today, some fans might feel like it's our job to win them over, but our approach is to let the music speak for itself. Entitlement is a bad thing and it starts when you accept the bottom line of "free." But there are still lots of fans who are happy to pay. They're just not as loud as the people who complain.

Overall, I think these changes are exciting and I think labels will still be around in the end. We are very far off from the death of the record label. It's not as if we will all just keel over like Blockbuster. We've had over a decade with piracy and we're still around. In some ways, the industry has thrived in this.

THEY DON'T HAVE A CHOICE IN THE MATTER

In every American city or college town it used to be a given. Walk the main drag and you soon came across a messy storefront covered with album art and tour posters. Turning a doorknob caked with multi-colored layers of chipped paint, you entered to find a provincial mecca of creative culture; a microcosm of local personality on display. The customers milling about offered a quick reading of the surroundings while, for his part, a cranky purveyor offered unimpressed glances from behind the dusty checkout counter. The independent record store existed as a singular cultural institution at the turn of the millennium and felt the impact of file sharing up close. Their existence is no longer such a given.

Hundreds upon hundreds of record stores closed in the United States during the Decade of Dysfunction, leaving fewer than 2,000 stores in existence by its end. Milwaukee's Atomic Records was a favorite store of mine growing up, a place where music culture wasn't just a peripheral curiosity, but a *raison d'etre*. Atomic closed in the late 2000s, but I didn't find out until a visit home one summer. Rounding an adjacent street corner, "Atomic" was still spelled out across the long dark storefront, but the word "Glass" replaced "Records." Atomic had turned into a head shop, representing an illicit industry (marijuana) consumers were still very much obliged to pay to play in. I popped my head in through the door to see its former maze of CDs and vinyl succeeded by darkly-lit displays of byzantine bongs. The musty smell of used records was a memory, masked by nauseating wafts of cheap incense.

If Atomic—located next to a college, near a main thoroughfare, isolated from any real competition—could close, it suddenly occurred to me that the extinction of the independent record store was a realistic possibility. So, when I came upon the empty storefront of one of my favorite stores in Brooklyn a few months later, Sound Fix Records, I immediately assumed the worst.

Luckily, the store had only moved down the street to a smaller retail space, on the ground floor of one of Williamsburg's rising condominiums. The landlord of their original building had forced them out, replacing the space with yet another hip, European-style bistro. People, after all, were still obliged to pay for their food.

One cloudy afternoon in Brooklyn, I spoke with Sound Fix owner James Bradley, baby-faced with prematurely graying hair, and with Mike Wolf, one of his staff and formerly a professional music journalist for *Time Out New York* magazine. Sitting from their vantage at the checkout counter, behind the clear glass of a brand new storefront, the pair considered how piracy had affected the industry and its fans, as they saw it. Mike Wolf, aside from his journalistic credentials, offered perspective as a former employee of Rare Book Room, a small Brooklyn record label that had recently put out the debut LP of a local psych-punk band, Talk Normal.

James: *We opened in 2003 and wanted to create a new kind of record store that would form a nexus of the music community in Williamsburg, and for a long time we were probably one of the few record stores that had increasing sales. Then the bottom dropped out in 2008. Our sales literally dropped by 40 percent in the span of a week. Our gross went from $1,000 a day to $350 and I was like, "What is going on? Where did everyone go?"*

Record stores are not needed anymore, really. We have the Amazons, downloading, and of course music piracy. But we think of ourselves as people with good taste who can do some vetting of the music for our customers. It's worth mentioning that people want to get out of their house. They want to go to brunch, see other people, go to the park, or pop into a store. Not everybody wants to sit in front of a computer screen all day long and there is no substitute for human experience. That kind of stimulation is not possible to replicate online.

I see why fans have become so turned off to paying for music. The bottom line is that record labels made a lot of money putting out a lot of crap in the '90s and they thought, "We could just do this forever." But that's not any kind of excuse for piracy. I think a lot of people are just cheap and they'd rather take something for free than pay for it and the misdeeds of the major labels is their convenient rationalization. There are others who genuinely think these are evil corporations and deserve to be destroyed—and I think those people are just misguided. Major labels do have a purpose to serve in the grand scheme of things. I'm glad the indies came along to push them, so the Majors would consider signing The Flaming Lips and Built To Spill and

The Magnetic Fields. The money the Majors can generate helps musicians, it helps people in the industry. So I think people should wait and think before they say that the getting rid of Universal or WMG will make the world a better place. It might make it worse.

Mike: *People have really convinced themselves that there are absolutely no moral ramifications to downloading something for free. There are a lot of regular people being put out of a job with these businesses going under. And yeah, there are lots of examples of major labels screwing over artists and stifling them creatively, but there are also examples of major label artists making money and building exciting careers.*

Personally, I don't think there's much hope. I hate to be the pessimist. There's a whole generation of younger people—I'm in my forties—and they don't have the experience of going into places and buying something and having a chance of injecting cash into an economic system. They don't have that experience. James and I grew up with these bizarre and intense experiences in record stores and comic stores, so we already learned that there is a payoff.

James: *I'm not as down as Mike. I don't think these things are so ingrained that they can't be reversed. I've had a number of young people who shop here tell me, "I used to pirate music when I was a teenager but now I have a few dollars in my pocket. I really enjoy coming here and feel a stronger connection to the music."*

Look at the resurgence in vinyl. Like a lot of stores, we've seen an explosion and it's great for a vinyl lover like me, very gratifying to see. But vinyl is not going to save the music industry and I couldn't operate an all-vinyl store. As much as I love vinyl, there are some problems with it. It's heavy, has a high rate of defective product and labels are not making enough of it or making it quickly enough. The new Flaming Lips album came out in September and we didn't get the vinyl until November—they can't keep up with the demand. CDs are quick, efficient and light and you can bang them out. They are still 60 percent of our business, whereas five years ago they were 95 percent. The funny thing is, people will spend anything on vinyl. I've never heard anyone complain about the price of a record—not once.

Mike: *In the early days of piracy, I knew I didn't like the tone and the nature of Metallica's response. But they were reacting in a very primal and animalistic way. They were threatened at the very core of their survival and they were fighting back with teeth and claws bared.*

James: *I remember people telling me, "This is going to help you, James. This is spurring greater interest and creating more music fans." There was a feeling that increased exposure was always a good thing. People were making* the library analogy to me or saying bands were going to make up for lost sales by earning more on the road.

But I don't think excessive touring is good. It's something that artists need to do, but I don't think it's good idea to do it out of financial necessity. I always think of the Beatles who stopped touring in 1966. Where would we be if they had to tour seven or eight months out of the year rather than be in the studio working on Sgt. Peppers and Revolver and everything else? These things have been thrust upon musicians. They don't have a choice in the matter and that's what I don't like. I heard this guy on the radio saying that it was "good" that musicians aren't so sheltered anymore and they have to go out there and connect with fans and I thought, "You know what, asshole? This not your decision to make. Don't tell people how to live their lives. If they want to tour, tour. If they'd rather spend time in the studio, that's fine too. There's no superior version of these things."

That really annoys me when people talk that way, "Isn't it great people are touring again!" Well there are also a lot of hazards to touring. It's physically exhausting and people get on each other's nerves being stuck in a van for eight hours every day.

This idea that everything should be free seems to infiltrate the music industry in many different facets. I get some kids here that I just want to punch after a while. They ask, "Is this for free? Is this for free?" They seem to be very young. I don't see people in their thirties saying these things to me. Once you're out there in the world and have to make money and recognize the importance of being compensated for your work, you're less likely to feel that entitlement.

Aside from touring revenue, you see much more willingness to sell a song for an ad. I think artists realize that they're struggling and if they can make money on a car commercial or beer commercial, then more power to them. I even heard Beirut[1] in a car commercial.

Mike: Definitely, it's an alternative revenue stream. Go figure, the last people on the face of the earth with money to spend are car companies and liquor companies. Every other licensing opportunity that comes along seems to involve a car. A lot of the stigma is gone, but there's still a big difference between licensing an ad for Hummer and licensing one—although this may only be perception—for a Volkswagon commercial. I know a lot of people who used to produce bands and be in bands who now work at music houses—which help place songs in commercials but more often that not they're making new music with established artists and creating new music in a matter of days.

James: *Think about what Moby did with Play. Every song was licensed to a commercial or a movie. And that's, of course, electronic sample-based music which seems to work really well for commercials. Artists who are electronic or rhythm based I think are going to be very successful in that model. I don't know how many other people can really make money through that route. I think you still need some record sales and label support.*

Mike: *The problem is that a lot of fans don't really consider how much labels actually assist bands in their careers and there is this idea that music piracy is something that hurts bigger bands, bigger labels. It is not only them. When the Talk Normal album came out, it was a little surprising for us.*

From the day our advance copies went out to press, we started seeing people posting it via Mediashare and Rapidfire—it was going up all the time. Basically, three or four days a week, I'm writing emails to Mediafire, Rapidfire and Megaupload saying, "You're in violation of the DMCA." Usually, in twenty-four hours they'd remove that link. Then someone else just reposts it. It happens to independent bands… it happens to unsigned bands… it happens to everybody. So if a major release would have sold 500,000 copies, now it only sells 150,000. You scale that down to an indie release where you were hoping to sell 2,000 copies and it is just as devastating in that case, if not more. People say, 'It's promotional.' No, that's a load of garbage. Most of the people who post these things don't contribute a thing. It's a jpeg of the album cover and a link. "Two girl punk band from Brooklyn. Grab it here." They don't care.

James: *I fear a lot is being lost. People are embracing low quality and compressed MP3s. It's one of the reasons why kids are getting into vinyl these days. It's so great to hear them come in and say, "I've never realized how great this record sounded, I can hear the instruments better. It's a whole new experience."*

Not enough people are talking about this because they are afraid—there's a culture of fear. No one wants to be associated with the Metallicas of the world. It's a curious position, because photographers expect to be compensated for their work, filmmakers expect to be compensated—for some reason musicians are supposed to work for free and if they object to this then they're greedy and letting commerce overwhelm their art or something? It really annoys me when I hear that stuff, that people aren't entitled to have some financial compensation for the work that they do.

Everybody has to realize we have a stake in this, it's not just the CEO in a Manhattan skyscraper. We all have a role to play and we all will benefit by preserving what we have. A music industry has a role to play in the culture that we have created and if you like these artists a lot, you have to support them. Eventually it's going to come back and haunt us if people can't make a living doing these things. Eventually, they're going to stop doing them. People need to have some money to pay their rent, to own a few nice things, practice their craft and make a living. That's why I get so angry when I read these blogs that are dismissive and crack jokes about it all the time. Pitchfork is glib about piracy. I want to say, "Hey guys, you review records! If there are no more records what are you going to do? Review MP3s? Is that what you want?"

So, we need to just get perspective on what our responsibilities are and how we're supposed to understand the complete package.

THEY ARE GOING TO NEED HELP

As independent record stores struggled with the effects of digital technology, entirely new types of record stores popped up online. Matt Wishnow worked at Elektra Records in the mid-'90s as the World Wide Web was just gaining its sea legs and finding a popular base of users. With two business partners, he founded Insound, an online mail order store that centralized distribution of music, band merchandise, fanzines, and books that primarily dealt in independent culture and independent labels. It was a website where fans could find items too obscure for their local record store to carry, delivering on the Internet's promise of convenience.

From his office in Insound's Greenpoint, Brooklyn loft space, Matt explained how his business had intersected with the rising tide of digital piracy through the 2000s, where he saw the digital retail business heading, and whether the direct-to-fan possibilities offered online meant that DIY was the future for serious artists.

When MP3s were brand new, I knew that our business benefitted from file sharing. At the time, I was interviewed a lot and I'd say, "I'm going to speak out of both sides of my mouth on this."

On the one hand, I can't imagine Death Cab For Cutie, The Shins or Modest Mouse being what they are without some version of file sharing. Insound has some of the most motivated music consumers in the world and we just did a survey of our consumers. The low-end spends $40 to $60 per month, the high-end spends hundreds of dollars every single month and obviously a lot of that is physical music. So I knew that the crossover between Napster, Audiogalaxy and Insound was that we had people who were becoming more motivated to buy specific things. Obviously, the ratio of downloads-to-buying was nowhere near one-to-one, but we were getting business from that discovery of music.

On the other hand, I realized piracy was socializing a way of music consumption that was going to have potentially devastating impacts on music listeners and musicians. I didn't totally know what it would mean, but I knew that it was pretty scary.

There are music businesses forming—one is for ubiquitous product that people want to pay nothing for, and even if they pay something it's not because they think it's something worth paying for, but because it's convenient. Then there are the people who will want to develop that relationship with a band and will pay hundreds of dollars for vinyl, tickets, something limited edition. Those are the two businesses that are being hatched that I see.

Vinyl was less than 10 percent of sales when we started and CDs were 90 percent. We also had a small business of 'zines and books—but that whole business became blogs. Vinyl went from 10 to 20 percent the first few years. Then, five years ago in 2005, vinyl jumped close to 30 percent. We were about to launch our digital store and I thought, 'Hmm, something's happening here…' Today, we are 60 percent vinyl sales—the biggest vinyl store in America and probably the world. CDs have dropped from that high of 90 percent down to 12 percent, two-to-three percent is digital sales, and the rest is merch, turntables, and books.

I think 360 deals are a necessary step for the industry, because the artist's direct-to-consumer relationship is going to be a bigger part of the artist revenue stream. Artists will require labels or other companies to shepherd that business. Some artists can do DIY stuff, but if you're talking about millions and millions of dollars a year… artists didn't get into music to run the best artist web store or the most streamlined t-shirt printing company. They're going to need help doing that. And I don't believe that perception that major label artists don't get royalties, it doesn't apply to indie artists very well. I see that many major label artists don't recoup their advances, but that's because they get enormous advances! And advances basically are royalties paid before they've even recorded anything. The idea that the artist isn't getting any money is a fallacy, total fallacy. That's especially true for indie bands who don't get those big advances.

Insound used to own an indie label called Tigerstyle Records until 2000, and we cut royalty checks to bands to this day! We gave very small advances, so if one of our bands sold a few thousand copies they could be recouped against the advance very quickly. Historically, especially in the '50s and '60s, there were fly-by-night labels who wrote onerous contracts or just flat out never paid artists, but record companies today are public companies so they get audited and have a responsibility to their investors. Royalty administration is incredibly important. There is definitely a perception that record companies are bloated, overspending and overstaffed. They are easy targets. A lot of their expenses can be recouped against royalties, so in the '80s and '90s when videos were expensive, radio was expensive, getting a record into retail was very expensive.... The cost base was so high that it was very hard for an artist to recoup.

But the industry has changed. Thousands of people have lost their jobs, MTV and the role of the music video is nowhere near what it used to be... so you don't see those million dollar videos anymore unless a corporation is sponsoring it. I know so many indie managers where the most important relationship they have is with advertisers.

And look, if the advance is big it takes longer to recoup—period. Without royalties and without label advances the future generations of bands' careers in music become a lot more suspect. Again, most musicians don't decide to form a band so they can run their own LLC.

Harder and Better

Working at the Greenpoint Coffee House, my fellow coworkers and I kept close tabs on blogs like Pitchfork and Brooklyn Vegan, naturally driven to learn which bands were getting hyped or who was worth paying attention to. The name "Yeasayer" began appearing in headlines on such websites in 2007, and broke further into the consciousness of plugged-in fans when their debut album, *All Hour Cymbals*, was released later that year by the tiny label You Are Free. The album harvested reams of positive press, led by the single, "2080." The song contrasted with the minimal, crudely-recorded garage rock and bedroom pop that was fashionable at the time, catching consumers off guard. The lyrics, "I can't sleep when I think about the world that I'm living in/I can't sleep when I think about the future I was born into," shrieked and moaned by singer Chris Keating, were a tribute to post-millennial dread. But the song's anxiety was softened by a danceable, eastern-inflected groove by guitarist Anand Wilder and the band's propulsive rhythm section, led by bassist Ira Wolf Tuton.

Ira, it turned out, was a regular customer of the Greenpoint Coffee House. I asked about the band's early success at the time of that first wave of buzz as he transitioned from his day job, as a carpenter, into the life of a full-time professional musician. I was jealous, of course. But my base envy mixed with genuine admiration for Ira and hope for myself as a writer. At least such a leap was possible.

In our brief talks, in between coffee orders and dropped checks, I obtained few details on how this transition was actually going for Ira. At Greenpoint's Pencil Factory bar, sitting next to a floor-to-ceiling window that framed a passing parade of young artsy pedestrians and industrial semi-trailers, Ira discussed his journey as a musician and its inherent difficulties. How did a band that never knew an industry without rampant digital piracy approach that reality? Ira, who bears some resemblance to The Clash's Joe Strummer, was plainspoken about the band's long-term strategy as they attempted to turn their debut album buzz into something sustainable. Yeasayer was in the middle of promoting their second album, *Odd Blood*, just released by Secretly Canadian, one of the largest and most successful independent labels in the US.

For a while, we weren't shit, no one gave a shit about us. I had this perception where I'd see other bands around me having some success—it's very easy to have a chip on your shoulder after spending ten years working on this—and say, "Their music isn't forward or challenging enough," or you just don't like it as music and talk shit and are generally resentful. I think that's the natural, sixteen-year-old, I-know-everything-about-the-world mentality. I bet there are people who look at us that way now. But I know that we worked our asses off and no one knew who the fuck we were for two or three years. We were playing random shows, but still living in New York, having to make rent and struggling.

It's still a matter of perception. It's not like I'm sitting pretty and don't have to worry about making money. Jon Pareles just interviewed us for the New York Times. To my family, that means, "Oh he's made it." Meanwhile I'm on the phone with my manager 'cause we're out of money, since we haven't toured in a while, trying to scrounge up some money that we're owed through ASCAP. We are not going back to our jobs, because we can't—we are doing this full-time.

There was a period when we were doing this full-time and not making any money. That was not too cool. We all had jobs before and got to the point where we thought, "If we want to turn this into anything more, we're going to have to tour a lot more, whether we're making $50 or $100 a show or not." To end up doing it for a living you have to go through that year or two years of grinding it out, not getting discouraged and believing it will pay off. You get to a point where you get a little more money from shows, not necessarily making a living but incremental steps of improvement that give you hope that this is turning into something. You've got to bust your ass. It's expensive to tour… it's expensive.

For some people, the more something turns into a job, it's natural to treat it as such and forget why you pursued it in the first place. But that isn't a rule and I hope we would realize it if we ever became jaded. We've been trying to do this full-time so we can do it harder and better. It's not like we are sitting amidst mounds of cocaine. Today, I don't have the distraction of doing carpentry 9-to-5, or 8-to-4. Some musicians, when that happens they get caught up in certain things—the old romantic idea is drugs and women—but there are lots of things to get caught up in. Your own ego, for example. Either you can check yourself or you can't. But I think most artists want careers just so they can pursue their art in a more intense and better fashion and not have to worry so much about making rent or being late for your morning shift because you were up recording all night.

Everyone knows the music industry is changing, and in some ways I feel consumers have more attachment to the bands they like and they do want to support them on some level. I think for us that means coming to shows—that supports us. You can no longer 'sell out' as a band. Name any band and it's seen as totally legitimate to be on a Honda commercial. Yeah, we're trying to make a living and it's not seen as evil anymore. It's not seen as greedy anymore 'cause everyone knows the money is less.

I know our record company, Secretly Canadian, they try to keep a smaller roster, focus on trying to develop those bands, whereas the old major labels snatched up as many bands as possible. Columbia tried to do it, signed MGMT and then signed all of their friends. But not every one of those bands is going to be an MGMT. And if a major label doesn't see that potential at the very beginning, that band is fucked.

Looking out for yourself—not signing a shitty major label contract—that is very much the band's responsibility. Our awareness has grown so much as to how the industry works that people are more suspicious when a major label comes and offers a lot of money. The only person who is looking out for you is you. You can't trust anybody. There are a lot of good people out there, but they don't take away the bad.

Still, it's not true that artists can do it all themselves. There's this idea that labels are dead. But there still is a music industry and there still are all these different moving parts to it. Right now, people are just scrambling to find the most successful part. Distribution still exists, publishing still exists, promotion still exists, sales still exist... That's why we signed with Secretly Canadian, because I trust them to know what they're doing. I see who they're working with and respect those people. I think there are some things that are better left to those people to figure out and I'm happy to give them a percentage of what we're doing. You can do it as DIY as you want but you're going to find limitations at every step. This idea that a band can just do everything from their MySpace page is just not true unless you're Justin Bieber and Usher takes a liking to you. Just like Bill Clinton coming out of poverty—it is the glaring exception. It's a nice story.

The whole question of music being "free"… I guess it all depends on what it's worth to the person listening to it. There's a salvage yard in Queens and I pay fifty cents for maybe fifty records. Beautiful records. For me, that's worth a lot more than fifty cents, but to the guy who's selling them, they are worth fifty cents. I value music, I just want to know where my money is going. If I'm spending money on a record and I know it's not going to an artist or the guy who's running a salvage yard—it's going to CBS or Comcast—I'm going to be more reticent about it.

But to produce stuff isn't free. I'm right in the camp of thinking that musicians and labels at the top of their game have been making too much money for a long time—I don't think that's fair in the same way I don't think hedge fund salaries are fair. But that's very different from people being able to make a living doing something, which is something I think we all deserve a chance at. I still need to pay my rent. I still need money so we can buy gear and record albums. It takes money in order to spend the time to make this stuff.

Oh yeah, "musicians and labels have felt entitled to gargantuan amounts of money." But I don't think we are entitled to that. Now, I definitely think we're entitled to something. And if you're not even going to come pay for a ticket to our shows and you want all your music for free, that doesn't make much sense. You need to be supportive in some way.

To record music and distribute it is not free, but you put your own value on it—that's the world we're living in. And in some ways, it's not really my concern what's happening with labels. For me, either way, we're going to have to figure out how to get people to listen, which will get people to shows and that's a model. And hopefully we can make more money touring so we have to do it a little less and can spend more time recording and developing in an artistic way when we record.

I'd be interested to hear the same conversation with Chris Swanson, our Secretly Candian guy, and hear what he has to say about it.

They Want to Participate

Chris Swanson started the record label Secretly Canadian with his brother, Ben, in 1996 in Bloomington, Indiana. Over the years, the label grew into an immediate family of three labels, with Dead Oceans and Jagjaguwar (home to Bon Iver), and a much larger extended family related by SC Distribution, Secretly Canadian's distribution wing that handles distribution for Asthmatic Kitty, among many others. Secretly Canadian developed into one of the keystones of independent music in the 2000s. Like Chapel Hill, North Carolina's Merge Records, New York City's Matador Records, and Seattle's Sub Pop Records, Secretly Canadian is known as one of the "major indies," independent labels who stand alone in their sustained success and influence.

As the co-founder and head of Secretly Canadian and Jagjaguwar, Swanson shared his observations of music's contradictory, chaotic digital age from his office in Bloomington. How did the head of a successful independent label, a perspective sorely missed through the Decade of Dysfunction, digest the state of digital music?

I was in college in '94, so I missed Napster. I didn't have high-speed Internet. I didn't understand it, either. We started in '96 but we didn't get our first digital distribution deal until '99. We didn't think anyone would ever pay for MP3s. We were all reared in the Touch and Go, Dischord record-label universe. We were naive—we thought people who liked our kind of music wanted it on vinyl and CD, not as an MP3.

Metallica was such an unsympathetic band. I felt when The Black Album came out that they were creatively dead. They became the thing that metal was originally rebelling against, because they had become so successful. They were no longer a revolutionary band. It felt lame—it just felt lame when they were fighting Napster. I didn't think about it much more than as the dismantling of an age-old infrastructure.

The value of the recorded master decreases every quarter. There's still money to be had—the pie is big enough and we're enjoying growth in this period—but the total pie is definitely getting smaller. It's not as if we were planning to become a major label, but the shrinking pie does make me wonder…. I think it will shrink another 60 to 70 percent when all is said and done.

But there are also huge upsides to what is happening. It's a more direct conversation between artists and fans. The thing that drove me and my peers into the music business was a desire to participate in rock culture. It's a culture you've been consuming your entire life and people want to participate—that drive is an important thing to reckon with. I don't think people are purely selfish. They will pay for things if they think they're getting something of value. I also feel like artists need to find ways to demonstrate the value that they're bringing to the community.

This reminds me of a similar conversation that's been had regarding NPR and the National Endowment of the Arts. It's a question that now hangs above rock culture, "Why should taxes go to this? Why should my money go to this?" It's kind of a liberal conceit. I don't know, maybe private individuals stop paying and it goes back to benefactors. I was talking to a film producer at SXSW and he was lamenting that he got into the film business too late. "No one is buying DVDs," he said. "Yeah, we need to accept the fact that it is changing, we have to accept the fact that we're not rock n' roll anymore. We are jazz."

Maybe those large sums of money that were made just aren't an entitlement, maybe music or film become more like poetry. I'm hoping it won't. There's still some money to be made, just not as much. Today, you have to be a hustler. I think that's one way to look at it. The really serious and talented musicians are in a better position today—and in general musicians are in a better position. I work with a lot of frustrated musicians who see their peers blow up in one album, meanwhile they are on album four, getting a pittance. And I think those frustrated musicians are a little bit wrong in how they think the hyped bands are doing. They aren't getting a ton of money either.

It's tough, man. Dog eat dog. Nobody's entitled to it. If that sounds unsympathetic, it's important for artists to just understand that fact. And labels, too. The music industry is not fair. It's subjective and it's fashion. You have one band who's king of the world one moment and the next one flops. And it's all about how you roll with those punches. Some people resent leaking, piracy… all of it. The happier, healthier industry people I know—rather than taking that curmudgeonly, old-man vibe—if you can survey the reality and make it work for you, you're going to be happier. You'll be having fun, rather than living in this weird fiction.

Leaks are a necessary part of the thing now. Some albums leak too late! We could leak them ourselves, but that feels too weird. You want to perceive that fan and blog chatter. You don't want it to be too early, where the album feels too old by the time it's released. Some bands don't want it to leak, but we explain to them that the leak is important. That leaked record has become part of the ecosystem.

That said, there is definitely the hope on our part that these things will be purchased. I also buy, share files, and have two subscriptions on eMusic. I buy liberally from iTunes and I buy tons of vinyl. Part of it is a sense of duty. I want to support it. I want to be part of the consuming end still—I just think it's important. There's nothing I enjoy more than filing my records or listening to them with friends. I haven't truly enjoyed a record until I've put it in the sleeve and put it away. People strive for high-quality experiences and vinyl feels like the return to a very high-quality experience. You sit in a chair, read the lyrics, look at the artwork and hold it…. There's still that desire among consumers for depth, but you have to fight for it. You have to earn it. And you have to pay for it.

I was seeing a rock show at a small club here recently. I was watching a cluster of fans enjoying the shit out of this band. And I looked over at these fans and thought, "They're not thinking about a critique on the industry or what the digital revolution means—they're just watching three gods on stage making magic." I think that experience for a fan is what this is all about, and it's a constant pursuit to not be jaded or take it for granted.

I feel that jadedness when I see the blogs where all they do is post the album art thumbnail and a link to a free Mediafire download. I think that's scummy. They're not adding anything to the process at all. Critics, for instance, they're not buying music but they're adding something. Those types of blogs want to participate in rock culture in some way but don't add anything to it. I find that annoying. That said, I still download from their sites.

Another thing that annoys me is some pirates' false revolutionary vibe— this anarchy vibe. If those people disappeared, that'd be awesome. To me, as long as you're adding something to the culture, at least that's some argument as to why you should be allowed to put up these links to free albums. But to say that labels and musicians don't deserve to be paid because everything is just 'free' now? That is not much of an argument.

It's easy for people to incrementally justify selfish actions, rationalize things by creating degrees of separation between you and the creator. What they don't realize oftentimes is that there's a great deal of collaboration between the record label and an artist. It's not just funding. Having label support behind you allows artists to focus on being creative, not just shilling with a day job. The creative process usually flows way more smoothly when funding is in place. We share a great deal of dialogue on these projects—we are a team. Oftentimes, the label is actually in the inner circle of creative brain trust with the artist. It's the same thing for book publishers. The publisher is supplying an editor, and that may be the difference between a good book and great book.

The argument is kind of dumb. Go dine and dash—"This restaurant is exploiting the farmer!" Stealing is stealing and I assume the only people who would actually try to make that argument are of weak character. Whether someone thinks that starving artists make better art—it's none of their business! What if it was their family member or them struggling? What if their employer paid them less because they thought hunger made workers more desperate and made them work a little harder? It's arrogant. Either you want it or you don't. And if you want it, you can steal it or pay for it. For people of low character, the deciding factor is whether you'll get caught and that's what the Internet allows. Everyone has their rationalization for stealing—either you want to be a part of the culture or be a parasite upon it. Do you want to contribute or not?

These same folks should keep in mind that 98 percent of bands lose money on tour. They are either losing money and subsidizing it with savings or a day job—they are sacrificing time going on road—or it's being funded by a record label. One of the reasons they can tour is tour support. Only about two percent of bands have a strong enough audience to break even or make something on the road—that's just the truth. It's revolutionary to go on the road and not lose money, because it costs a lot. Also, a lot of bands are making less money and want to be on tour more, which creates a glut in the market. Some big bands who you think are making money actually lose money.

In the future, some musicians will have careers, but there will be room for fewer of them. How much room there will be is dependent upon more people paying for music than are paying now. It will depend on people paying for digital subscriptions—casual listeners spending $15 a month rather than $15 a year.

Things are definitely changing. Bands started to be okay with car commercials ten years ago. I'm not sure why. Maybe the music supervisor for an ad or film used to be a Replacements fan. Maybe old punk rockers got jobs at these companies and used their tastes and improved the products and presentation. Maybe ads became less gross and as tastemaker bands did it, it didn't feel so taboo. At the same time, the DIY universe no longer needed to distinguish itself by the need to be poor. It was no longer a punk rock thing of rich-versus-poor, but more of an aesthetic distinction. Indie was no longer "independent," but based on aesthetic context or listener experience. I mean, Nirvana was the punkest band ever and they didn't compromise their work. Through them, punk was co-opted but everyone saw that it didn't compromise Nirvana's work. Pre-Nirvana, we're talking about 'sellouts.' Post-Nirvana, people realize that some art is more durable than that.

Now, the sentiment is like, "Yeah man, go make some money." People would rather see Neon Indian on a billboard than Fergie. Now, we realize that we can control our culture. We're not outsiders anymore.

THE WRITING WAS ON THE WALL

For the few record labels in the independent world that rose to the levels of a Secretly Canadian, there were dozens, if not hundreds or thousands, of less successful stories. As with Mike Wolf's tale of digital piracy's effect upon Talk Normal, these smaller independent labels with few promotional resources were disproportionately threatened by a mentality on the part of hip digital music fans that paying for their music was now optional because artists no longer needed labels, barely received any money from a purchase, or that pirating an album aided small bands by "promoting" them. New York City label Social Registry was one small label that arguably paid the price for such attitudes.

When I moved to New York City in 2004, I quickly fell in love with Social Registry's urban-psychedelic aesthetic. Bands like Gang Gang Dance, Psychic Ills, Blood on the Wall, and Sian Alice Group blurred the boundaries between accessibility and experimentalism. The label seemed more focused on turning the anxieties of modern life into transcendent art than in partying or making money.

All labels need money to survive, though, regardless of their artistic sensibilities. As I began to write and think about digital piracy in Brooklyn, I began picking the brain of another one of the Greenpoint Coffee House's regular customers, Joe Gaer, who happened to be co-owner of Social Registry (also distributed by Secretly Canadian, the Social Registry office was in the same loft building as Matt Wishnow's Insound). Joe came in each day to quietly have an espresso and work on the *New York Times* crossword puzzle, but when I began asking how piracy had affected his business, he had a long list of grievances. Joe visited my apartment in Greenpoint one day to speak at length about the problems facing the independent industry, expressing his frustration with seeing his labor of love suffer from them and his inability to identify potential solutions. Small, critically acclaimed artists and labels were thought to be the resounding winners of file sharing. Joe Gaer dispelled this myth as little more than wishful thinking.

_____

We really started to see a downturn in 2007 or 2008. The writing was on the wall, but we always hoped one of the bands would hit. The bands were doing okay, making some money, but after awhile we realized it just wasn't happening. In 2008, our landlord was going to jack up our rent 50 percent. We were like, "That's insane! We're paying too much for this space already. We're out of here." That office space has been empty ever since.

The Social Registry started in my business partner's apartment, then moved to another apartment, then to the office space, and now it's back to the original apartment. If the label had had one relatively well-received album we could have cushioned through it. But the attention of the label was always more than what the sales figures would have you believe. We have a lot of critics and a lot of fans, but the vast majority of people got their music for free. That's basically what it comes down to. The label was hurt buy the ability to download music without having to pay for it.

You'd like fans to be supporting the labels but it's what the music industry has turned into, a situation in which you can get music for free. Kids who have grown up with it, they have no intention to pay. They assume they aren't doing anything by taking it for free, but they're destroying the industry as it is. But what can you do about it? The music industry has done a number of nasty things to their own fans, and that's coming back to hit them. There's an App on Google phones where you can scan the barcode and it will search the Internet to find a free download and will download to your home computer in about three minutes. That is the point to which we've gotten. This is the stuff I hate: there's one blog in particular where if you go to it on Monday you see links to download every single indie release. It's like, "Wow you're obliterating the chance for anyone to make money from this." It's automatically free. And you can bust them, but someone else is going to put up the exact same stuff.

You can look at the label as a bank in some ways. We're investing in you guys and hopefully we both can profit from it. The reason bands want labels is that they don't have the money to put up for production costs and they don't have the reputation for a distributor to take them on. It's true you can do that stuff for free, but the idea that the label is "over" is only an idea because people have no idea or concept of what happens otherwise.

Let's say, two years ago, if you were a major music critic you probably got 150 to 200 CDs a week, and a lot of those are from labels. So, if you're somebody that has no label? The chance that anyone will listen to your music is close to nil. Labels are an editor. We look for what's out there. We find these things. We pick what we think are the best ones and put them out. And hopefully you trust our taste enough to at least give it a listen. That's what it comes down to. Otherwise, there's just too much for the average person to sift through.

So, go to the Internet. "Let's go to the Internet store and look under the section for artist names that start with M. Oh, there's 5 million names here!" How in the world can you separate one from the other?

The labels themselves are editors, finding what they think is popular or in some ways imposing what they think is popular. But the idea that piracy is going to get rid of that—the chaos that erupts when they disappear really isn't good for the artist. New bands—how are they going to get people to know who they are? I'm not saying it can't happen. If you want to do the crapshoot we'll see what happens. Ingrid Michaelson, some important person heard her on MySpace and about a year later she's playing Webster Hall. If you hear her music, there's nothing heinous about it, but it isn't anything unique from what a thousand other singer-songwriters are doing. There's nothing special about her, so that game is just a crapshoot. If you think indie artists are going to be helped out by a level field, think of what that's like in reality. In reality, if you're trying to see what's out there, with the label apparatus you look out and see peaks and valleys. You have some perspective. But if it's flat, you can only see so far until everything becomes nothing. Eventually it all merges together and you are lost.

People have to realize when they pirate songs that they're not just taking money out of the label's pocket, but taking money from the artist's pocket too. Why are people going to invest money into an artist's career if there's no hope of making money? A lot of well-known bands still have day jobs, but fans don't want to hear about that stuff.

Artists definitely need income. That excuse about money dirtying art, so art should be free—that's just full of shit. That's an idiotic thought as far as I'm concerned. There's no doubt that money changes what people do all the time. Money also gives opportunities to do things you never could have done before! The idea that getting rid of money is going to make bands any better is hilarious. You can hear the difference between hearing a band's demos and what they can do with some recording money behind them, with a real studio. I'm not saying it's always better, but you can hear the difference. And if a band is *making money from music, that means they can make more of it, rather than "I gotta go to my job, then go to my second job and then practice."*

The anarchic idea that, "Oh you take away the monetary system and everything will be, like, groovy"—it's just not true! There's always gonna be a hierarchy, no matter what. Okay, no money for music, no money to artists, painters, sculptors.... The idea that all of a sudden there'd be all this new art? No, there wouldn't be! People are doing as much as they can already. There's plenty of people who are artists who make money and they make complete schlock, but they make it only because people are willing to pay for it.

I don't see any way that you can guarantee a music industry even of the size we have now unless some miracle happens where people are forced to stop file sharing or start buying directly from the labels and musicians. Bands like Radiohead can go out and do whatever they feel like. New bands can say, 'Pay what you want!' Most fans are going to pay zero.

They have no loyalty.

THIS IS ABOUT CREATIVITY AND ART

The potential for direct connections between artist and fan that the Internet offers inspired a renewed conversation about the potential for DIY: Do-It-Yourself. Artists could supposedly build their own careers, using little more than PayPal and a Twitter account. So long as the music was good, it was argued, anyone could do it.

One concert promoter in Brooklyn earned the brand of DIY more than any other. His name is Todd Patrick, but within the music scene, he is known as Todd P. Todd moved to New York City in 2001 and began setting up concerts for up-and-coming or unknown punk, hardcore, pop, electronic, noise, and experimental acts in empty loft spaces and in the back rooms of Brooklyn dive bars. Over time, his website (toddpnyc.com) became a go-to spot for people who wanted to see new or emerging artists in unconventional, DIY performance spaces. As media outlets like the *New York Times* and MTV began covering Todd, his reputation as an indie rock kingmaker grew. Bands like Wavves, Best Coast, Vivian Girls, Matt and Kim, Dan Deacon, Deerhunter, High Places, No Age, and Vampire Weekend all crossed the threshold of Todd P-promoted shows and landed record deals with respected independent labels, built careers for themselves, and even found popular success.

Todd P shows were a touchstone for my own early years of exploring Brooklyn's cultural scene. In his mid-thirties and fighting a few grey hairs, Todd struck me as a serious music fan, a hard worker, and an honorable idealist. The first time I met him was in 2005, at the Asterix Art Space, a second floor communal living and event space between the lumber yards and supply warehouses of East Williamsburg. I was there to interview a since-disbanded psych-rock group named Gris Gris. I showed up to the space a few minutes before the show was slated to begin. In other words, much too early. The dingy, railroad style space was empty, except for a couple of young folks canoodling on a ratty sofa. I waked past them to find Todd Patrick working alone in the next room, kneeling on the floor amidst a rat's nest of sound cables, surrounded by amplifiers. By the time I finally obtained my interview, after the show was finished at around 3:30 in the morning, the space was again deserted. As I walked out, I found Todd in the same position, breaking down that which he had built up, a ritual he no doubt had repeated hundreds of times.

"You get your interview?" he asked, smiling.

At another Todd P show, at Bushwick's Market Hotel, I watched Todd deal with all-out chaos. On the bill were the hardcore group Aids Wolf, punk rockers Titus Andronicus, and the infamously rowdy garage rock revivalists Black Lips. The crowd was young, drunk, and drugged—potential problems for Todd's shows in unsanctioned spaces, which could be raided by the NYPD on any given night. Before Titus Andronicus took the stage, Todd appeared before about four hundred young scenesters to politely ask them to walk around the block if they went outside, because clusters around the door attracted attention from the NYPD. When he also reminded everyone to smoke their cigarettes in the back room of the space rather than the main room, boos rang out from the audience. I was struck by this expression of nihilistic, superficial rebellion. The crowd was heckling the very person who had organized the show for them. Todd seemed completely unfazed by it. Later on, as the Black Lips played, I watched from the back of the room, where the members of Titus Andronicus sang along to "Dirty Hands" and fell over one another, wasted. A shirtless twenty-year-old, probably on ecstasy, suddenly hugged or tackled me from behind. Once I realized what was happening, I pushed him off of me and he stumbled on into the sweaty, festering, hedonistic crowd. In less than a minute the shirtless kid had climbed onto the stage. Now he was harassing the band members, who, even with their reputation of vomiting and performing fellatio on stage, seemed a little taken aback by his presence.

"Is Todd here? Todd!?" their singer Cole asked from the microphone. "We really need some water up here."

Todd was nowhere to be seen and the crowd was in their own glorious world of celebratory self-destruction. Standing alone near the back and having my full wits about me, I walked to the back room and found Todd talking to one of his interns, unaware of the situation. I told him about the plea for water and he snapped into action, fighting through the damp crowd to bring a few bottles of Poland Spring onstage. All this for Todd's stated goal of providing cheap all-ages concerts for the NYC music scene and providing spaces for new bands to play. Months later, Market Hotel was raided repeatedly by the police and shut down. Todd began an initiative to turn the space into a non-profit community arts center, which he finally succeeded at in 2012.

I spoke with Todd at a café just a few blocks from Market Hotel in the Bushwick neighborhood of Brooklyn, where many of the artists that "pioneered" Williamsburg and Greenpoint for later gentrification had fled to for its cheaper rents and sense of possibility. Over coffee, looking out the window to a pothole ridden Myrtle Avenue and a brightly lit 99-cent store across the street, I asked Todd, so enmeshed within the burgeoning realities for young musicians, for his thoughts on digital piracy and its consequences. Was the tag of DIY, given to him and the artists he worked with, appropriate? As he did personify many of the ethics of early punk culture, which eventually morphed into the concept of indie rock, I was also curious what he thought of the corporate branding and sponsorship that seemed to be playing an increasingly important role in "independent" music, anathema to both "independents" and major artists of the '80s and '90s.

Almost no one goes anywhere with their bands. You'll spend three years ramping up to getting somewhere, if you're lucky. It'll go somewhere for maybe three to five years, but you'll spend some of that time and a couple years afterward in a depressing decline where nobody gives a shit about you. And you start thinking about going to real estate school. In that time, you probably dropped out of college and you don't have any insurance at all. You haven't saved shit, because when you were in the middle of that, when you were making $300,000 a year, you financed something or made a bunch of crazy purchases, like that gravy train was going to last forever. But it doesn't.

The label support is usually what pushes people over that line of success— it's true. I've seen people who were complete unknowns be signed to a hot shot label of some kind, get the right publicist, and they are suddenly something that everyone pretends to have been into. That certainly was the case with No Age. That certainly was the case with Prince Rama, who suddenly got label interest from Animal Collective's label and now they're a big deal. A lot of times you find someone doing something interesting who's not been noticed and you start to work with them thinking it would be cool for the band to get a legit, sincere following. But then, before anything else happens, they're managing their career because they've been inundated by all the levels of indie-management bullshit.

The indie system has become a lot more like the old Majors, which is good and bad. It's good because it brings more professionalism into how people move forward. The people making decisions are people who have too office-y lives to really be engaged in the culture. Though you can argue that there is no "counter-culture" anymore. There is no "underground." It's really just a different flavor of the product. But hey, there are great products in the world that are wonderfully made. Music being considered as such isn't necessarily a bad thing.

From my point of view—I see myself as a businessperson—there's a challenge to creating sustainable change through the landscape that exists, which is the process of generating income… using that to change the world. Can you do that in a way that is not predatory, evil or suffocating to the art form? I think that if you really want to make a point, the way to do it is to prove you can do things right, without having to be a martyr.

The non-profit model that's paid through the community by taxes or by wealthy individuals is one model. But I'm more excited in opening a for-profit club to show that you can do this in the right way. And my agenda is the fan paying less money, the club can make money, and the artist can make more money. 'Cause what we really have is a monopolistic system in this live scene. The players are a very small group of people who have a lot of collusion and work to drive up prices. So, there's an activist moment and agenda moment for me to prove they're ripping people off by starting a venture that makes more money by charging less money. And the beauty of the marketplace is that those guys have to lower their prices, or they go out of business.

Whether music is more or less commercial in the wake of piracy, I think it's a wash. Partly more, partly less. You look at a scene like Canada or New Zealand, they consume a whole lot of American culture but have very strict content laws. If you're a broadcaster in Canada, you have to play 75 percent Canadian music. A&R guys have to look harder to find that 75 percent content to fill the airwaves. So, it's possible to be a household name there while being smaller and maybe less shiny and less fake. In this country, you're not getting on the radio, you're not getting on the TV, unless you're created in a lab, unless a board room came up with you. But up in Canada, Broken Social Scene, Feist, and Arcade Fire are basically winning Grammys.

Because of the media blackout of anything real or sincere or grassroots in this country, a lot of artists will say, "Fuck it, I'm going to make what I want to make," or something closer to it. Whereas up in Canada, you see talented, intelligent people making watered down art and they do it because the urge and temptation is so great. I think that's starting to be true here, but it's not because of content laws, it's because of the direct connection bands now have through the

Internet to their audience. It makes it much easier to see what gets attention, and they can then pander to that.

When we talk about punk or indie, most of this music used to appeal—and I say this from experience—to social misfits of suburban America. People growing up in high school and college who were too smart for their own good, too interested in intellectualism to be socially effective. This music was a way for people to feel less alone. It wasn't always heavy or serious. Sometimes it was a lot of fun. Bands like Pavement or Dinosaur Jr were fun and irreverent. It became a way for those kids to find themselves. It was an identity thing—that's what subculture always is. But the great thing about this subculture is that it was intelligent and intellectual and literate. The problem now is that I don't think kids suffer the same variety of alienation that maybe defined post-war America for most of us. To most kids today, their social life—especially the more nerdy and awkward you are—hugely takes place on the Internet or on your phone, so I don't think kids feel alone in their tastes for too long. I'm not saying they can't still find themselves through music, but they can't lay any claim to its obscurity. They can't believe, "This is my thing no one else knows about it and this is me." No one defines it that way anymore because it's too easy to get. There's nothing romantic about finding things on the Internet.

I think one of the worst things a band can do today is be forced to tour for a year-and-a-half straight without any breaks. It's a terrible idea and the reason bands do it is… the moment they're asked to do it is the same moment they get "big." Their first "bump" moment in popularity. At that moment, everyone descends upon them. The label, publicist, booking agent, management… Those people don't think—and I'm being very sincere—they don't think that band is gonna last more than a year and a half so they want to squeeze as much out of them as they possibly can. And the band, of course, just got bumped up to being big and they're like, "Shit, I don't know what to do next. These guys are insiders. They're giving me good advice."

The musicians who are really savvy, you see them making more and more boring music. The reason—though not across the board—is because of that "I'm a little businessman" mentality. Everyone is their own cottage industry now. You've also got these little boutique marketing companies who convince big corporate behemoths, "We can take your product and make this cool!" And that means things like the Scion phenomenon. Somehow I haven't seen any hipsters driving Scions. The strategy is to convince middle-America that hipsters are driving Scions by showing how much cool art Scion is involved in, then convincing people, who secretly follow anything hipsters do, of that appearance of influence.

Bands can just say, "But we don't make any money selling records anymore. We have to do this Scion ad." True? Not true? Who's to say?...

Regardless, I have seen the advent of this corporate money starting to be something that makes bands cater. As savvy as corporate marketers may be compared to fifteen years ago, they're still not that savvy. They will approach a band and they'll be like, "We really love you guys. That one hit song you have is great!" They have no idea about the band's back catalogue. Because they have to be up on so many trends, they only know about the one catchy song. These corporate people appreciate you as a two-dimensional cartoon character. So to stay in favor with those people is an even bigger compromise.

You know, FADER magazine is really Cornerstone Promotions. VICE magazine is really Vice Marketing. Both of those magazines exist to demonstrate their marketing savvy and cultural cache, not to be great magazines. The point is to have a following so they can point and say, "See? You should hire us, Colt 45." Colt 45 and Scion are both clients of Vice Marketing. I've met those people. They're not the savviest people in the god damned world. But it doesn't matter if they're the savviest people, because they're the only ones, frankly, who are cheap enough to do that work.

I don't talk about "sellout" and shit in those really old-fashioned terms. It's about a practical effect on artistic output. On a practical level of business, I think these things are corrosive and I've definitely seen a lot of people—coincidence or not—get more boring after taking that money. And it's not just being in commercials or video games or writing jingles. It's about being flown in to play events that are basically product launch events. That's a huge part of a lot of people's income now. To me that's even more like, "Let me buy your subculture. Let me buy your audience base. We really want them to come out and dig this."

When we have a new starlet actor coming up, someone we take seriously as an actor—ten years ago and we're talking about Juaquin Phoenix—and let me also say that acting is definitely the lowest form of art in the world. I mean, sure, it's art. But Hollywood acting? It's the most compromised of all art forms. Anyway, if Joaquin Phoenix ten years ago had started appearing in ads for Coca-Cola, we'd have looked down on him. Movie stars have to fly to Japan to make money doing commercials that way. We don't let those guys sell out. We consider it cheap. It would ruin their career.

How is that true in a Hollywood world where there is zero integrity—none—and yet music made by small groups of people who are not wealthy, are not world renowned, have very little power and authority—it's not selling-out when they're doing it? I think that's a very opportunistic attitude on the part *of consumers, musicians, labels, and especially those marketing companies. And to say it doesn't compromise their art is to be lying.*

All commercialism compromises art—you can't get around it. It's a capitalist system, period. I'm not fighting that. I'm not a Marxist. But some commercialism is really egregious. It's one thing to play live shows and charge money, it's another thing to play live shows only in casinos and charge $200. You see the difference. One is cheap and tacky and clearly not about art on any level. The other is doing a reasonable amount of commerce that supports the work you're making. I wouldn't say all commercial appearances are bad. I wouldn't say that playing in a sponsored festival is bad. I'm not some purist.

People used to be way too doctrinaire in saying it was or wasn't selling out. I mean, Jesus, when Yoko sold "Revolution" to Nike in 1987 people were fucking pissed off.[1] The Beatles! The most commercial, richest musicians on earth. McCartney is a billionaire. We've gone way more the other direction. It's interesting to me that nobody else is talking about this—and I mean nobody.

It is about taste. The shit is tacky and crass and I don't think it has to have a deeper ideology than that. To me that's a strong enough argument. This is about creativity and art. You don't see branding in art museums. You might see sponsorship. You don't see branding in art galleries. You just don't see it in other forms. Why is it so accepted in music?

The reason is that people feel guilty about downloading.

ANGRY ARMCHAIR QUARTERBACKS

Yeasayer represented a band on an independent label trying to turn debut album buzz into a career-sustaining audience, but I also sought the perspective of an independent band that was a few albums deep and had found that sustaining, if not gargantuan, audience. Fortunately, the streets of Greenpoint offered me another band that fit the bill: The Hold Steady.

The Hold Steady, a group of Minneapolis musicians who had moved to New York City in the early 2000s, formed in 2003 in an attempt to recapture the unapologetic fun and bombast of classic rock, the spirit of which members Craig Finn, Tad Kubler, Bobby Drake, and Gailen Polivka had found sadly lacking in the fashions of independent rock. The group's ambitions were limited to playing shows in and around New York until their second album, *Separation Sunday*, became one of the most critically-acclaimed rock albums of 2005. The band moved from their label French Kiss to the larger independent label Vagrant Records for their next albums, *Boys And Girls In America, Stay Positive,* and *Heaven Is Whenever.* Along the way, the band performed on *The Late Show With David Letterman* and *The Colbert Report,* and lead singer Craig Finn, who released a solo album in 2012, became something of an icon within the sphere of "indie rock." Finn introduced himself to the world as a normal thirty-something guy in glasses with thinning hair, and fans adored him for it. Finn juxtaposed his unlikely-rock-star appearance with live demonstrations of sheer exuberance each night on stage. He spat and shouted out his lyrics. Standing behind the microphone, he spastically shot out his arms like an untrained cheerleader, overwhelmed with rock spirit.

Craig Finn and I met at Café Grumpy in Greenpoint one afternoon, and then walked through the pouring rain to his apartment nearby. He spoke from the couch in his sparely decorated living room, between taking incoming calls from The Hold Steady's manager and record label as they finalized the release of their album, *Heaven Is Whenever*. Like some other musicians, Finn had accepted the fact that, for many people, music was now "free" and nothing could be done about it. Yet he continued to put out new records through Vagrant and showed disgust with those who share files, then try to rationalize their actions as being somehow righteous.

When iTunes came out and became a robust thing it fit my needs way more than Napster did. I don't mind paying $10 for a record and I definitely don't mind paying 99 cents for a song. To buy a song for 99 cents seems like, you know, leave a tip for your drink.

As an artist, it's not so much the file sharing I think about but the leaks. It's an applicable time to talk about it, because we're working hard on the artwork and the credits for our new album right now. It's six months of culmination and the past couple of weeks we've been listening to the record and having these passionate arguments about the sequencing. You want to unveil what you've been working on to your audience. So, to have a couple of tracks leak, people getting six out of ten songs, listening to them in any order... I don't know, I have a hard time respecting the mindset of, "I need it now!" You know? Or that "I had it first" mentality.

I remember the last time we put out a record and it leaked. There was a blog where some kid, probably, posted the first review of the record. He was very proud of the first review of Stay Positive *and... so, you downloaded this leak and you listened to it and spouted off this review. And yeah, you're first, but in this application, is "first" of any value? What about the most thought-out? What about the best written? First is good for an Olympic race. I'm not sure how it relates to art.*

It took six months to make the record. For some of these songs, I remember writing the lyrics as much as a year ago. So to have it all consumed like a McDonald's cheeseburger, like, "Okay, checked it off my list. It's on my iPod so I'm done with it." It's almost like people want to capture it rather than experience it.

There's this weird—I think about it but I can't really put words to it— there's an emotion that's out there that's almost angry. You know? The tone of some Internet journalists. "Oh, I got the new Spoon record and the production's shit!" And it's like, "What? You're a seventeen-year-old kid. You're failing out of your freshman year in college. What do you know about production?"

There's definitely this armchair quarterback thing that the Internet has brought out. And it's not just with the music but with the industry, too. "Well if the industry hadn't charged $17 for CDs…" That's the thing that infuriates me, this kid in his dorm room in Kansas saying that the music industry is run by a bunch of idiots. 'Cause I know the people who work at my record label and they're really smart, passionate people. They're not "music industry idiots." The technology has changed and they're trying to adapt in a way that's fair to both the fans and to the artists. They're not idiots and they're not abusing expense accounts. They're not exploiting the artists. They are working people.

I never post comments to articles or blogs on the Internet. I find that most people I know and respect don't, and haven't, and wouldn't. The people who do, I question what they're doing with the rest of their time. So the angry people in front of their computers skew everything because their voices are going to be heard loudly. The people who are making records are busy making records. Also, I think if you took any music blog and looked at their comments or read a message board, what percentage of those people are in some ways artists themselves? How many of those guys have a band that they're trying to get booked at Maxwell's?[1] There's definitely a part of it that seems like sour grapes.

I don't think a lot of those people understand how difficult it can be to establish yourself as a full-time musician. What happened to me—and I'm almost positive that it happens with most bands that have to work for a living—I became "unemployable" before I was making a living with music. Meaning, I was taking so much time off for gigs that I couldn't sustain a job. So there was sort of a leap of faith that we all had to make.

It was right after our album Separation Sunday. *I think that came out in April and was getting crazy reviews. By the fall, I was pretty much unemployable. I had a really cool CEO at my company who was bending over backwards to make it work, but it wasn't fair to the other employees to let me leave and come back again and again.*

It was a leap of faith, like, "If we go for this we can float it at least until it stops." We played hundreds of shows that year and I think all of us went through scary, rough times. Funny thing is, from the outside, there is an idea of the record label handing you a check, you put it in the bank, you quit your job…. But in this day and age no one is selling enough records for that to work.

I think there were also personal things wrapped in to why that period was a struggle. I was married at the time and I'm no longer married. "Scary times," meaning quitting your job with the idea that hopefully you've got a couple months you can survive for. Hopefully, if you stay on the road, the shows will keep getting bigger and you can keep touring and it will be sustainable, because every record has a cycle and you can't just keep touring. You have to go back, write a record, record an album—in which case you're not getting that income from the road. I gave up my apartment and stopped paying rent for a couple of months 'cause I was just going to be on the road, but then I had to figure out a place to land when the tour ended. I'm thirty-eight years old and I got this place in May of this year. The four years before that, I was renting a bedroom in a house with three other roommates. It wasn't really how I imagined I'd turn thirty-six, but it was all part of the sacrifice.

In the end, it's all about priorities, you know? It's something I chose to do and obviously something that I want to do. I've known people in bands, especially back in Minneapolis, who would say, 'Well, we can't really tour 'cause we have real jobs.' But that's your choice. The reason why I can tour isn't because I can't get a real job; it's because this is what I want to do. It's certainly what I've chosen, so I wouldn't want anyone to feel bad about it, but it is absolutely something that isn't always comfortable.

When we started, we put our record out through French Kiss which is a vibrant indie label and still is. Then we went on Vagrant after Separation Sunday *and it was really just so we could make the record the way we wanted to—to spend the time from an artistic standpoint. It was really just the recording that they could help us more with. There were things that* Vagarnt *could do that we hadn't thought of. Stuff like retail marketing, getting your record in Best Buy. That makes a big difference. Talking to the armchair quarterbacks out there, there is an art and a science to what labels do. I don't profess to understand it, but there are people who do a good job at it and that can be the difference between 20,000 and 60,000 records sold. Vagrant helps us to make the record as good as it can possibly be. Labels absolutely still provide a lot of investment and a lot of support.*

I don't know if doing things in a truly DIY fashion is possible. There's this whole other class of musicians that are sort of post-label. Like Radiohead. You get the benefits of being on a robust major label for five albums, then you have a chance to go out on your own. That's very different from a guy who's nineteen and just starting out with no money or audience. In all of this, it needs to mentioned that we're a five-piece band. That's five mouths to feed and five rents. A singer-songwriter acoustic guitar dude could easily do it, I think. A five-piece band is gonna have a much harder time.

I really don't understand why people are angry at record labels. People pump up the idea of Touch and Go and these labels with 50/50 deals.

Then there are these more major label deals when you're paid a small royalty but the same expenses aren't included. In my experience, they end up roughly the same. In 50/50 deals you start to see line items like, "These are our office expenses, divided by our total number of releases, applied to your release." I think a label, at least in an ideal situation, is excited about music and is there to support you. They have expenses and mouths to feed, too. I think a fan or someone who is pirating music has absolutely nothing to do with that—it has to do with the artist and the deal they sign.

I don't know why the angry armchair quarterbacks would pick this issue. I mean, what about credit card companies or auto financing? Are you mad about them? Should we be taking them down, too? When you buy a Dell computer do you need to know their deal with Intel? Music is being separated from the rest of commerce. When you a buy a painting do you need to know what the artist paid for the canvas? Say Lost—lots of indie rock people watch Lost—I never hear any discussion of what their deal with ABC is. Or, "That actor just renewed his contract so his parts don't seem as believable." They are able to enjoy that and suspend themselves in a way that they aren't able to in music. It doesn't seem like the terms of Death Cab For Cutie's deal with their record label should matter. Either I like their music or I don't. I have a hard time wrapping my head around that. There's an illusion of more awareness about the industry among consumers today, but I'm not sure if there actually is more awareness.

Or this thing, like, "If the labels had only made a deal with Napster..." Everyone's got an answer for how to change the record industry, but I'm not sure what they think they would do. As if the music industry is so lazy, but I don't see where these people are working. It's not like someone pirating music is being so proactive.

I get way more upset with the discourse around piracy than with people who take my music, because the people talking about it are usually such idiots. If someone buys my record and rips it for ten of their friends, I'd be excited for their enthusiasm for the record. But if they went online and talked about how they're going to pirate the album because Vagrant is ripping us off anyway, then I'd just want to kill them. The self-righteous justification drives me crazy.

It's funny, because people get more hung-up on artists having money, meanwhile there doesn't seem to be any sort of stigma anymore as far as selling-out. If I had to guess I'd say the lack of record sales has made artists more amenable to licensing their music. Now that we've seen so much of it, we just accept it. It seems true that corporations and brands are probably going to provide more and more support to art and music. Modest Mouse had this photo book—they got this sunglasses company, RAEN Optics, to do it. I don't know what this sunglasses company got out of it, but it's a really cool thing and I enjoyed looking at the book. The fact that it said "RAEN Sunglasses" on the last page? I don't really care. And now I know there's a sunglasses company called "RAEN" and they like Modest Mouse too, so they must be cool. And there's fake blood all over the photo book, so it's not exactly safe. Then again, that's probably what the company is going for—that's the image they're trying to build. And here I am talking about this company I never would have heard of otherwise.

Cigarette companies can't advertise as much as they used to, but they have marketing budgets that are still pretty big and they throw that money around. I don't know how many people they can actually turn into smokers, but I'm glad they rented out my friend's bar, because he made a whole bunch of money from it. We've done a lot of sponsored shows, mostly for alcohol companies. We've done a bunch of shows for Jim Beam, Jack Daniel's, Southern Comfort… It's funny because two days later we can never remember what liquor it was for. It's just a normal show for us.

No matter how we do it, it's definitely crucial for artists to be able to make some money. It allows you to focus on what you're doing. I don't mean money at the Madonna-level, I mean the sustenance level. It allows you to take your work seriously and function as an artist.

In politics it's way easier to be conservative if you have something to conserve. I see how Metallica might have looked at Napster as taking something away. While I do think the industry is filled with smart people trying to come up with a reasonable solution, I'm less alarmed because so little of our money comes from sales. There's this movie, Festival Express. They film a tour with The Band and The Dead and Janis Joplin. It is 1970 or something. The first show goes fine, but at the second show all the students are demonstrating that the music should be free and they shouldn't charge anything for the show. Now, that would infuriate me. That would hit me where it hurts and I'm sure I'd have a very different reaction.

COMMON GROUND

It would be difficult to imagine the independent music scene without Matador Records, which gave us luminaries like Pavement, Liz Phair, Guided By Voices, Interpol, and Yo La Tengo. The same can be said of 4AD Records, home to The Pixies, Cocteau Twins, and Throwing Muses. Rough Trade Records buoyed the careers of The Smiths, The Slits, and The Strokes. XL Recordings dominates the contemporary independent music industry with artists like Vampire Weekend, MIA, The XX, and 2011 success story Adele. True Panther Sounds, only in operation since 2004, is supporting new crop of bands, like Girls, Unknown Mortal Orchestra, and Glasser. These labels, with their cumulative histories and continuing impact upon music culture, today share office space, ownership, and distribution under the umbrella of Beggars Group.

As a confessed fanboy of labels like Matador, it was a bit surreal to sit in the Beggars Group offices in Tribeca in the late winter of 2011, waiting to speak with the company's vice president of marketing, Adam Farrell. When Adam met me in the office conference room, he fit the role of "guy who works at a cool record label": ripped t-shirt, closely cropped dirty blond hair and an easygoing demeanor. My time with Adam was enlightening, as he offered a comprehensive take on where the music industry had gone wrong, what the value of record labels was in the age of rampant piracy, the prospects for emerging models for music consumption, and why Beggars Group was finding success in a period when most independent and major labels were struggling.

———————

The thing the music industry did—the mistake was to reapply the rules. They thought it was a new format and they could take it over and make money from it, but all they did was create this global game of whack-a-mole. I think the biggest mistake was taking 25 million people that were actively engaged in music and dispersing them. They let loose a virus, in a way.

They should have figured out some way of licensing it, but there are still problems with that today. Labels don't want to license to Spotify right now. There's the problem of going from analog dollars to digital pennies—it is a reality that most companies can't get their head around. It's a shift that's going to require some patience. Unfortunately, music labels went from being owned by music guys to being owned by finance guys who just aren't going to wait three quarters to see a profit.

The ability to make the natural way people consume and behave online work for you is a challenge, because you can't control it. The music industry was built upon control. But for labels like us, there's a tremendous flip side to this. Music discovery is chaotic and unknowable. For Beggars, the thing we focus on is putting good stuff out there and hopefully the cream rises to the top. As opposed to the '90s, where you could ship a million records if you had enough money, you could have a top-ten hit if you had enough money to control those channels. And that just doesn't work with new technologies online. So the Majors started suing people because they wanted to make examples of fans and instill fear. At the time, the general consensus of consumers was, "There's gotta be some way that downloading this free music is all right." When I first used Napster, I remember being at my computer and thinking, "This has to be okay, somehow." But absolutely, it is theft. It is a violation.

An artist comes to us with this thing they've created, right? And they, for the most part, are horrified when it leaks. I don't know where this started, this idea of artists making albums just so they can go on tour to sell merchandise. I don't know one artist that thinks that way, I really don't. They care about the way an album is sequenced. They care about when you flip from the a-side to the b-side, how the album transitions. They care about the artwork. They take pride—and we take pride—in our ability to sell something that people don't have to buy. It blows my mind every week that we are able to sell something that people don't have to buy.

The last few years have been incredibly strong for us. Not only as far as revenue but also profit margins and relative marketing costs. We're sitting in a meeting for the finance board for Beggars and the finance guy says, "You should be spending more on digital marketing!" The reality is, you don't have to do that much money-wise. There's no co-op for iTunes—they don't charge for positioning. It's not like Target where you're spending $50,000 to be in their circular. I find that very interesting, because our business is growing and it is growing in a more profitable way. For us, occupying this world where we are selling to people who buy 25-30 albums a year, they go to Amoeba at least twice a month and walk out with four records. This whole thing works very well for us. Just putting out good music and not relying on commercial radio to sell records. It's not even part of the mix. I had a meeting last week and a guy said, "I think we can do something with commercial radio." We didn't even know how to talk about it. It was like, "What do we do?"

The business is super-healthy. We're getting more songs in film and TV. Revenues shifted from 40 percent performance (commercial licensing, placement in film, streaming) and 60 percent sales to the other way around. The way things work now benefits someone like us. And, sure, we have our gripes. It's a pain in the ass when an album leaks early and throws your promo plan askew. The free full-album downloads are a bummer, but at the end of the day, if you want free music you can get it. Who are we going to fight? We'd much rather focus our efforts on the people who buy music and enrich that experience, make it better for them, care about them so that they don't get disenfranchised.

With blogs, we try to have an open dialogue with them. "We've put out this single as a free MP3—totally cool to post—but we'd like you to keep it to that." Initially we got some resistance because blogs were like, "We just wanna write about songs we love." It's like, "All right, but if everyone did that then you'd just have the whole album out there. Do you support us? Are you with us or are you against us?" I think most were like, "Well, we understand." In exchange, we don't really fuck with them.

Today there's such a premium placed on newness that it's tough if you're a band that's five or six albums deep. It's hard to get that attention. And people say, "Oh! Music discovery is so fluid" and blah, blah, blah. I talk to people at small labels and they say it's fucking impossible to get noticed, even by music blogs. You have access to everything today, but because music discovery has become so chaotic, it's almost forced people to focus on this subset of artists that are so-called in "our" world. It's fascinating to me because, in the '70s, the radio sultans came in and said, "You can't just play the forty top songs, you have to micro-serve your audience. People can't pay attention. You'll have much more stickiness if you pare it down to twenty songs." So they moved to playing twenty songs with a power rotation of ten songs, which is kind of where we've gotten today. You could almost say the same thing is happening today with Pitchfork and the likes of Stereogum. They super-serve a certain kind of thing. If your album has been produced by the bass guitarist in Grizzly Bear, you'll have a lot of attention paid to you. If you don't have an easy way into that discussion, it's a pretty hard world to penetrate.

As for piracy, there's almost a need for a moral obligation or higher calling. To say that music is like a garden—if we don't care for it, it's gonna wither and die off. The world will be an uglier place. I think if we're not developing another generation that has appreciation for arts and culture, then we are fucking out of business. You're only gonna have a Katy Perry, a Taylor Swift and a Black Eyed Peas. You're not going to have anyone coming up who is interesting. You're not gonna have the superstars that take five or six albums to develop. I mean, how many albums did it take REM to break through? How many albums did it take U2? These are big, huge bands and it took time for them to develop. Probably only The National have developed like that—sold 5,000 copies, then 20,000, and then had a breakthrough album four albums in.

Bands are absolutely making more money on the road. If you're selling 20,000 records, you're not getting a ton of money off of that. The problem is that we've created a real glut in the market of bands who can play the Bowery Ballroom—we've created all these blog buzz bands that can get 500 people to sell out the Bowery before their album even comes out. It's hard to make money on tour, so you've got to get above that 500-capacity room to play bigger rooms before you can make much money, and you need a record label to get above that point. Bands that get a ton of buzz—most of those bands aren't making a ton of money, especially now. Last year (2010) was the year of the reckoning and this is the one of reality. You'll see less $42 tickets to see Jonsi.[1]

For us, recorded music and live music are more in alignment. For a few years, you could put any band out there and they'd sell out Webster Hall,[2] but that's no longer the case. There's been a huge correction. I do know that a lot of the bands that we work with make a pretty good living—with what we offer their live business, the merch, and stuff like that. There are the elite ones: The National, The New Pornographers, Belle and Sebastian. I think they are making a really good living. But they also do it worldwide—they can tour everywhere. We have a worldwide network, offices in twenty-seven countries. That's where you really grow the business.

My colleague Nils Bernstein will say that 30,000 in sales is the new 100,000. It's funny, a "Best New Music" designation on Pitchfork, some decent touring in Webster Hall-type rooms, a feature in SPIN, NPR supports you—that's good for about 30,000 in sales. You can almost track it to a 't.'

That's a Titus Andronicus, an Ariel Pink, a Girls...That's about as far as it gets you. After that, you're dealing with more casual fans. Ten years ago 100,000 was that good buzz, the sweet spot. There were probably lots of bands that could sell that number of records then.

We are filters. A record label is fifty percent editorial and fifty percent marketing. We're there to commit to a John Darnielle,[3] who's doing his own thing and touring all right, and see that he's an amazing talent, and take him over the course of five albums to the point where he now has a successful career. He makes money on the road now. He sells his songs in films. He has a career, whereas ten years ago maybe he wouldn't. That's the record label commitment. And now John can go out and get people into Kaki King—he's become part of that editorial voice. That's great for music. And we absolutely pay him royalties. He makes money—he makes most of it on the road—but the experience and promotion we're bringing to his critically-acclaimed albums, I think, he would say is invaluable. If we're not seen as valid by the consumer, if they're not supporting us, then they're not supporting the artist and they're not supporting the whole ecosystem that will give them back more of what they want: good music.

I mean, when was the last time you saw an artist that got any degree of buzz or hype that didn't sign with a label? Clap Your Hands Say Yeah, they made a decision to do it themselves and just sign a distribution deal and for their second album, they just didn't have enough experienced people around. They went with a producer (Dave Fridmann) who turned them into a science project and they didn't make a great record. We think we help artists make great records, but we also make sure the record is heard and bought by as many people as possible.

Look at top-ten, top-twenty, top-thirty best album lists at the end of the year—all of those artists are either on labels or have been snatched up by one. If you look at reader or critic polls as a kind of barometer for what's good, you might find some self-released stuff. There are definitely more artists now doing things by themselves and people say, "Look, you don't need a record label anymore!" But meanwhile, that artist has been on record labels for twenty years with millions and millions of dollars put into their careers.... and now they're "DIY." Radiohead or NIN are bands that have the luxury of not needing a label anymore because they already have a huge fanbase to access. So, the idea that they're doing it "DIY" is kind of bullshit.

The great thing now is there are so many options available to you as an artist. It's not like, "Okay, my career is going to come down to getting a $250,000 advance. I gotta write a single and then I'll have it made for the rest *of my life." There are a number of ways to go about your career. And the same goes for us—there are a number of ways to break an artist.*

We have a lot of heated debates around here about what personal situation makes for an artist doing their best work. My feeling is that a single artist makes their best work—as in not married. I don't know, I think inspiration and songs come from a number of places and I'd never try to boil it down to one factor, especially not money. Take Ariel Pink. He's been a starving artist for a long time and finally we got involved with him and Ariel finally said, 'I want to do it.' He had a recording budget and a marketing budget for the first time and he made an amazing record. He had resources. I definitely think that, with money, some artists can get a little lax. But I've also seen artists get money and then become more focused and goal oriented than they've ever been.

People in this industry get excited about new models that are out there, but I think their potential is a bit overstated. Subscription and streaming services like Spotify, Rhapsody, and Pandora… I think they're just gonna be part of the mix. Again, you're talking pennies. If you can go out and license that consumption and add it up in aggregate then maybe it can be a thing. The reality is that there are two models involved: subscription base and percentage of advertising.

The percentage of advertising is just going to always be limited because music is already so commoditized that the CPMs[4] are really low, on aggregate. So there is a very limited pool of money on that side and that drastically limits the potential of streaming revenues. There's just only a certain amount of money devoted to that stuff via ad budgets on a year-to-year basis.

On the subscription side, the challenge is more related to user experience. These services have been around for a long time now and haven't been terribly successful—it's just not a great user experience. I think Spotify and the likes of Rdio are great but for your average person you still need a pretty good filter to make those things work. You need pretty good editorial to get those things to work. For most people it's pretty daunting. You may think you want music discovery and everything, but paying $10 a month to be daunted is something people won't get excited about.

I think, potentially, an entertainment tax on Internet Service Providers, where we re-imagine music as a utility—I think there's some potential there. But even when they run the numbers on that, it doesn't make up for the decline in sales. Those more passive ways of monetizing the consumption just aren't as substantial as direct sales. At the same time, all these things potentially add up to something. There is no set model anymore. We can have *an artist post a video of them playing a song live. It goes everywhere and a music supervisor comes to us and says they want to put it in a Reese's Pieces commercial. For us, we hope if we just keep putting out good music that the Reese's Pieces person will see it and we'll make some money that way.*

We have an artist who is very punk rock in her ethos and a phone company wanted to license a song for good money. She said no. So our A&R guy asks why and she said, "It fucks with my fans." So we said, "Well, why don't you ask your fans?" She goes on Twitter and says, "Guys this company wants to use my song in a commercial what do you think?" Responses were basically, "Go get yours...You should take it!... Why don't you donate 25 percent to this charity?" The fans don't care anymore. Before, artists worried about the perception of selling-out. "Will my fans abandon me if I do this?" And the reality is, the fans could give a fuck. In the end, she did the ad.

Once putting music in ads becomes common, the stigma goes away. The perception among fans is that sales are down so they think, "I want you to make money and pay your bills." There is some connection there between what's happened with file sharing and this rise in commercial licensing.

Corporations have also gotten savvier and savvier in how they work music into their marketing. Mountain Dew is doing the Green Label Sounds record label thing. Whereas Mountain Dew used to pay $60,000 to license a song for a commercial, now they're putting out an exclusive 7-inch that makes their brand look really cool, for only $5,000. So, what they're telling bands is, "We're going to do all this promotion for it"... blah, blah, blah. But what they're doing is figuring out how to make themselves still look really cool while doing it for cheap.

Today, people idealize erasing the middleman, but we think the middleman is vital. We think the Other Music and Amoebas of the world are vital to create the value of consumption. Any day of the week, I would choose to do anything that benefits independent retail. They are serving a community. They are where music gets real. They promote our shows. It's a place for our fans to get excited about music and talk about it and engage in that community. It's part of the experience for the type of consumer we want. If any of these things go out of business, we're fucked.

In fact, we own the Rough Trade record stores in the UK and over the next year or so we'll probably bring a store here to New York. So we're actually getting more involved in retail as a company—which definitely bucks the trend. It is strange, because everyone says digital is the big thing, and I just spent all that time talking about how the margins on digital are great, but we want to get back into physical retail because we think it serves a great purpose for our business. Target and Best Buy are expensive to get into, but they're still vital. If you want to sell 200,000 copies or 100,000—or even 50,000—you've got to be in those places. The idea that it's all going to be iTunes and digital isn't realistic.

I just think it is important for consumers to hear a guy who works at a label say, "Hey, this is actually okay. There are some companies who are actually doing really well in this period." But the dialogue has been so heated and vitriolic that it's hard to find common ground.

SOMEBODY FED JESUS

As the major label system appeared to be unraveling through the 2000s, and self-satisfied blog commenters counted down the days until the antiquated industry's final collapse, one phenomenon seemed awfully out of place. Despite all the bad vibes and fatalism associated with the "old" music industry, indie artists continued signing record deals with major labels. Artists like Interpol, LCD Soundsystem, Modest Mouse, Yeah Yeah Yeahs, Iron & Wine, and TV On The Radio took their turn in pivoting away from independent labels and digital DIY opportunity, toward the traditional, corporate, major label universe that, in many people's minds, the Internet was supposedly doing away with. What was happening? What calculus was at play when bands that one wouldn't expect to embrace major label culture did just that?

I was admittedly a bit star struck when Kyp Malone walked into the Greenpoint Coffee House during one of my first shifts behind the bar. Kyp played guitar and sang in the Brooklyn-based TV On The Radio, a band that dominated the indie realm through the mid-2000s after critics fell head-over-heels for their debut *Young Liars EP*, released on Touch and Go records in 2003. After their first full-length album, *Desperate Youth, Blood Thirsty Babes,* was released in 2004, the band switched labels, from the beacons of independence at Touch and Go to Interscope Records, a major label home for artists such as Nine Inch Nails, Eminem, and Lady Gaga. The band's first major label release, *Return to Cookie Mountain,* was an artistic triumph, featuring guest vocals from David Bowie and earning them a 2006 Album of the Year designation from *SPIN Magazine.* Their acclaim snowballed with the release of *Dear Science* in 2008. That album garnered nearly unanimous approval as being the best album of the year from *Rolling Stone, SPIN Magazine, The Guardian, Entertainment Weekly*, and MTV, among many others. By the 2011 release of their fifth studio album, *Nine Types of Light,* they had performed on *The Tonight Show, The Late Show With David Letterman, Later With Jools Holland, The Colbert Report,* and *Saturday Night Live.*

TV On The Radio's music was alternately angry and amorous; squalling and soulful; pretty and punk; atonal and accessible. They defined what it meant to be a progressive, pioneering, post-millennial rock band. Anyone who paid attention to contemporary music culture during this period saw the images of TV On The Radio via countless blog posts and magazine features. Kyp's image, in particular, became symbolic of Brooklyn's music scene. As a black musician, he stood out amongst his mostly white indie peers and fans, indie predominantly being the province of white suburbia's anxious children. Kyp cut a powerful, lion-like visage thanks to an incredibly thick beard and puffed-out afro, as if the hair was gobbling up his face from the perimeter on in. Kyp looked unique—certifiable catnip for image obsessed magazine and website editors.

Though I'd been somewhat brainwashed by the reproduction of Kyp's image to see him as more than a regular person, over time I stopped seeing him as a walking magazine cover or rock star. Rather, he was a soft-spoken, affable regular, always ready to talk about music, and in pursuit of new sounds. For myself, and the other staff at the café, he also represented real hope. He too had worked for years at a coffee shop (in Williamsburg) while pursuing totally unrealistic creative pursuits, and ended up "making it" after all. The fact that he made time to ask us how our writing, music, or plays were going validated our sometimes dispiriting days of the service industry. Kyp personified a sense of optimism, that the real, long-term risks we were taking on in pursuit of our creative ambitions were worth it, or might be.

But when I spoke with Kyp in his neighborhood apartment, he hardly painted a rosy picture of artistic success, and obliterated whatever misconceptions remained in my mind as to the glamour of pop life. Music, or any creative enterprise, is a desperate art, even for those who appear to have ridden such work to the apex of cultural power. Given such realities, Kyp was brutally honest about his unexpected journey from artistic obscurity to major label notoriety, the compromises he had to make along the way, and the naiveté of the "pirate mentality."

Being a musician on a major label was never inside my frame of reference. I didn't have a rule against it, but then again it didn't seem remotely plausible that it could happen. I didn't even know what Interscope was—which is kind of ridiculous. It wasn't music I listened to so I didn't have any preconceptions. Touch and Go brought a lot of music to me from my teens on. I didn't really mythologize it, though. I didn't think about "the label."

I certainly am not organized or interested enough in the minutia of the day-to-day of getting a record promoted to do it myself. I don't have the means. I don't have the skills. The reason we ultimately left Touch and Go was because we did the math of what we could potentially expect on a month-to-month basis if we stayed there versus going to a Major. It just was not sustainable to be living in New York while doing what we wanted to do. So, when there was interest, we said that we wanted to go. That didn't happen simply or easily. It was long, protracted, and ugly. A drag, ultimately.

At the end of the day, the differences between the indies and Majors are negligible in that they are trying to do the same essential thing. The big difference is that, with an independent label, when the money is coming in you can see where the chain stops. But Interscope just keeps going up to Universal, which probably is connected to some multi-national corporation that is accountable to stockholders and probably invested in all sorts of things that I'd hate to hear about. That's a huge difference. But I also feel like no one can get clean in dirty water—and we're all in it. In the meantime, I can't download my rent or my daughter's tuition.

I made the leap to being a full-time musician well before that was an advisable thing to do. I stopped working a day job about six months into TV On The Radio—not because we were making any money. I changed my life to accommodate the fact that I wanted to focus on the music and there was a lot of patience on my daughter's mother's part, a lot of initial consternation of roommates, then living with my girlfriend's parents for a little bit and bumming lunches—I owe the universe a lot of lunches. After we started touring, we toured for a full year and that sustained me 'cause our tour paid for itself. Even though it wasn't profitable, it was budgeted in order to sustain itself.

This was while we were getting a lot of initial media attention. It's a very funny and common misconception that coverage equals some financial success. For example, I've been looking for a new apartment. I'm three years from being forty years old and as a child I'm sure I thought, by this age, I'd own a house. Even if it was a tiny ranch house on a cul de sac. I didn't expect to be a renter my whole life. Now I look around at new apartments and at homes to buy in Bed-Stuy and think, "That could be nice." I'm at a point in my life where I'm considering it. So I was talking to my friend about this stuff and she was like, "What is your problem? Buy an apartment. Buy one now. They're not getting any cheaper than they are now."

And I said, "What the hell are you talking about? With what exactly am I going to buy an apartment?"

She said, "With your money! Buy an apartment!"

I said, "What the fuck are you talking about? The lowest end I could think of finding anything would be $500,000."

She's like, "You don't have that!?"

I said, "Do you have that? Why do you think I have that kind of fucking money sitting around?"

She said, "From your records...."

That was the "old days" for some people, but it is no longer the case. I feel like I've been fairly fortunate. I've been able to take care of myself and family, but I'm not buying a fucking house off of the music. I don't know how the paradigm would have to change for that to seem like a realistic potentiality, but now it seems like a pipedream.

For me, it's been a slow coming to terms with certain realities. Growing up, I thought that if a band had their music in a commercial, it was gross. I definitely still think it's gross, but if I'm going to continue making music, there's got to be more things that I'm open to doing. More compromises.

I was working with a young person the other day and we were talking about Cyprus Hill. I was talking about how great they were—the first two records. I haven't listened to them in a long time but I really loved them, the idea that you could rap for two whole records just about smoking pot and killing cops. Kind of like, "Somebody had to do that and they did it." My friend, who's much younger than me, thought I was being sarcastic, 'cause she couldn't imagine anyone liking Cyprus Hill. She said, "Their music is in skateboard videos," in some dismissive way. That automatically discredited them for her. And this person has an iPod and an iTunes library full of music and I don't imagine she has paid for any of it. In fact, I know that she hasn't.

So I said, "Maybe they want to feed their fucking kids."

It requires money to do this. It requires money to do this in the scene you think is so fucking "real." House parties and basement shows.... Somebody's paying for that house, someone's rich parents are. Even if you think you're creating on the fringe of society, you're still completely reliant upon that society and most of the models for independent music—which I'm not trying to attack—are still capitalism. It's still, "We give you money to make a record and then we press it, advertise it, distribute it, sell it." A lot of people are working to make that happen and they have lives and responsibilities. They have to eat and pay their fucking rent.

The idea that you can just follow this technology into this utopia where, "It's free!" It's the most shortsighted fucking bullshit I've ever heard. No one has shown me anything that implies a new paradigm that makes things more sustainable for artists and creative people. And the whole argument that, "Well, it's only the suits making money".... Listen, there's been a lot of exploitation in music, particularly in this country with black musicians, but people also have built real capital for themselves, so that argument doesn't work for me. I've been learning over the years to deliberate that relationship—what I agree to in a contract, what I don't agree to in a contract. So what business is it of yours as a consumer? It just seems like a copout. A pretty transparent excuse.

For me, it was already a nearly impossible tightrope to walk, the intersection of commerce and creativity. It was already hard enough to deal with trying to sell something. It was enough of a mind-fuck, selling something that was personally coming out of you and meant something to you. The popularity of selling music to commercials or TV shows or film.... I know it has some influence on people's writing and I feel like that makes the music industry even more commercial that it already was. That doesn't bode well for creativity, I don't think, so I'm not too hopeful about that model.

The anti-corporate vibe from people is hilarious to me. Downloading is only possible because of tools given to us by the corporate world. You are more tied into the corporate world by having a computer in your house than having a record player. Look, the major labels inflated the price of the CD and there're a lot of things about that medium you can attack and assail. But you can buy a coffee and a bagel for $7 and you can buy a CD for $12 and, in most instances, that will leave some margin of profit for the person whose music is on that CD. A small margin, but a margin. And you think about the amount of time it took to write the music, the time it took to record it or rehearse it. Even if it was done in someone's home—the price of the equipment and electricity, the price of not working your job. And add to that, it's a product you can return to again and again, which gives it its value as far as I'm concerned. The idea that that should be free is fine if my rent is free and my food is free. But none of that works. It can't be free. We can certainly examine another form of exchange or cooperation, but do it fast and make it not just about music.

The idea that artists don't get anything from record sales is totally false anyway. You have to recoup, but you certainly get something. A major label deal is about 85 percent to the label, 15 percent to the artist after recouping. Some indies are also 85/15 but most are 50/50 that I've come across. I'm still receiving quarterly statements and payments from Touch and Go, which is not even an active label anymore.

It was very sad when Touch and Go went under. I don't know what all the motivation was and no one that I've talked to out there seems to know why. But EMI is going under too. Lots of shit is going under. Is it as simply explained as, "People don't buy records anymore"? Well, I think that has something to do with it. They are record companies. I don't know what they're supposed to do about it, how they can "change with technology." I guess they could adopt it and become a cyber-terrorist group and figure out a way to disable the Internet, or something. Also, change to what? Fire almost everybody, put out your catalogue for free online and get some suckers who are still holding onto the dream to buy vinyl re-issues of something they didn't get the first time it was out? I don't know what the appropriate adaptation is.

I remember being at a corporate bookstore on tour and they had a table dedicated to Kindles and I went up to this kid who was working there and said, "Hey, I know this isn't your dream job, but isn't it kind of weird to be selling this thing that is going to destroy bookstores—in a bookstore?" He looked at me and said, "That's not gonna happen, that's not gonna happen…."

It doesn't bode well. No one who's pirating seems to have any kind of ethical dilemma at all about it. You know, I'm not a fan of Metallica, but I'm also not against them. I remember when Lars went off about Napster. He was basically panned as being this rich dick—and certainly they've done very well for themselves—but they also sacrificed a lot. It certainly seems funny to say that about Metallica, but those guys have dedicated their entire lives to playing music. They toured all the time and they didn't have a major machine behind them at first. They made their own machine. I think Lars has a right to say, "What the fuck? I did all of this, and now it's free!?" But he was so easily turned into this out-of-touch old dude. I feel like even if you do make the argument and break it down to: who's gonna pay for electricity in the studio, the engineer, the equipment, the Protools… People are still going to think, "Well, no one's looking so I'm just going to fucking steal it anyway."

I know that music seems so ephemeral to these people—it's just magically hanging in the air. "It's like water." Well, water's not fucking free either. Which is a much more important conversation than whatever might be happening to music.

I don't know what the future holds for me and I don't want to shit on anyone else's way of making it. There have definitely been times the past three or four years where I've thought, "Man, I could really use a job to come home to after tour." I want to be able to focus on creative work. I feel like everything *else I've ever done to make ends meet has been only that, or nearly. I mean, I like to cook and I like to make coffee for people. I did that for ten years. I like that culture, but it didn't fulfill my soul in any way and I started drinking myself to death in the process.*

We were talking before about, "Man, I don't have the money to buy an apartment," but neither do most people in the fucking world! It's obscenely expensive to live here. It is all right though—I've come to the point of acceptance of it being all right. My version of "making it" here has changed a lot in the last ten years. I don't think that music, even if it's popular, should mean free license to a life of excess. I don't think anyone deserves a perpetual blowjob in the back of the longest limousine. But I certainly don't think "for fucking free" is what I deserve or what other people deserve.

And the idea that having more starving artists around will improve music is ridiculous. The idea that the lack of resources is the main determinant of quality is a very convenient argument for capitalist exploitation. Especially considering the history of pop music in this country—the glamorization of the blues, the least glamorous music there is! People take it as a romanticized ideal, the starving artist. No one that I know who has been working for more than a couple of years will really believe that.

You know, I was really looking for counsel when TV On The Radio was debating whether to go to Interscope. I needed to hear the perspective of someone who didn't stand to directly profit, someone who was an older musician. The musicians who were older than me or significantly older were like, "Fucking take the money. I'm telling you now. Any opportunity you can. There's no promise it will come again. There's no guarantee of what hardships you will face later on. Don't pass it up because you want to be righteous."

It's very weird—the whole thing about getting clean in dirty water. I'm grossing myself out talking about it, but it's the reality that I'm living with and you're living with. It's our system. I feel like I don't believe in this system and don't like this system—but I can't change it single-handedly without doing something that's far worse than the status quo. I just hate to see us moving in the direction of, "Everybody can steal now, not just the guys at the top!" There's a whole pirate mentality that's in the fringes and counter-cultures of our society and it really drives me fucking crazy because ultimately that's not anarchism or anything challenging or progressive... It's just selfish, shitty greed.

People ask me now, "How do you hear about new music?" I go to the record store. I read music magazines. I ask people what they're listening to. I sometimes go to shows where I don't know what the band is about. I use the Internet and I like some things about it, but I also try to keep a healthy distance. I don't search for opinions of us or my friends on the Internet or read online reviews or watch performances on YouTube. I don't want to know what some anonymous coward has to say about something, in either a positive or negative way. That's a shitty way to say it, but it's often how I feel when I see anyone's comments about someone that I care about. "Who are you? You're hiding."

The idea of depending on social media or any form of patronage seem like models that lend themselves to the artist going, "Well, what do you want to hear?" Where art comes from and where ideas come from is not the result of asking people what they want.

I do feel like if there was actually some organization—some cooperation between musicians, which people feel is impossible because rock 'n roll is so ego-based—you could maybe make some demands or have some agency toward how the whole system works. To say, "For a year straight, we're not going to make records" or "We're not going to tour." But that seems like a pipe dream.

A lot of younger bands are of a generation that doesn't buy records. Getting some coverage or playing a talk show is reward enough. Fame is satisfying a lot of people and motivating a lot of people, but there's nothing more fleeting than fame. And when it actually comes down to making this work, you can't pay for anything with fame. You might get a seat at a restaurant or a free drink, but it isn't paying for anything.

Talking before about how difficult it is to walk that line between creativity and commerce, I almost think my frustration with piracy is secondary to my frustration with having to sell anything. The idea of selling yourself and the music… some of that is sacred. Being brought up in a Christian culture means that "sacred" equals "not-for-sale." It means Jesus in the temple, smashing the money changers. "Not for sale!"

But at the same time, somebody fed Jesus. He didn't starve to death in that story, and that's ultimately the thing. In my ideal society, that I'm not citing any study on, if you fulfilled this necessary thing inside this society and community and were earning your place, you were deserving of a dignified life. I feel like musicians are certainly doing their part and earning their place in this society. For people to suddenly say, "No, you're not earning your place. Just be a slave…"

That's not right to me.

PART 3

RESTORATION

HOPE

As many people I've spoken with agree, young consumers have passed the point of no return, as it applies to paying for music. To whatever extent the preceding voices from the independent music industry suggest that nearly all "successful" musicians live in a precarious financial state as a sacrifice to their music; that the support of editors such as record labels is crucial to the long-term creation and spread of such music; that fewer people paying for music didn't mean art was any less tainted by commercial compromise; that a profound and unnecessary disconnect between consumers and creators had manufactured an unbalanced understanding of digital piracy... it doesn't really matter. If one believes that the forces of technology, when mixed with human selfishness, stir a potent social concoction that is beyond reason, then there is no point to this search for the truth of digital piracy. As we saw in the vitriolic dismissal of my original writing, in the disconnection from reality that our digital gadgets offer, and in the Decade of Dysfunction that crippled any hope for reasonable discussion of the issues, it makes little sense to hold faith in the future. The fear mongering that took place during the SOPA protest was just one more symptom of communicative ineptitude. We are forever becoming more isolated and splintered away from our concentric communities—from our immediate neighborhood, from our nations, from our human species—isolated by and for technologic tools that numb us to reality. No longer counting on one another to do the right thing in service of the common good, nihilism and opportunism become the only reasonable courses of action.

Why the hell should I pay for music if he's not paying and she's not paying? I'm not a sucker.

In our cynical, media soaked world, there is no greater sin than to trust in the decency of your fellow consumer. The lack of faith in one another that results invites us to join in a culture of negativity, where we assume greed is too powerful to be fought and institutions are doomed to failure. Hope for a better future, for digital content or anything else, is stupid and naive. We are on our own, all of us.

That cynicism would all be fine and good, except for the fact that I have not been fully honest with you. Forgive me, but the tangled discourse of digital piracy is not as hopeless as I made it out to be.

Amidst the "kill yourself" hate mail and message board ridicule for my pro-responsibility piracy writing, described earlier on, other sentiments revealed themselves. One of these alternative sentiments forever shifted my assumptions for the possibility of changing popular attitudes. A few days after receiving the email that told me to kill myself, an antithetical message appeared in my inbox:

> Hey! I just read your article and it kind of blew my mind. I, a seventeen-year-old kid in the suburbs of Texas surviving on a small allowance and the occasional babysitting check, have always pirated music in the spirit of "hey, there's no way I could afford all the music I love, so I'm sure the bands would want me to listen somehow." I also justify this by buying the occasional record and pirating the rest, but with over 8000 songs on my iPod and a vinyl collection that won't even fill up a bookshelf, I have to realize that I could have bought more and supported more of my favorite artists, but due to the convenience and free-ness of the Internet, simply didn't.
>
> As someone who tries to support independent businesses over the Wal-Marts and Starbucks that cost less and are easier to find, this hipster "share-the-music" ideology really just comes down to being a load of hypocritical bullshit. So, thanks for the article, it was a big wake-up call, and I'll definitely show it to a few friends.

Hmm… I thought.

If my arguments had reached even *one* mind, perhaps change was possible after all. The letter stood in such sharp contrast to assumptions of teenage pirates: these digital natives who could never conceive of an analog, paid-for past long enough to alter their consumption habits. While such assumptions were presented by experts like Lawrence Lessig and Chris Anderson as proof that they alone were the unsentimental realists in the room, the idea that youths were lost to the idea of payment was, I now realized, alarmingly condescending.

This zombie-like teenage army was incapable of paying for content, supposedly, because they'd never been properly programmed. They could not be educated. Appeals to common sense or morality were above their limited capacities. As a result, because file sharing was the way they fundamentally "understood culture," digital natives couldn't be bothered to take responsibility for their actions. The mess in music was the responsibility of the government, corporate record labels, supposedly rich artists… anyone but people actually *doing* the downloading.

Digital natives served as useful boogeymen for those looking for means to stiff-arm piracy's critics. Because teenagers and college students would never pay for digital content, file sharing's positive or negative consequences were pointless for us to examine or discuss. A waste of breath. We would just have to deal with this new reality of free content, like it or not.

Digital natives themselves play this "youth card" in order to excuse their actions. The conventional expectation that their generation would never pay for digital music has become an easy rationalization for them to do just that. Making the claim that a generation would not pay for content implicitly consented to such a future, a self-fulfilling prophecy. This spirit of fatalism contributed mightily to the Decade of Dysfunction, lending the entire period an air of resignation and pessimism as to our capacities to do the right thing.

This teenager's letter exposed the fallacy of such assumptions, but it wasn't the only feedback to do so. The few pieces of hate mail I initially received were outnumbered by dozens of letters telling me, in various ways, "Thank you."

"I'm a teenager—apparently a member of a hopelessly self-entitled and over-privileged generation—whose sole income comes from working in an ice cream shop twice a week," another wrote me. "Beyond that I don't have any honest justification for the amount of music I download. I'm really conflicted about it."

"Thank you for writing this," another said. "I started downloading music this year and quickly realized that it was irresponsible. My policy now is to only pirate music that is out of print or music by dead people. I'm not sure whether the latter is sensible or not."

These file sharers were not "understanding culture" by way of piracy, they were anxious and confused about it. But rather than throwing their hands up in the air in surrender to their irrational desires for more, they matched their anxiety with honest self-awareness. People desired confidence in their choices—wanted to do the right thing—but the digital content debates had left them feeling stranded to work these vexing issues out on their own.

"I too, in the past, have fallen in with the hordes of pirates only to emerge with a different view," said one reader. "I've gone through cycles of this, several times deleting all my illegal music."

Another reader was remarkably evenhanded in his assessment: "In the end, to me, it's all about balance.... File sharing and supporting your local musicians can peacefully co-exist I think. Anyone who holds an entitlement attitude that they should never have to pay is just as greedy and unethical as the suits of the RIAA."

I checked up on the avatars attacking me on various Internet message boards. There, too, pleasant surprises awaited. On the Hipinion message board thread, the first few pages of comments were derisive, as expected. But at the juncture when I might have logged on to defend myself, other voices chimed in to challenge the file-sharing apologists. In the subsequent days, I marveled at a developing open discussion. I sensed a community of strangers struggling with the meaning of digital piracy in a sincere, intelligent manner. It was that rarity: a constructive online conversation. By the discussion's end, over a thousand comments later, the jilted originators of the thread had completely disappeared.

Other message board threads popped up where I grew to better understand this secret middle ground on piracy. Its members were by turns pessimistic ("I would like to think people will develop some morality upon being educated, but sadly that is unlikely"), confused ("Just for clarity's sake: I'm 100% ambivalent about illegal downloads. What I would like to believe is that we're just going through a paradigm shift that will eventually work itself out"), funny ("Imagine how much better The Beach Boys would've been if they worked 40 hours a week doing stupid shit"), passionate ("pay apple. pay comcast. pay a liquor store. pay a bar. pay a drug dealer. pay your taxes. but FOR GOD'S SAKE, DON'T EVER SPEND FIFTEEN FUCKING

DOLLARS ON A PIECE OF RECORDED MUSIC"), and clearheaded ("Being in cyberspace doesn't change the fact that you're taking something from somebody (usually many, many people at once) without their consent. No matter what arguments or justifications you might think you have, you can't argue with that"). Candor, hope and a sense of responsibility percolated from these message boards. In the midst of a long, argumentative thread, one post concisely summed up both digital piracy's status quo and the silent majority's simultaneous yearning for a more humanistic future:

> I'm profoundly conflicted about the whole situation we live in, because I don't feel like the world owes me free music, and I spend more than most on physical recordings, old and new, but at the same time, I do download records. If suddenly I wasn't allowed to, I wouldn't be particularly upset, but I do think that what we have now is an unsustainable situation, and instead of just saying "tough luck, musicians who don't make the kind of music that benefits from touring and live performance," it would be interesting to think of how things could evolve in a positive way, where we don't try to either put the toothpaste back in the tube or act like musicians must necessarily be hobbyists from now on.

The status quo of piracy *could* change. Perhaps James Bradley of Sound Fix Records was correct; reformed file sharers, a bit older and wiser, could help end the recording industry's depressing slide and usher in an inspiring renaissance. With this new hope, the truth of the Internet grew in its subtle complexity.

On the one hand, Marshall McLuhan was right. The further we stretch and stress our nervous systems through the mediated experience of gadgets and grow dependent upon them, the more we risk becoming numb to our real selves and interests. But the hypnotizing, hallucinatory qualities of digital media are a danger, not an absolute condition. As much as I harbored some curmudgeonly reflexes toward the Internet, I couldn't deny the ideals manifesting themselves in front of my eyes. The overwhelming majority of my reader reaction came in the form of diverse, gracious, good-faith reflections. A community of thought seemed to recognize itself for the first time, aided primarily by digital connections. When quality information is married to the radical efficiency of digital distribution, reality-based communities can build and affect positive change throughout the world at near simultaneous rates. Such is the true promise of the Internet.

In the overall reaction to my writings, I found plenty of reasons for hope in this regard, that consumers could place their rational visions for a better society above some itchy compulsion for free content. The question remained: was the largely positive reaction to my article truly representative of a silent majority that believed creators deserved to be compensated for their digital works? It was impossible to know for sure, although the results of one 2011 survey were at least encouraging.

In their efforts to combat digital piracy, the government of the United Kingdom controversially turned to the suspension of Internet service as a possible punishment for repeat violators in their Digital Economy Act legislation, which was seen as an extreme measure. In an effort to gauge where the UK stood on such enforcement, a regional law firm measured how many people were file sharing and where attitudes stood in 2011:

> The law firm Wiggin polled 1,750 "digitally active" UK con-
> sumers over 15 of all ages for its annual survey. 62 per cent
> surveyed agreed that it was right to suspend the Internet con-
> nections of persistent online copyright infringers. The same
> number agreed that more should be done to block pirate sites,
> but 61 per cent preferred site blocking to going after individual
> infringers…. A mere 11 per cent disagree with the statement:
> "It is important to protect the creative industries from piracy;"
> four per cent disagreed with it strongly. Around 25 to 30
> per cent of those surveyed were indifferent.[1]

Even when Wiggin restricted the question—of the importance to protecting creative industries from piracy—to confessed pirates, nearly *half* of them agreed it was important to protect such industries from piracy. When all participants were asked whether they pirated digital music regularly, only five percent said yes, with a total of thirteen percent admitting to unlicensed downloading on a rare to regular basis.

Judging by the survey, the core group of ideologically committed digital pirates is marginal—as little as five percent of Internet users in the UK. Reflecting the inner conflict many of my readers expressed, one-third of Internet users remained undecided on the issue, presumably open to new ideas.

If a sensible middle ground can be reached on how to deal with digital piracy, the Decade of Dysfunction may end up looking like nothing more than a historical anomaly on humanity's path to discovering an enlightened digital course. In this anomalous period, the loudest and angriest voices in the room, as noted by Craig Finn, drowned out the sensible among us and jerry-rigged public perception of the issue. Knowing that most people believed it was important to protect the basic legal rights of artists and businesses from sites like The Pirate Bay, this marginal group advanced shocking allegations, as with the SOPA protest, that any attempt at bringing fairness to the digital marketplace was an attack on freedom of speech; or that what rights holders *really* wanted was to shut down Twitter or Facebook. These claims, coming from hip young activists and entrepreneurs, confused most of the population, leaving them unsure what to believe.

During my time at the University of Minnesota, when the school hockey team won consecutive national championships, we students did what most drunk college kids do when they want to collectively express joy or anger—we rioted.

Though never a hockey fan, I got drunk and watched the team win the title game in 2004 at a friend's house. After the final buzzer rang and the championship title was official, we slammed one more beer and headed out to the main business district to see what was going to happen. The previous year a minor riot had occurred, so students were expecting and perhaps hoping for a follow-up affair. We walked down the street to a main intersection of the college district, called Dinkytown, feeling energized and curious. The streets were empty and ominously quiet. After one block, we passed a mattress burning in the middle of the street. There was no sign who had put it there. An angry flame cast shadows between the parked cars.

We walked on to the main intersection and waited. A few other students showed up and stood around as we were. Then, a few more arrived. And more. Then, some students started climbing the traffic poles while the crowd below cheered and rooted them on. When the traffic light turned red, the coalescing mob's more enthusiastic members recognized the open intersection and filled it with their jumping bodies and pumped fists. The crowd was now in the hundreds or thousands, moving between the cars, banging on windows and blocking traffic, unworried and exuberant.

Along with the great majority of the crowd, my friends and I remained on the sidewalk, watching the developing chaos. We smiled and laughed in nervous disbelief.

Where is this going to lead?

By this time, some in the middle of the intersection had taken wooden signs and garbage cans off of the sidewalks. They piled them up in the middle of the intersection and lit them on fire. The mob cheered and took pictures as the instigators in the intersection scavenged for anything new to feed the bonfire. More kids were hanging from the poles and climbing on buildings. The same unlucky cars were stalled amidst a scene of total chaos, beholden to the will of the mob.

After a few short minutes, the police showed up and prepared to disperse the crowd. Those like me, at the edge of the mob, could see the police preparing and shifted position to ensure an easy escape path. The True Believers wreaking havoc in the intersection weren't as aware. When the police finally charged, the passive element of the mob fluidly dispersed. Two True Believers were lassoed by the police near the bonfire, while the rest of them easily escaped. At another intersection, just two blocks away, the mob quickly gathered yet again. While the police were busy cleaning up the mess at the original staging ground, the True Believers, now acting with some experience, efficiently gathered dumpsters and material for a new, larger bonfire. Next to where I stood watching, four students flipped over a parked car. Again, after a few short minutes, the police advanced from down the street. This time they apprehended no one. The mob dispersed once more.

With thousands of my classmates, I wandered around Dinkytown that night, sniffing out new nodes of drama. I passed by a parking lot filled with students celebrating, encircling multiple overturned cars serving as tinder for twenty-foot high flames. I watched as True Believers methodically smashed the windows of a parking lot booth, setting it on fire before moving on to the next one. One half of a mile away from the original intersection, I witnessed a group of three male students—all the students destroying property were male— smash the windows of a liquor store and dash in, exiting with armfuls of liquor bottles. I eventually became disturbed by the destruction, but I must say it took awhile. I felt very alive, watching these scenes from a comfortable distance. On my way back home, I ran down an embankment with scores of others, hiding under a bridge and covering my face as policemen lobbed pepper spray canisters in a last ditch attempt to restore order.

The following day it occurred to me that the True Believers were, in fact, a tiny fraction of the mob that night. On a normal evening, the few dozen of them who were actually setting bonfires, harassing drivers or looting stores would never have acted in such ways or considered acting in such ways. Ultimately, it was the passive crowd—the thousands watching from a comfortable distance and milling about, drawn in by the drama—that gave the True Believers their perception of power and influence. I may have felt as though I was merely watching that night. But without me—and the rest of that crowd who watched, shocked and curious, as the property and welfare of our community was set in flames all around us—the riot and its consequences would never have come to pass. Ultimately the unthinking crowd was just as responsible for providing an aura of protection, if not acceptance, to actions and attitudes of a marginal and extreme core of individuals.

Digital piracy has enjoyed massive popularity for an obvious reason: pirated content is free and easy to find. Millions of passive consumers—the digital natives—were used as props and powerful proof that destructive actions of True Believers like The Pirate Bay were expressions by and for the masses. The passive crowd lent power to ideas and ideologies that, when examined, were ill-conceived notions that merely eroded the foundations of open society and sowed the seeds of destructive chaos. The crowd was entertained by the actions of the True Believers. However, once peeled off from the mob mentality, as my early articles did for those who responded to me, the dark assumptions and misunderstanding that girded digital piracy was exposed in the light of day. As a result, the True Believers setting the fires became a bit more marginalized; a bit less powerful. In an effort toward common sense and marginalizing the forces of self-destruction, it is time to aggressively reconsider the many assumptions that emerged throughout the Decade of Dysfunction.

The True Believers of digital piracy might be delirious with illusions of their own power or opportunists in search of action—but mostly they are well meaning people who have been temporarily led astray by their own insatiable desires and can no longer objectively perceive the truth of their own actions. If everyone seems to be setting the fire (or encouraging it), it begins to feel as though no one is truly responsible for the blaze. Ultimately, is the public of individual citizens whose choices and attitudes will determine how many more fires will be set and how far the blaze will spread.

A Failure of Memory

As Adam Farrell himself implied, the original sin of the music industry was to shutter Napster rather than figure out a way to monetize it. In the RIAA's inability to understand where technology was taking the distribution of recorded music, the labels sealed their own fate. The "global game of whack-a-mole" that commenced after Napster's decline and music fans' refusal to pay for their content were just punishments for major labels' own ineptness. But Farrell also admitted to the deep feelings of many Napster users, that downloading music files for free "had to be okay somehow." The combination of these two sentiments transformed into a conventional wisdom that formed a foundation for rationalizations of piracy. Rather than the individual choices of millions of consumers driving the spread of piracy, it was merely the *new thing*; an innocent phenomenon of technological progress. Thanks to Napster, the labels had their chance to ride the wave of innovation. Having foolishly pissed away their opportunity, those same waves were fated to crash into these bygone industries, eroding them until nothing was left.

Amidst the assumptions of original sin revolving around Napster, Lars Ulrich was the perfect foil to Napster's image of grassroots, collegial sharing. As many of my interview subjects pointed out, he was easy to vilify. As a wealthy artist, he was in a terrible position to advocate for the rights of struggling artists. Due to the lack of small artists standing up to draw ranks with him, he appeared to be using the idea of the struggling musician as a prop to justify his own money grab, as major labels were also accused of doing whenever they tried to argue that copyright protected all artists. But as Kyp Malone and Andy Falkous pointed out, Metallica had every right to stand up to what Napster was doing. It was pure and unadulterated exploitation of other people's work. Ulrich's relative wealth, or shrill style of speaking, shouldn't blind us from the fundamental strength of his arguments. Reading his testimony before the US Senate again, Ulrich doesn't sound so dissimilar from the indie voices we heard from:

I do not have a problem with any artists voluntarily distributing his or her songs through any means that artist so chooses. But just like a carpenter who crafts a table gets to decide whether he wants to keep it, sell or give it away, shouldn't we have the same options? We should decide what happens to our music, not a company with no rights to our recordings, which has never invested a penny in our music or had anything to do with its creation. The choice has been taken away from us.

Lars Ulrich's tone was annoying, sure, and showing up at Napster's offices in a limousine was a monumental PR blunder, but in hindsight he was correct. Ulrich deserves retroactive credit for standing up for artists' rights at the time, and also for noting the glaring hypocrisy of Napster. The file-sharing company made hay by dancing around the sanctity of copyright when it came to the recordings flying back and forth across its servers. But at the same time, in the user agreement on Napster's own website, one legal subsection read, "This Web site, or any portion of this Web site, may not be reproduced, duplicated, copied, sold, resold or otherwise exploited for any commercial purpose that is not expressly permitted by Napster. All Napster Web site design, text, graphics, the selection and the arrangement thereof, and all Napster software are copyright 1999/2000 Napster Inc."

Napster wasn't a company based upon revolution or innovation. It was based upon opportunism, employing the legal protections of copyright when it suited them, ignoring them when it didn't. The company wasn't the band of young do-gooders some remember it as, but shrewd businessmen who sought to manipulate public opinion in order to expand their user base.

Remember Chad Paulson, who helped Napster to remain on university broadband networks when the RIAA/Metallica lawsuit was first filed? His view of Napster changed soon after their mutual success. Only months later, Paulson strongly criticized Napster's status as the "cozy middleman" for mass piracy in a public letter on the Students Against University Censorship website. "Napster is giving the MP3 a bad name," he wrote. In what would become a familiar reaction to anyone who voiced criticisms that the True Believers of the file sharing mob wished to silence, the website was quickly hacked and a fake letter was posted, labeling Paulson a "back-stabber." Rather than address the issues Paulson raised, it was easier to personally attack his character and sabotage his website. Similarly, when the British pop star Lily Allen started a blog in 2009 to serve as a forum to express her own critical views of file sharing and invite perspective from other artists, she quickly decided to shut the website down because "the abuse was getting too much."[1]

"I've never stated I'm all for Napster," Chad Paulson told *Salon* in 2000. "I've always had concerns about piracy and have a huge education section on my site on how to use MP3 responsibly. I've been the open-minded one. Now I'm branded a traitor."

Paulson became further disillusioned with Napster when company co-founder Sean Parker phoned him about his open letter. Paulson recounted the conversation to *Salon*: "[Parker] said, 'The technology can't be stopped.' He said that like fifty times…. Some employee was screaming at me in the background, yelling about how Napster is the plight of the record industry and they can't stop the revolution…. And I said, 'When are you going to start promoting local music?' He said, 'That's not a priority right now.' My jaw dropped to the floor. I got in contact with Napster when the university thing blew up in February. They told me, 'We don't like piracy…we promote local artists.' I was all excited. Since then I've realized that was just a façade they put up so they could build up their user base. Now, they're trying to build up a user base with the attraction of, 'Download any song you want!'"

In *Appetite for Self-Destruction*, Steve Knopper's essential history of the music industry and its digital downfall, Paulson's disillusion finds further support. As reported in the book, an internal email from Sean Parker to Shawn Fanning, revealed later in court proceedings, included the admission that the entire basis of their company was fans "exchanging pirated music." They knew full well that they were violating the rights of creators. In the meantime, Napster acted coy in public on the realities of copyright. When music industry professional Ted Cohen showed up at the Napster offices to interview for the CEO position in the midst of the RIAA litigation, he saw dry-erase boards lining the office walls. One was labeled, "How to talk to the press," and read, "If they call to say, 'Don't you know this is illegal?' say, 'We didn't know it was illegal—we think it's fair use.'" Cohen described the messages as "all deflection points" from the truth.

Shawn Fanning may have been responsible for dreaming up Napster in his college dorm at Northwestern University, but his uncle, John Fanning, was critical to the company's early financing and long-term ambitions. According to Eileen Richardson, an employee of Napster at the time, John Fanning was known to declare, "We will take down the music industry! And give away free stuff!" When RIAA representatives first discovered Napster in 1999, they sought a meeting with the Fannings to discuss how to move forward, but were repeatedly given the runaround. Lydia Pelliccia, then spokeswoman for the RIAA, said, "Our urgent requests for a meeting were not taken seriously. We really had no other option but to file litigation."[2] After the litigation was filed, Shawn Fanning appeared onstage at the 2000 MTV Video Music Awards wearing a Metallica t-shirt, openly mocking the RIAA and Lars Ulrich, who sat in the audience.

With such public and private gestures from Napster, relations with the RIAA were sure to sour. How was an agreement between the two parties supposed to take shape when Napster took such glee in antagonizing the music industry? A potential deal between the parties was explored, but even as those negotiations began, John Hummer, a venture capitalist who financed Napster and owned 20 percent of the company at the time, told *Fortune*, "I am the record companies' worst nightmare."

Some members of the RIAA believed in making a deal. Edgar Bronfman Jr., the head of Universal Music Group, publicly called Napster "both slavery and Soviet communism" in *The Atlantic*,[3] but privately thought it was very much in the interest of the industry to take the uncertain leap into the digital marketplace, as did the head of Sony at the time. "Here was an opportunity to maintain a large customer base, potentially, and over time migrate it to a commercially viable system," Bronfman said in the book *Fortune's Fool*. Others in the RIAA were wholly against dealing with Napster, but nonetheless the two sides seriously explored an arrangement in which the Majors would own between 50 percent and 90 percent of the company and have significant involvement in all company decision-making. Hummer and his Napster partner Hank Barry were indifferent to making such a deal. Reportedly, Hummer concluded that a deal wasn't worth it after Andy Grove, the head of Intel, convinced him that copyright would not be protected online. Operating under the assumption that free, unlicensed content was destined to become the digital norm, Hummer saw no reason to make a deal.[4] Indeed, why on earth would he?

But that changed in 2001, when the Ninth Circuit US Court of Appeals ruled Napster to be illegal. Suddenly, Napster was keen to work out licensing deals with the major labels. It was their only path to survival. Ted Cohen, the same digital executive who interviewed for a position at Napster, was privy to the terms of discussion and described them in the 2011 book, *The Future of the Music Business* by Hal Leonard. According to Cohen, Napster offered the major labels a $1 billion flat fee for all future rights to their music with—no royalties. This offer came even though, at the time, the record business still brought in over $14 billion a year. The proposed deal was a joke.

Says Cohen, "Everybody said no. I mean, if I said to you right now… 'I will give you $200 for your car. Ok?' Will you give me your car?… But I made you an offer, you turned me down? How short-sighted of you. I mean this is basically what it was. So again, in the legend of Napster, Napster tried to be nice, but the stupid label people wouldn't listen. It's not true."[5]

Even if a deal had been reached, would the record industry's problems have just flittered away? Probably not. In a *Wired* magazine article at the time titled, "Napster May Not Matter Anymore," writer Brad King noted, "If Napster strikes a deal with the recording industry or users are charged a fee to trade files, the company could quickly lose its outsider status—the very thing that gave it cachet with its members."[6] A software consultant named David Weekly admitted to King that he had found the source code for the Napster application and published it online, so that new services could easily copy the protocol and develop new "Napsters." With decentralized file-sharing services like Gnutella, Grokster, Audiogalaxy, and Limewire popping up left and right, the idea that significant numbers of early adopters would have chosen to pay $10 each month for a major label-backed Napster is dubious. If a deal had been made, it's quite possible that the sordid history of piracy might not have looked all that different.

Regardless of what could or would have happened, we know what *did* happen. Tens of millions of consumers suddenly felt an infinite entitlement to download unlicensed music and movies. It was the mark of a historically bleak and foreboding decade, for America and for the world, that in the 2000s the entitlement to trample upon the legal rights of others became so unquestionably in fashion.

CREATORS' RIGHTS AND THE SLIPPERY SLOPE

Lawrence Lessig's charge that copyright laws "criminalized a generation" was publicly lanced by none other than Stephen Colbert, when Lessig appeared on Comedy Central's *The Colbert Report* to promote his book *Remix*. Colbert asked, "Isn't saying that copyright laws are turning our children into criminals the same as saying arson laws are turning our children into pyromaniacs?" Lessig changed the subject, conflating attempts at enforcing copyright with the Iraq invasion of 2003: "a failed war." But Colbert's satirical jab rang true. What about the law? Weren't citizens still responsible to respect the rights of creators, within reason?

Such questions were rarely asked during the Decade of Dysfunction, mostly because Metallica and the RIAA were so seared into the public mind as the sole beneficiaries of copyright enforcement. The RIAA mass lawsuits were arrogant, nefarious and cruel. They permanently blighted the reputation of record labels. A sad consequence of that action was, over the long-term, the way in which the outrageous lawsuits poisoned any attempts to reasonably view the nature of copyright and how it functions, in practical terms, to protect all individual creators and incentivize a creative culture worthy of the public.

Copyright as we know it, the exclusive right for an author to his or her works for a limited time, was born in 1710 at the dawn of the Enlightenment—the age of reason. That birth, via England's Statute of Anne, came as a result of the mass exploitation of creators. The Stationers' Company, a printing union sanctioned by the crown, had been publishing and distributing the works of authors, then selling the books with no obligation or intent to compensate the creators themselves "to the great detriment of [authors] and their families," as the statute read. Granting authors the right to their literary property (for a maximum of twenty-eight years) not only protected against the unjust exploitation by printers and distributors, but it ensured that men of genius had the opportunity to make a living from their work, develop their ideas and share them with the public, for the benefit of all. Allowing authors and other professional creators the right to distribute their work as they pleased was an ingenious means of engineering incentives for the spread of independent wisdom and creativity in consumer society. The limited copyright terms that created a public domain perfected a balance between ensuring a fair marketplace for creativity and wisdom, while recognizing that, as social beings, we all benefit from the spread of knowledge and understanding through science and the arts.

Critics of digital copyright through the Decade of Dysfunction argued that copyright was no longer necessary online, because artists had so many new opportunities to distribute their works and profit from them. To them copyright wasn't rights or property-based, it was a utilitarian method for incentivizing new creative works. So long as it could be shown that new works were being created, as they still were, digital copyright could be abandoned with a clear conscience. Through the decade, fears were also expressed that copyright could be used as a tool to quell freedom of speech or "chill" speech. During SOPA, the ideas that protecting copyright would violate freedom of speech or bring about "censorship" were presented as plain fact.

As Terry Hart has exhaustively explained on his legal blog, Copyhype, copyright has existed in tandem with the freedom of speech and the First Amendment for over two hundred years.[1] The Founding Fathers were explicit in labeling literary works an author's "property"[2] and decided against including utilitarian provisions in federal copyright laws, such as limiting the price at which books could be sold, despite those provisions having existed at the time in some of the states' copyright laws.[3]

Between passage of the Statute of Anne (1710) and the nascent United States of America's first federal copyright law (1790), the Founders had eighty years to measure whether or not copyright was truly useful for their nation. So, what did they do? They first placed a copyright clause within the Constitution and then *expanded* copyright from just authors to include mapmakers and illustrators. All but one of the original States adopted their own copyright laws before our Constitution was even ratified. An often ignored fact is that the essential principle of copyright has been ratified by the

United Nations as a human right, summarized within Article 27 of the Universal Declaration of Human Rights: "Everyone has the right to the protection of the moral and material interests resulting from any scientific, literary or artistic production of which he is the author." That individual creators have the exclusive rights to their work, have the legal and human right not to be illegally exploited for their labor, is fundamental to who we are as a civilization of open, democratic societies.

The rights of creators are so engrained into our culture that we have no remote idea of what life would be like without it. As much as The Pirate Bay talked about all of the "new authors" that were being created because of digital technology, the vast majority of content driving users to their services was created through the rights-based *mechanism* of (supposedly illegitimate) copyright. The True Belivers were like a rebellious teenager who sees their parent only as a constraint on their freedom. The teenager fails to recognize that the parent is also feeding, housing and clothing them. The teenager takes the parent's existing support as a given, having never known anything different.

If the Age of Enlightenment gave us copyright that elegantly balanced the rights of creators versus those of the public, the Age of Entitlement gave us discontents who wanted to have their cake and eat it too, infinitely, and were willing to make any argument to protect their have-it-both-ways status quo.

One argument was that file sharing or online streaming caused zero harm because users were not using the content for commercial uses. Let us recall, from Part One, how Lessig wrapped his idealization of read-write cultural participation in John Philip Sousa's recollection of a past age, of "children singing the songs of the day" together on front porches and street corners throughout the land.

But Lessig's romantic association was a fallacy. In the early 20th century, no one was selling ad space on the front porches where these singing children performed or charging pedestrians for access to the children's front laws, but that is precisely the model upon which YouTube and the Internet were built. A non-consenting artist absolutely had the right to be dismayed at their toil and labor being distributed by Google or an Internet Service Provider in order to drive demand for access and advertising revenues. These Internet sites were inherently commercial in a way that children singing on porches were not.

Because the Internet's basic architecture was initially predicated on paid access from ISPs, content being "free" and selling advertising to make revenues, nearly every corner of the Internet was commercial, with flashy banner ads taking up more and more screen space. But this essential truth never made it into Lessig's lofty rhetoric of a culture that needed to be freed from the onerous chains of its nasty, corporate, rights-holding overlords.

In fact, the sentiment that the big corporate record labels and movie studios were the problem, not the artists, was wishful thinking that shooed away copyright's fundamental mechanism of placing the legal rights to their work with artists alone.

Record labels and publishers have no inherent right to exist in the marketplace. The only reason they do exist is that creators in the past and present have chosen to extend their rights by legal consent. The existence of the creative industries is an expression of multitudes of artists having extended their copyrights to them, and multitudes of consumers having respected an artist's choice by paying for content if asked to do so and the price is worth it to them.

But copyright does not *demand* payment to artists or their "gatekeeping" legal partners; only respect for an artist's implicit wishes. Copyright equally protects an artist's individual choice to give their work away for free as it does the choice to charge a fee. The point is that it is *their choice*, not that of a consumer or unlicensed distributor, no matter how easy the Internet makes it to ignore or rationalize away. The question is, are we prepared to respect that choice? At issue today is whether we see ourselves existing within the construct of philosopher Immanuel Kant, who believed that all human beings are capable of reason and free will, and therefore deserving of common rights and common respect. We may not like a certain record company's litigious actions or believe they are pursuing idiotic business practices, but copyright demands that we acknowledge their legitimate rights, extending from the artist. So long as piracy is easy and punishments are rare, people will certainly continue to do it. Instant gratification is a difficult urge to fight. But that shouldn't excuse us from being honest about our actions or dismiss the knowing violation of creators' rights when it occurs.

Certainly, copyright terms are grotesquely long and Fair Use law can be confusing, but our criticisms of one or the other have nothing to do with knowingly pirating an album or film that has been recently released. And, in fact, the Fair Use controversy surrounding the remix artist Girl Talk, who uses recognizable samples of popular songs, demonstrates the inherent flexibility of copyright. The funny thing is, though he has been used as an example of what is wrong with copyright, as of 2012 Girl Talk has never been sued. He has released and sold copies of two albums and built a nice career, touring clubs around the world, without significant rights-holder protest. In this sense, Girl Talk is an example of the positives of copyright law. Just because rights holders *can* sue perceived infringers or charge for content, there is nothing about copyright that says they must. Once more, we see that copyright is conditional upon the wishes of individual artists, not merely a corporate bludgeon.

Through the Decade of Dysfunction, the essential muddiness of Fair Use law was sometimes conflated with all of copyright policy in an effort to portray the entire system as unworkable. But we ought to separate the two when we discuss digital piracy, at least in regards to music, movies and books (it is quite relevant to protections for visual art in the age of Google Images, and journalism in the age of aggregation). Sampling policy is important, but is has little to do with an online storage locker or torrent tracker knowingly and serially violating the rights of creators for financial gain. Oddly enough, the existence of Lawrence Lessig's Creative Commons made the free choice of creators to protect the distribution of their works from such violations all the more clear.

If, by choosing a Creative Commons license, an artist was expressing their desire that a consumer could enjoy the work without paying or redistribute it without their permission, then clearly an artist who *ignored* Creative Commons to retain their normal copyright protections was also making a choice. By their actions, if not always their conciliatory words to young fans, artists implicitly asked that their intentions be respected. A knowing digital pirate was blatantly contemptuous of those wishes. But those in the open culture crowd played a double game in which creators' choices were sacrosanct when they chose a Creative Commons license or Kickstarter campaign, but somehow misguided when an author or musician chose to sell their work through a partnering company and enforce their traditional copyright. Respecting the legally held rights of all individual artists is essential to keeping some perspective as we negotiate the uneven terrain of digital piracy.

———————————

Imagine a free weekly newspaper that takes articles from the best newspapers and magazines in the world, reprints them without permission or payment and charges advertising on the strength of such infringing content. In each issue, one or two original opinion pieces appear. When legal action suspends the publishing operation of these knowing actors, should we call that "censorship," as some label attempts to shut down P2P services that knowingly enable infringement while charging advertising?

Certainly, not all uses of P2P technology are infringing. But when a company intentionally sets out to start a business upon a model of attracting users to unlicensed material, that is a case of callous illegal exploitation of creators with no sensible justification. It is a backwards ignorance to call punishing or blocking such sites "censorship," as if the sacred doctrine of free speech is being violated. Some, like Techdirt's Mike Masnick, suggest that attempts to punish or marginalize sites like The Pirate Bay are pointless and only end up stifling useful "innovation." When such notions are repeated with a straight face by intelligent people, we have already skipped into dystopia. If "innovation" means excusing obvious cases of illegal exploitation, I'm afraid freedom has become slavery.

Copyright was traditionally understood as a property right. Just as tangible property rights prohibit our Freedom of Assembly from meaning we can trespass a private home or business to hold a rally, even if the property is unharmed, Freedom of Speech does not mean we can "trespass" upon another person's rights as a creator along our path to personal expression. Even the most staunch libertarian agrees that we ought to be able to do as we please as free citizens only so long as we do not harm or infringe upon another citizen's equal rights. Otherwise, the concept of legal rights would be meaningless.

The problem for those who would rather not deal with creators' rights, because of the way they dirty a self-evidently pure and innocent technology like the Internet, is that they know the law is not on their side. When Lawrence Lessig argued before the Supreme Court that the Copyright Term Extension Act of 1998, which extended terms to their ridiculous current state, was unconstitutional, he decisively lost. When the P2P service Grokster was taken to the Supreme Court in 2005, and the service claimed that they couldn't be ruled as secondarily liable for the infringement of their users, because they didn't have specific knowledge of infringement, the court ruled *unanimously* against them. The decision was a withering repudiation for those who claimed that, like the VCR, any P2P service was legal because it *could* be used for non-infringing purposes:

> The question is under what circumstances the distributor of a product capable of both lawful and unlawful use is liable for acts of copyright infringement by third parties using the product. We hold that one who distributes a device with the object of promoting its use to infringe copyright, as shown by clear expression or other affirmative steps taken to foster infringement, is liable for the resulting acts of infringement by third parties… And although the networks that they enjoy through using the software can be used to share any type of digital file, they have prominently employed those networks in sharing copyrighted music and video files without authorization.

In a lesson for those who assume aged Judges are incapable of adequately relating to new technologies, the decision demonstrated an impressive grasp of the intersection between P2P technology and its practical use. Though Grokster was not aware of every specific instance of infringement by their users, the court chided, "a few searches using their software would show what is available on the networks the software reaches." Given the evidence of up to 90 percent of files being on Grokster being infringing and billions of files being shared "the probable scope of copyright infringement [was] staggering." The court acknowledged the advertising that appeared on Grokster's pages as users browsed for files and sardonically noted that "while there is doubtless some demand for free Shakespeare, the evidence shows that substantive volume is a function of free access to copyrighted work. Users seeking Top 40 songs, for example, or the latest release by Modest Mouse, are certain to be far more numerous than those seeking a free Decameron, and Grokster and StreamCast translated that demand into dollars."

The court directly confronted the difficult nuances and tensions between copyright protections and allowing new technologies to develop. But where copyright critics like Cory Doctorow accepted the ease with which digital works can be perfectly copied as the sign of a natural and unstoppable force, the court instead recognized the existential threat that condition presented to the very survival of copyright and a corresponding need to identify appropriate courses of punishment:

> The more artistic protection is favored, the more technological innovation may be discouraged; the administration of copyright law is an exercise in managing the trade-off. The tension between the two values is the subject of this case, with its claim that digital distribution of copyrighted material threatens copyright holders as never before, because every copy is identical to the original, copying is easy, and many people (especially the young) use file-sharing software to download copyrighted works. As the case has been presented to us, [the legal protections afforded to rights holders] should…be offset by the different concern that imposing liability, not only on infringers but on distributors of software based on its potential for unlawful use, could limit further development of beneficial technologies. The argument for imposing indirect liability in this case is, however, a powerful one, given the number of infringing downloads that occur every day using… Grokster's software. When a widely shared service or product is used to commit infringement, it may be impossible to enforce rights in the protected work effectively against all direct infringers, the only practical alternative being to go against the distributor of the copying device for secondary liability on a theory of contributory or vicarious infringement.

Determining secondary liability would be dependent upon evidence that the administrators of any digital service or website demonstrated awareness of likely infringement and made no reasonable effort to address it. The supposedly "vague" language in the SOPA and PIPA bills—describing sites "dedicated to theft," that served no significant purpose other than infringement or its facilitation, and failed to take "reasonable" actions to address infringement on their sites—was largely based upon the language of the unanimous Grokster decision by the Supreme Court. Another major US P2P service, Limewire, was also conclusively ruled against in 2010. Meanwhile, in Europe and other nations around the world, courts were taking action against The Pirate Bay or other services they determined to be in violation of copyright. In a landmark decision in 2012, the United Kingdom High Court ordered six ISPs to block The Pirate Bay. Precedents for determining what constituted fair Internet commerce were becoming more and more clear.

In regards to SOPA, it bears repeating that it was not applying US law to other countries, but applying it to domestic ISPs and companies that were serving as middlemen between American Internet users and foreign "rogue" sites that would have been held liable as dedicated to infringement if based on US soil. SOPA didn't affect "rogue" sites or their ability to reach their foreign consumers; it sought to ensure that the US consumer market was not being easily targeted by such sites.

In any case, with the illegality of sites "dedicated" to infringement becoming clear, those who desired an "open" Internet, free from the supposedly "chilling" effects of copyright enforcement, were running out of arguments, and their responses to rights holders' interests being legally upheld became ever more dubious.

After the UK High Court decision against The Pirate Bay was announced, the Executive Director of the Open Rights Group, Jim Killock, told the BBC that it was "pointless"—a tacit admission that he did not view the serial violation of creators' rights with much seriousness. "We should keep blocking them," countered analyst Mark Little. "They are stealing music illegally."[4]

UK Pirate Party leader Loz Kaye utilized another argument in the same BBC report. He couldn't very well call the UK High Court decision "censorship," as they had clearly found the actions of The Pirate Bay illegal. "The truth," Kaye said, "is that we are on a slippery slope towards Internet censorship here in the United Kingdom."

Yes, the slippery slope. The same argument used by Google's Eric Schmidt against SOPA months before the legislation was introduced, implying that to block sites like The Pirate Bay meant that the United States would be encouraging or drawing closer to the real, content-based censorship of China or Iran. During SOPA, tech bloggers began calling it the "Great Firewall" of the

United States. But the argument was based on an enforcement measure to be used consistent with established law, as we see in the Grokster decision. There was no especially good reason to believe the slippery slope would come to pass, given the Bill of Rights and the paranoia of the technology community. But the argument wasn't a matter of solid reasoning; it was propagandist, baseless fear mongering. After all, any law enforcement measure could be construed as leading to a slippery slope in the hands of the wrong government—be it site blocking or something else. Are we to stop arresting criminals, merely because authoritarian regimes happen to arrest artists, lawyers and activists they don't approve of? The slippery slope strategy is a simple-minded, last ditch effort at protecting the knowing enablers of file sharing.

However, slippery slope arguments succeeded in the case of SOPA because the propagandists behind the blackout had a trump card— popular mistrust of both entertainment companies and a government awash in campaign donations and lobbyists. One didn't need to justify arguments that SOPA was a censorship law that functioned only to preserve Hollywood fat cats, but only remind consumers of how evil the RIAA and MPAA were. After the Decade of Dysfunction had built, maintained and amplified irrational biases against creative industries and for "technology," all the anti-SOPA brigade had to do was exploit these biases. No evidence, nuance or good faith was necessary. We neglect to correct the Decade of Dysfunction at our own cost, because it has left a population (the young, especially) without the conceptual tools to grapple with piracy, and an uneducated population is an easily manipulated population.

Now we see how categorical attacks, that digital copyright enforcement is "censorship," are baseless when applied to exploitative online businesses like Grokster or its modern equivalent, The Pirate Bay; that record labels, publishers and film studios are really just extensions of creators' individual rights to choose how their work should be distributed; that the categorical denunciation of "gatekeepers" or "middle-men" of the creative industry is really a cowardly attack upon creators' rights which are fundamental to such industries; that The Pirate Bay isn't so different from past entities that exploited the hard work of creators for financial gain, like the Stationers' Company; and that copyright is an Enlightenment-based idea central to the ideals of an open democracy while also enshrined within the Universal

Declaration of Human Rights. Looking at the law helps us to see the importance of creators' rights, and how those rights have been ignored by those who would prefer to go on exploiting artists for pleasure or profit.

There is another sacred framework, within which those in favor of exploiting today's creators have hidden their true intentions, from the public if not from themselves: economics.

Markets, Morality and Incentives

The legal protections afforded to individual creators and business through copyright are no longer up for debate—at least as it pertains to the Napsters, Groksters and The Pirate Bays of the world. The lack of hope for challenging digital copyright through the law resulted in the movement's greatest advocate, Lawrence Lessig, announcing in 2010 that he was effectively putting the brakes on his campaign for copyright reform. With the legal thicket of the Decade of Dysfunction cleared, those unwilling to acknowledge the legal and human rights of individual creators fled for cover in the thicket of economics.

Those who mask their support of the illegal exploitation of creators in economic principles maintain that the logic of supply-and-demand means that the abundant supply of digital content drives demand for such products to zero. Creative goods are scarce in the physical realm, but the Internet had changed that and the illegality or immorality of infinite goods is immaterial. As Chris Anderson noted earlier, piracy is analogous to the natural force of gravity.

However supply-and-demand curves may be used to justify piracy, there is a more fundamental question that must be addressed. After all, the lower costs (approaching zero) of any unsanctioned black market also operate on "post-scarcity" principles. All market scarcities are somewhat "artificially" upheld by the law, through threat of criminal punishment.

For a commercial market to exist in the first place, it must be sanctioned under law, by consent of producers and consumers within a functioning citizenry. Otherwise, the lack of trust results in chaos, preventing the market from functioning fairly or to its full vigor. Digital piracy is not the same as theft, but it is a clear violation of the fair commercial market, which producers and consumers enter under good faith that they will not be unfairly exploited. Just like serial shoplifting by consumers or price gouging by business trusts, the unequivocal injustice of serial and knowing copyright violation erodes this sense of good faith. And it isn't just some naïve Brooklyn hipster who believes this, but the father of capitalism.

Before Adam Smith penned *The Wealth of Nations*, he wrote a less famous but also important work called *The Theory of Moral Sentiments*. Smith sought to explain the sympathies of man and how such individual sympathies combined to form an acceptable social code for society. Quite the opposite of what Chris Anderson would have you imagine, *The Theory of Moral Sentiments* was chock-full of morality and value judgments. "How selfish soever man may be supposed," Smith wrote, "there are evidently some principles in his nature, which interest him in the fortune of others, and render their happiness necessary to him, though he derives nothing from it, except the pleasure of seeing it." Smith may have been lecturing the many digital pirates among us when he proclaimed that "to restrain our selfish, and to indulge our benevolent affections, constitutes the perfection of human nature." But Smith knew that such perfection, though a wonderful thought, was impossible to achieve as practical reality. He reasoned that, though lacking perfection, men acted with "tolerable decency" in most everyday interactions and this natural code was good enough to prevent injustice in most instances. "Without this sacred regard to general rules," he said, "there is no man whose conduct can be much depended upon. It is this which constitutes the most essential difference between a man of principle and honour and a worthless fellow."

We might expect one of these "general rules" to mean both respecting the dignity of a person's labor and their equally held legal rights as common citizens. Without such respect, what market-based society can hope to function? As Adam Smith makes clear, we cannot simply wish the contributions of moral character away by hiding behind the perceived logic of the market or wishes of technology. At the day's end, we face ourselves in the mirror. Have we contributed to ensuring a fair society or not? Smith writes:

> The characters of men, as well as the contrivances of art, or the institutions of civil government, may be fitted either to promote or to disturb the happiness both of the individual and of the society. The prudent, the equitable, the active, res-olute, and sober character promises prosperity and satisfac-tion, both to the person himself and to every one connected with him. The rash, the insolent, the slothful, effeminate, and voluptuous, on the contrary, forebodes ruin to the individual, and misfortune to all who have any thing to do with him.[1]

One form of "ruin" that awaited those who turned a blind eye to "insolent" and "slothful" digital piracy was the harm done to new and innovative means of artists to distribute their work. Will Page, of PRS For Music, observed this subtle threat in a 2010 interview with none other than Mike Masnick:

> The best way to approach the unlicensed services is to think of it this way—we're all chatting about whether Spotify will sink or swim, right? That's the hot debate at the moment. Well, I would argue that at the margin Spotify would have far more chance of swimming, or up selling the subscription service, had they not had to face this unfair competition of illegal free. That's a powerful argument when you run it through, as it moves away from the old arguments and towards a more plausible observation: what opportunities are being foregone in the legal digital market due to the unfair competition of illegal free?[2]

Those who dismiss the importance of digital copyright or gatekeepers, the evangelists of New Media, speak of the emergence of digital piracy as a sentinel of technological innovation, but in reality nothing could be less innovative. Perhaps it was fair to gang up on the "legacy media" industry in 2000 or 2002 for failing to adapt, but does that sentiment hold any weight whatsoever today?

For all the real or imaginary misdeeds of the content industry in the past, a continually expanding array of licensed digital services are being offered around the globe: digital sales, free streaming, paid streaming, online radio and consumer-direct services like Bandcamp. Does anyone really believe that the widespread use and acceptance of knowing distributors of unlicensed content, like The Pirate Bay, is helping any of these sanctioned markets to grow or develop? True innovation lies in these markets, sanctioned by law that fulfills Adam Smith's baseline of "tolerable decency." As noted in *National Review*, the idea that the entertainment industry must "innovate" and compete against "illegal free," as they would with any other competition, rather than pursue law enforcement strategies, is a fallacy:[3]

> When brick-and-mortar bookstores complain about the threat they face from Amazon.com, they are complaining that

customers will leave them for a superior alternative; when Hollywood complains about piracy, they are complaining that customers have left them for an illegal alternative. They have stopped paying for Hollywood products yet are still consuming them. These are not even remotely similar situations—morally, legally, or economically.

I can hear a few readers scoffing about the copyright industries' historic attacks on new technologies and innovations. We are told the music and film industries tried to stifle the spread of innovations like radio, motion pictures, the VCR and MP3 player. But if they tried to choke the use of these technologies, they didn't do a very good job. Their apparent incompetence wasn't because of fuddy-duddy economic theories or the power of technology being a force "like gravity," it was because they were on the wrong side of the law which ultimately regulates the market. Those controversies were settled in the *courts* just as P2P has been settled in the *courts*. In the case of P2P, the True Believers simply would rather ignore the court decisions and go on believing that Internet "openness" means we must allow an unfair marketplace that excuses illegal exploitation.

Businesses are keen to give away limited amounts of free products or services when they see an opportunity to attract customers, just as marketers continually seek new ways to attract attention to promote their clients. But for the supreme difference between these classic cases of "freeness" or "innovation," and what Masnick and Anderson wrote of, we return to the matter of rights and consent.

Musicians and their record label partners are free to give their music away if they perceive they can make more money in the long-term by reaching a wider audience. Beggars Group has used this very strategy in the past. The label consortium temporarily offered free downloads of albums by both Titus Andronicus and Kurt Vile to reach new customers quickly. There is no conflict between an artist holding on to their exclusive rights of distribution and choosing to give their work away. There is no conflict between copyright and artists such as Josh Freese or Amanda Palmer looking for new ways to "connect with fans." Can't we approach the digital age with respect for all creators' rights, no matter how they may be executed?

Carving out a career as an artist of any kind is difficult and desperate. As consumers and fans, it is not our role to arrogantly tell creators what they can and cannot do with their own works, while simultaneously exploiting their labor for our own amusement. We are here to support those creators whose work speaks to us with our attention or, if we are asked and we feel it is a fair price, with a few dollars. The merchants of creative industries are not entitled to our money. If for any reason we feel offended or apathetic about a particular author, magazine, or musician it only makes sense to take our dollars elsewhere. What they *are* entitled to, if we are to consider ourselves members of a "tolerably decent" society, is only our basic respect for their rights under the law.

In an attempt to bridge the extremes of the piracy debate, it is crucial to acknowledge the exploitation inherent to piracy, but also the violation of the public's right to a public domain of our creative heritage. There is no "tolerable decency" to be found in the near-perpetual copyright terms we have in 2012 and any fair push for common sense copyright enforcement must be paired with a radical reduction in the length of copyright terms. The piracy debate is dominated by extremists on both sides, while "tolerably decent" society is imperiled in the middle.

As Adam Smith, the great capitalist, wrote:

> Society... cannot subsist among those who are at all times ready to hurt and injure one another. The moment that injury begins, the moment that mutual resentment and animosity take place, all the bands of it are broke asunder, and the different members of which it consisted are, as it were, dissipated and scattered abroad by the violence and opposition of their discordant affections. If there is any society among robbers and murderers, they must at least, according to the trite observation, abstain from robbing and murdering one another. Beneficence, therefore, is less essential to the existence of society than justice. Society may subsist, though not in the most comfortable state, without beneficence; but the prevalence of injustice must utterly destroy it.[4]

In the interest of justice, we ought to stare one of the prime tensions of the digital era straight in the face: where does progress reside, if the same technology that offers creators radical new choices for distribution simultaneously democratizes consumers' ability to disrespect those same choices—in other words, to rip them off? Where do we draw the line?

The author Daniel Pink studied the relation between incentives, motivation, and results in his book *Drive*.[5] When examining how economic incentives operate in work environments that require cognitive skills and creativity, he found some surprising results, which bear on our discussion of professional artists. As those still resentful of Lars Ulrich will feel vindicated to hear, the higher the rewards people are offered in creative work environments, according to multiple studies, the worse their performance becomes. But in direct conflict with the starving artist mythology, he also found, "If you don't pay people enough, they won't be motivated... The best use of money as a motivator is to pay people enough to take the issue of money off the table. Pay people enough so that they're not thinking about the money, they are thinking about the work." This aligns with the real ideal of copyright, that creators are able to make a comfortable enough living so that they can focus on giving us more of want we want—their music, prose and expressive visions.

Interestingly, in Pink's studies, once the thought of money was taken off the table, creative workers performed *even* better when they were offered the opportunity for autonomy, mastery, and purpose: essentially the ingredients for being an independent artist who has found a supportive audience—the ideal of copyright that's as good of a "reason to buy" as anything else.

But the reality of copyright's incentives have been lost amidst the cacophony of insults and accusations. Content revenues statistics are parsed and manipulated by one side of the debate or the other in order to justify pre-existing attitudes. It is impossible to say just how harmful digital piracy has been to the entertainment industry or to artists. There *is* the fact that the global record industry is less than half the size it was in 2000 and it stands to reason that the corresponding emergence of digital piracy had a fair amount to do with it. Regardless, endlessly debating whether piracy was responsible for 40 percent of industry losses or 60 percent seems to miss the real point.

Artists aren't stupid. They come to understand very quickly that to pursue a career as an artist is to ask for a lot of hardship, failure and uncertainty. It is a sacrifice, especially when one considers the stability and pay of non-copyright-based professions. But the risk of that sacrifice is usually considered worthy because the artist is somehow compelled to pursue their work *and* there is some possibility, even a remote possibility, that their risk might eventually bring a financial reward. If modern civilization wants to have full-time artists as part of our cultural milieu then it stands to reason that these artists will need to pay for food, shelter, clothing and perhaps put some money away for the future. In the interviews from Part Two, Kyp Malone, Ira Wolf Tuton and Craig Finn all alluded to long difficult periods where it was unclear whether their music could sustain them financially. They had to take a leap of faith—quitting their day jobs because turning their art into a career required a greater commitment. Implicit in their choices to take that risk was the prospect of reward.

So, if one is a fan of creative culture and has enjoyed professional works released through record labels, movie studios and publishers—in other words, if a fan has reaped rewards from the copyright-based industries in the past—where is the wisdom in stripping that tool away from the most ambitious creators? It only makes the creation of new *quality* works by professional artists that much more unlikely. In a world without copyright, would Kyp, Ira or Craig have continued to pursue their art, or switched gears toward making money through conventional means and treated music like a hobby? There is no way of knowing what might have been—just as there is no way of knowing what young artists might have benefitted from greater respect for digital copyright in the past decade. Has the stress put upon the music industry meant great bands having gone undiscovered or deciding against dedicating themselves to their art? Again, we'll never know.

When Kyp, Ira and Craig were taking risks to pursue music full-time, their bands were still building an audience. They needed support, and that support largely came from their record labels. Without a respect for copyright from consumers, such record labels and their support won't exist. As Joe Gaer of the Social Registry stated in our interview, "Why are people going to invest money in an artist's career if there's no hope in making money?"

Yes, the efficiency of the Internet can make an artist's marketing and promotion far less expensive if they already have an audience to build from. There are new ways for artists to engage with their audience and build their business. But when Chris Anderson writes that the solution to "illegal free" is to "[s]imply offer something better or at least different from the free version"; or when Mike Masnick tells artists that they need to "add value" if they expect fans to give them any money for the music they have illegally downloaded, I question their basic understanding of copyright. The wisdom of copyright is to focus the incentives, like a laser, upon the creative work itself. If our shared interest is the creation of more and better art, then why take away the fundamental legal right that incentivizes it, while setting artists off on a wild goose chase to find the best marketing scheme rather than to write the best song? The only true way of "adding value" to art is to make *better* art of *higher* quality. And that takes time—years in the cases of many creative works. That time means a need for money to live. As was the state of affairs in the United Kingdom before the Statute of Anne was passed in 1710, most people are not going to give you their money for a product or respect your exclusive right to sell it in the absence of some law and punishment that compels them to do so. Hence, copyright.

When faced with the easy option of piracy, of course that temptation is difficult to resist. This reality was captured by the online comic "The Oatmeal" entitled, "I Tried to Watch *Game of Thrones* and This Is What Happened." The main character attempts many different legal options to watch the first season of HBO's "Game of Thrones" but ultimately pirates it because the only legal means available involves the inconvenience of signing up for an HBO subscription through a cable service.[6] The comic was an insightful examination of the frustrations that occur when a consumer is conscientious of doing "the right thing" but also knows that a perfect, free copy of a television show or album can be had with a simple Google search. It also lays bare the absurdity of calling illegal exploitation of creative works "file sharing" or "remix culture" or "free culture." The character is perfectly aware of what he is doing but does it anyway because it is easy.

The comic inspired a minor debate online about HBO not having given non-cable subscribers a way to pay for the show, and effectively blamed HBO for people's choices to pirate their material. But the reason HBO was able to pour money into a project like *Game of Thrones*—a show millions fell in love with—*is* their restrictive policy that guarantees a return on their investment.

It is a difficult tension—when we love what a content creator has made for us so much that we can't resist violating their legal rights and undercutting the very infrastructure that brought us our art, on our path to illegally downloading it for free. I don't have an answer for that tension. As I have stated, so long as unlicensed downloading is as convenient as it is today, that temptation will be difficult to fight.

But we *can* be aware and honest about our actions and wonder what it means to be "tolerably decent" as it pertains to copyright. We can take note of the creative works that we love and note whether they were produced with the support of copyright. Whether we pirated that album or not, perhaps it will become clear just how much we benefit from the existence of copyright and the incentives it creates for high quality content.

There should be no question about what it means when we accept the illegal exploitation of creators, or the pathetic white-washing of that exploitation in vague concepts like post-scarcity, innovation, sharing, freedom, free speech or Internet openness. To undercut respect for copyright or pretend that it no longer matters is an attack on all creators, from the poorest to the richest. And it is an attack on us. Each time we consent to piracy, whether in conversation or in action, we do our little part to lessen the chances of our most beloved music, films, books or television shows being made in the future. As a society, will we actively value high quality art, creativity and communication on into the 21st century? Will we make the market more fair or increasingly unwelcoming for artists? The choice in what kind of incentives we provide for independent creativity is ours and ours alone, and it starts with respecting the legal rights of creators to choose their own path.

TRAGIC IRONY

From the early days of the Decade of Dysfunction, the apologists for piracy reliably presented file sharing as an action that hedged, in one way or another, against media corporation profits, corporate musicians, or corporate control over culture. Corporations were succeeding in their efforts to assert their will over the future of creativity, the thinking went, and that sin far exceeded whatever transgressions were inherent to piracy.

In regards to creative industries, we know that this anti-corporatism was misplaced in many regards. Corporate record labels and film studios only existed as a function of individual artists choosing to partner with them and in some cases these corporate entities invested in beloved content and helped artists build serious careers. However, the RIAA lawsuits were forever relevant to public attitudes of the biggest content companies. At the same time, income inequality in the United States was yawning just as the influence of special interests in government grew. Neither public nor private institutions were held in particularly high regard in the 2000s (or since). In the context of the times, piracy felt like a vote of "no confidence" if not an outright protest of the world as it stood.

The problem with a vote of "no confidence" is that it ends up being a vote for the side you oppose, the side happy to pursue its own goals motivated by power or profit. Blame it on the novelty of it all or the confusion spawned through the Decade of Dysfunction, but digital pirates' misunderstanding of and disregard for copyright led them toward creating a fertile terrain for the very corporatism in art they claimed to abhor.

As discussed in the last chapter, one of the strengths of copyright is the way it efficiently engineers incentives for creative works. But it also provides an answer to the problem of how keep creativity as independent as possible in the midst of private or state power which might have their own interests in mind.

In the 2000s, as people entertained the notion of music and art regressing to the days before copyright, the idea emerged that we might return to a patronage model, like the one that supported the composers and artists of the Middle Ages and Renaissance. If consumers were going to stop spending money on creative works, choosing to believe that copyright no longer mattered, this prediction made some sense. Without the incentives secured by copyright, labels and publishers would eventually disappear without consumer support. Artists, desperate for financing, would be gradually drawn by this desperation to those institutions and individuals in society who still had superfluous money to spend. As Jaron Lanier observes, "What free really means is that artists, musicians, writers, and filmmakers will have to cloak themselves within stodgy institutions. We forget what a wonder, what a breath of fresh air it has been to have creative people make their way in the world of commerce instead of patronage."[1]

In the market-based capitalism most of the world lives under today, the new nobility and monarchs are still found, to some degree, in government grants, but mostly in the forms of the multinational corporation, whose patronage is facilitated through advertising and marketing companies. The acceptance of "free" does not encourage creative independence or cultural democracy; it is effectively a surrender of power on the part of consumers, leaving a vacuum for other more powerful institutions to fill. To decide that creative culture should now be "free" is not a rejection of the commercial market, it is a rejection of one's own potential influence upon that market: self-disenfranchisement by the dollar.

In the music industry, the shift toward corporate patronage was observed and felt.

In the UK, where the music industry actually experienced growth in the late 2000s, the shift toward methods of patronage was seen in an increase of Business-to-Business revenues (B2B) versus Business-to-Consumer (B2C) ones. In 2008, total UK music industry revenues grew a full 4.7 percent despite the ongoing problem of piracy. In a report written by Will Page for PRS for Music, their chief economist, he found that business-to-consumer (B2C) revenues (consumer spending) had risen slightly, by about 3 percent, over 2007 figures. But B2B revenues, such as corporate sponsorship and the licensing of songs for advertisements, jumped a full 10 percent. Page noted that the B2B went from comprising 20 percent of total revenues in 2007 to 25 percent in 2008. B2B revenues rose again in 2009 and 2010, even as B2C revenues shrank, in signs of an ongoing shift between consumer and corporate patronage. In a separate report by IEG, North American marketing companies planned to spend over $1.09 billion to sponsor music venues, festivals and tours in 2010, a year-on-year increase of 4.2 percent, and then $1.17 billion in 2011, a 7.3 percent increase.

We have discussed various "new models" for creative commerce in the digital age. In 2009, Sean Adams, editor of the UK music blog *Drowned In Sound,* articulated his view of where the music business was headed in the event that sales disappeared. "I think corporate patronage is the only viable model," he said. "Something that mashes up Levi's ads in the '90s and the Starbucks label."

"At the end of the rainbow of open culture," warns Jaron Lanier, "lies an eternal spring of advertisements.... Any other form of expression is to be remashed, anonymized, and decontextualized to the point of meaninglessness. Ads, however, are to be made ever more contextual, and the content of the ad is absolutely sacrosanct. No one—and I mean no one—dares to mash up ads served in the margins of their website by Google."[2]

As digital piracy took hold through the 2000s and sales revenues sank, the American independent music scene became ever more branded and used as a sales prop for car companies and banks.

Beloved Pacific Northwest rockers Modest Mouse lent one of their most beautiful songs, "Gravity Rides Everything," to be used in a minivan commercial in the early 2000s, setting the stage for what was to come. Torchbearers of anti-corporate punk, Sonic Youth, signed on to release an album through the Starbucks' record label, Hear Music. Chicago post-rock legends The Sea And Cake sold one of their songs to appear in a Citigroup ad in 2009. Neon Indian, far and away one of the most hyped new bands of 2009, followed up their critically acclaimed debut album *Psychic Chasms* with a highly anticipated single in 2010. The song was released by Green Label Sounds, a "record label" which is in reality a branding vehicle for Mountain Dew. Grizzly Bear, another highly-touted young band from Brooklyn, enjoyed a wildly successful 2009 with their album, *Veckatimist*, and its lead single, the irresistibly catchy "Two Weeks." The song found its monetized success as the soundtrack to a Volkswagen ad. Then, Grizzly

Bear released a new single in April 2010 as a jingle for a Washington State Lottery commercial. Vampire Weekend did a Honda commercial, Karen O of Yeah Yeah Yeahs recorded a cover for Chipotle burrito, Phoenix broke though to a far wider audience only after lending a lead single to Cadillac, and every week or two another "Indie" band was announced to be partnering with Taco Bell, Bushmills, or Chili's restaurants. Green Label Sounds, Mountain Dew's "label" handled by the marketing agency Cornerstone Promotions, was just the first corporate label looking for a foothold in the indie rock demographic. Vice Marketing client Scion announced their own label in 2011 and Converse shoes (another Cornerstone Promotions client) built a studio in Williamsburg, Brooklyn, and invited bands in to record for free. The young hip-hop duo The Cool Kids' own Green Label Sounds release even included a Mountain Dew logo within the album cover art. If The Shins, Death Cab For Cutie, Broken Social Scene, or The Rapture had done anything like the above in the early 2000s, the music scene's eyebrows would have collectively been raised. After the Decade of Dysfunction, fans barely noticed.

For such a shift to occur in the realm of independent music was noteworthy, because the subculture traced its "independent" lineage back to the stridently anti-authoritarian, pro-community, self-determined movements of punk rock, hardcore, and college rock. Certainly, consumers' knowledge of piracy's harmful effects for bands, combined with the identification of the indie rock demographic by marketers, combined with the artists' desperation for money equated to the paradigm shift in this unlikely corner of music culture.

Ben Sisario of the *New York Times* noted in a 2010 article that "lifestyle brands are becoming the new record labels."[3] He documented the construction of the recording studio in Williamsburg, Brooklyn by Converse. Josh Rabinowitz, music director at the Grey Agency, told Sisario that "Indie-inflected music serves as a kind of Trojan horse. Consumers feel they are discovering something that they believe to be cool and gaining admittance to a more refined social clique."

Artists like Neon Indian, Wavves, Best Coast, Bon Iver, Gorillaz, Vampire Weekend, Kid Cudi and many others had signed up to represent the "Trojan horse" for one brand or another. If young music fans felt under a pre-meditated marketing attack after reading Rabinowitz' quote, Zach Baron of the Village Voice provided a reality check. In the past, he said, consumers could "vote" for the major label machine or the independent music scene with their wallet:[4]

Fast forward to 2010. How do consumers vote with their dollar? By not spending it at all. Ask Ted Leo—people are no longer buying enough records to support musicians, period. Major, independent, whatever. No wonder then, as Sisario puts it, 'lifestyle brands are becoming the new record labels.' Someone has to pay artists, and increasingly, we're not doing it. So who is the enemy in 2010? We are. Not the majors. Not Converse. Us.

The link between digital piracy and a rise in corporate patronage was also acknowledged by the owners of Cornerstone Promotions, Jon Cohen and Rob Stone. The game of linking corporate brands to edgy young bands was pioneered by Cornerstone, a Manhattan marketing agency. Along with Converse and Mountain Dew, Cornerstone counted Bushmills, Levi's, Nike, TDK and Fiat among many other clients.

"Cornerstone is benefitting greatly from some of the turmoil in the music industry," Cohen said on the Fox Business cable channel in April of 2008, above an info banner on the screen that read, "Spinning Radio Jams into Corporate Jingles" and "Cornerstone uses strategies to target 15-34 year olds."[5]

Asked by the Fox Business anchor whether Cornerstone was in the business of helping artists to "sell out," Cohen again alluded to the effects of music piracy in the music business, explaining, "The artists tend to do very well. The record labels do very well. The publishers do very well. And in a very tough environment in the music business this has become a big source of income."

Cohen also illustrated the major difference between consumer patronage and corporate patronage. For music supported by fans, through the mechanisms of a record label and album sales, the idea for a song can come from anywhere. The artist has the freedom to explore, to change and to challenge themselves along with their audience. As described by Cohen, corporate patronage begins and ends with the "brand," with a client looking for sales of their product:

> The way we put our deal together is it starts with the brand and the idea. They come to us, give us some information, and Cornerstone is very much rooted in music and the culture that surrounds it so our job is to come up with some good creative thinking and then figure out, who is the best fit? Who are the right artists to work with? Do those artists show

a passion for that brand? And can we bring everyone together to have one strong common goal, to really expose what the brand is trying to achieve?

We can view corporate patronage through the prism of incentives. Under such a system, artists are given incentives to pander and give corporate brands the kind of music that they want. Music fans become incidental. And we get watered down, cross-genre collaborations like the ones sponsored by Converse, which result in songs about having *fun*, acting *crazy* and—more than anything—being an *individual*! Bethany Cosentino of Best Coast participated in one such corporate patronized collaboration with Kid Cudi and a member of Vampire Weekend. The song was called "All Summer."

"We just made something that is a fun song," Cosentino told the *Times'* Sisario, "that will hopefully make people dance around in their Converse during the summer."

Art is a sloppy, unhinged search for the truth—shared with an audience. Corporate patronage hems in that search and controls it, ensuring that artistic expressions fit within certain boundaries that are helpful to sales of soda or cars.

But the reach of the facilitators of corporate patronage, like Cornerstone, is not confined to music. It affects music journalism as well. Everyone knows that bands are desperate for cash for their recordings in the wake of music piracy, but online websites and blogs that depend exclusively on the low advertising rates of the web are just as desperate. The media website Gawker has reported on numerous examples of bloggers who have failed to disclose the fact that they have received advertising money in exchange for their positive coverage.[6] The clear label of "sponsored post" used on Gawker or The Awl for content that has been sponsored by an advertiser is a gesture toward the limits of normal advertising revenues in digital media. But are all sponsored posts labeled as such and what happens when the same patron that is funding the band is funding a music blog through advertising?

———————————

The music website Pitchfork emerged through the 2000s as the premier tastemaker for young music fans of the era. Over time, the website grew and developed their business, even getting into the business of producing music festivals in Chicago and Paris. Some questioned whether Pitchfork was undermining their journalistic credibility. Wouldn't they be tempted to promote the bands that played their festivals, in the interest of driving ticket sales, while ignoring those artists who didn't play ball?

When the site announced "Pitchfork.tv" in 2008 (an online television feature) Jim DeRogatis interviewed Pitchfork founder Ryan Schreiber for the *Chicago Sun-Times* and held his feet to the flame on the direction of his increasingly powerful website.[7] Schreiber easily dusted off DeRogatis' insinuations that a conflict of interest was emerging.

"I don't want to sound over-sincere," Schreiber said, "but it really is completely about the music we like and the music we're into and music criticism in general, and so far that's worked, so it would be not wise to suddenly be insincere… Our advertising department is completely separate from editorial and also from Pitchfork.tv. These things are totally independent of one another. We see where the conflicts of interest could exist, and we try to think about that so that it can become a non-issue."

Jim DeRegotis cited Bob Pitman, the former head of AOL Time Warner and his strategy of corporate synergy: "The idea was that a band signs to Warner Bros. Records, its song is used in the soundtrack of Warner Bros.-produced movies and TV shows, it's championed in Time magazine, it plays at Warner Bros.-owned theme parks, and AOL sells the music and the videos. They called him 'Bob Pitchman' and it was all about sell, sell, sell."

"Right. Exactly," said Schreiber. "That to me is the whole problem. I don't know… I see where you're coming from, but it's not like we're doing what we're doing just for corporate expansion or more money or something like that. It's a new model; we're just kind of testing it out and seeing how it goes."

DeRogatis noted that *Sound Opinions*, his radio show with Greg Kot, would never get in the concert business because they "wouldn't be journalists or critics anymore."

"I think there's more flexibility than that," Schreiber responded, "provided that you are being true to your ideals."

And what were the "ideals" of Pitchfork? As a reader of the site since 2000, the attraction of the site was its independence from the traditional music press and music industry. You could trust the site to promote the music that they sincerely believed to be good.

As noted by Todd Patrick in our interview, Cornerstone Promotions had a cozy relationship with *FADER Magazine*, one of the most stylish and hip chronicles of edgy culture. It turns out that there is barely a line in which Cornerstone stops and *FADER* starts. In an interview found on YouTube, Cornerstone co-founder Rob Stone described the relationship with *The FADER*:[8]

> Cornerstone is a standalone company from *FADER*. Jon, who is my partner on the business, we own both companies outright. But without a doubt the ability to be on the pulse of what is happening on the *FADER* side with emerging artists and Indie bands and the world that's around *FADER* definitely helps us with the work that we do at Cornerstone.

So, *The FADER* helped to keep Cornerstone "on the pulse" of music trends, which they could then use to convince their real audience—corporate brands—that they were cool enough to market their products. Stone could claim the independence of the two entities all he wanted, but *FADER* was founded just two years after Cornerstone, held the same two owners and shared the same office space on 23rd Street in Manhattan. And it is apparently taken for granted by employees that *FADER* belongs to Cornerstone. In two separate interviews found on YouTube, Cornerstone employee Kevin Nicholson respectively describes Cornerstone as "a lifestyle marketing company and we also have a magazine called *The FADER* which is— we keep it two separate entities but it's still the same company"[9]; and "we also own a publication called *The FADER Magazine*."[10]

As much as *The FADER* employed many talented writers, designers and editors who covered emerging culture with aplomb, Todd Patrick was correct that it didn't exist "to be a great magazine" as other publications might. *The FADER* was a crucial tool in Cornerstone's business of facilitating corporate patronage.

On Wednesday, December 3rd 2008, a press release appeared in the inbox of music journalists:[11]

> PITCHFORK AND *FADER* MEDIA ANNOUNCE STRATEGIC PARTNERSHIP: Leading Voices In Emerging Music And Culture Join Forces To Offer Enhanced Opportunities For Advertisers and Readers
>
> New York, NY: *The FADER* and Pitchfork, the two leading voices in emerging music and culture, have announced a partnership designed to extend the reach and enhance both brands.
>
> The deal will include integrated advertising and sponsorship opportunities across all properties and platforms, including print, online, festivals, events, and unique content exchanges.
>
> "We are extremely excited to be working with Pitchfork," said Andy Cohn, Group Publisher and Vice President of *FADER* Media. "We know that the ability to leverage both properties will offer great value to our readers and advertisers alike."
>
> "We love *The FADER* and are continually impressed with their ability to navigate the ever-changing media landscape in a way that always stays true to their unique vision," said Pitchfork's Publisher/COO Chris Kaskie. "We believe this partnership will complement both brands and enhance what we can offer our advertising partners, and most importantly, our readers."

Though the press release made zero mention of Cornerstone, the email was sent by a Cornerstone employee.

As much as Pitchfork's Ryan Schreiber was conscientious of his site staying true to its independent ideals, what followed from this "strategic partnership" suggested otherwise, that corporate patronage from Cornerstone meant less freedom for Pitchfork to cover the bands and issues they thought were important and less ability for them to be honest with their readers. Advertising is a reality of nearly all media, of course, and its danger of shaping and influencing editorial content is nothing new. But in their embrace of corporate patronage, Pitchfork crossed a line.

Before and even shortly after the ostensible partnership with Cornerstone, Pitchfork had covered examples of corporate patronage in independent music, sometimes with disdain. When *Rolling Stone* and Camel cigarettes were implicated in an attempt to pass off a Camel advertisement as an editorial feature on "Indie Rock," Pitchfork noted that "*Rolling Stone* has come under fire from bloggers and message board pundits who believe the publication complicit in an alleged scheme to dupe lovers of indie rock."[12] In January 2009, the month after signing the "partnership," Pitchfork wrote that a Pepsi commercial featuring Bob Dylan and Will.i.am was "pretty gross."[13] When Pitchfork posted news articles on an artist partnering with a shoe company, for example, the brand of the patronizing company was nearly always kept out of the headline and sub-headline.

Days after the *FADER* deal was announced, Pitchfork posted a flurry of internship openings, on December 11th 2008. The next month a news story appeared about DJ Shadow designing a shoe through Reebok. Reebok, a Cornerstone client, was mentioned in the sub-headline. The same month they posted an interview with Matt & Kim, in which they spoke approvingly of Cornerstone's *Green Label Sounds* and the *FADER* label. The article conspicuously linked to both Converse, whom the band had done a song for, and Green Label Sounds.[14] Already, Pitchfork's integrity was compromised. The article mentioned Cornerstone related Converse, *Green Label Sounds* and the *FADER* label—and Pitchfork had just signed the "advertising and content" partnership—but there was zero disclosure of this, nor was there any mention of Cornerstone.

That interview, which appeared in the "news" section of the site, would be just one of dozens of Pitchfork "news" articles on Cornerstone-backed projects like Green Label Sounds, Levi's Pioneer Sessions, songs commissioned by Nike, Converse's Three Artists One Song campaign, and the Bushmills Since Way Back ad campaign. These "news" items usually featured the involved brand in the headline, linked to the ad campaign's homepage, featured embedded videos or songs created by and for the advertising campaign or printed sizeable excepts from press releases. Essentially, that is what corporate patronage turned the Pitchfork news section into, a surreptitious space for Cornerstone to promote its projects while enjoying Pitchfork's "Indie" stamp of approval among young *influencers*. Why try to convince an influential music site that they should cover your campaign when you can just as easily pay them to do so?

What's more, the approving tone of the articles bordered on self-parody. In 2010, Pitchfork wrote of Wavves' "Mountain Dew-tastic" single released through Green Label Sounds.[15] When they announced another Green label Sounds single from Neon Indian that year, the article finished with the aside, "Have you guys tried that Mountain Dew Game Fuel stuff yet? Terrible name, but that shit is really good. Best New Sodas."[16]

In 2009, Pitchfork.tv followed Wavves at South-by-Southwest. The video included over six minutes of Wavves hanging out at the Levi's *FADER* Fort, playing in front of the Levi's logo, picking out Levi's jeans and holding a Levi's bag. This, on an "Indie Rock" standard-bearing website that was covering the breakout "DIY" star of 2009. Credits at the end of the video went to the Levi's *FADER* Fort, *The FADER* and Cornerstone Promotions.[17] The video was inked and embedded on the *FADER* website under the headline, "~~FADER~~ Pitchfork TV: Daytripping with Wavves." A strange post followed:[18]

> Full disclosure: Some of us used to work occasionally for Pitchfork. None of them have ever worked here. Now we are kind of working together but not on anything fun. All of us apparently love Wavves, which is why it's hilarious that when Pitchfork TV recently filmed an episode of Daytripping with the band while in Texas, most of it ended up being shot at The *FADER* Fort.

In the case of the Bushmills campaign in 2011, it was common to be reading a "news" item on Pitchfork about Bushmills that included a video produced by Bushmills, while that "news" item was surrounded by ads for the very same Bushmills ad campaign. Bushmills produced a lengthy documentary on Pitchfork's Paris music festival in 2011 and sponsored the site's South-by-Southwest coverage in 2012.

After looking through the news archives, going back to 2007, the effect of Cornerstone seemed to be reflected in the number of news stories directed toward Cornerstone clients year by year. In the summer of 2008, the *FADER* website gave repeated coverage to a Converse campaign featuring Santigold, Julian Casablancas and Pharrell. Pitchfork gave this campaign zero coverage. The first Cornerstone-related story appeared in November 2008—one month before the partnership was announced—a brief mention of Matt & Kim's forthcoming album on the *FADER* label. So there was a single Cornerstone-related article in 2008 and none in 2007. I found four such articles in 2009, along with Pitchfork.tv features branded by Cornerstone clients like Levi's and Southern Comfort. In 2010, the amount of Cornerstone content peaked to twenty-two articles, then the number dropped to ten articles in 2011. Seven such articles appeared in the first two months of 2012.

I found no evidence of the Cornerstone partnership having any influence over reviews of albums that were released through Green Label Sounds or *FADER*. But the point is that corporate patronage prevented Pitchfork from deciding, for example, that Green Label Sounds was bad for music culture and to boycott their campaigns or albums, as they could have easily done if they were as independently-minded as the Pitchfork "brand" suggested. This association also made it less likely that Pitchfork would explore the interplay between fans not paying for their music and the rise in corporate patronage. Pitchfork had a historic opportunity to remind their readers that the artists covered on Pitchfork needed support from fans, but instead was curiously silent on the issue throughout the Decade of Dysfunction. The *FADER* Media partnership required a heightened amount of self-censorship and readers suffered as a result. Meanwhile, Pitchfork played a significant role in spreading widespread acceptance for corporate patronage because they were benefitting from the very same system.

In a 2011 interview with *SPIN Magazine*'s Eric Magnuson, Damian Abraham of the band Fucked Up was forthcoming on the influence of corporate patronage upon music. When Magnuson asked whether the term "selling out" meant anything in rock anymore, Abraham responded[19]:

> It still does. I'll admit it, I've sold out. I'm not saying I've sold out to the level of some other people. But as soon as you take money, you are selling out. Like, you have taken what you've created and you're lending it to someone else. That

doesn't mean that you're a sellout forever and everything you do is now tainted. But you've made the decision to take that money… I think that's the reality. It's kind of sad that it's gone this way. But you can't rewind five years, or ten years, or now twelve years ago. Not that I would want to because I think there's been a lot of amazing cultural developments. But you can't go back and get people to buy records again. We love talking about this kind of stuff but it can get a little heavy.

Abraham captured the sense of resignation many music fans and journalists seemed to feel toward corporate patronage or the fact that people no longer were buying the records they loved. But the strong, "heavy" opinions and feelings hiding just behind the surface of this resignation suggested an alternate path. Why couldn't credible voices like Abraham organize themselves and communicate to fans that there were consequences to piracy, that if they wanted independent music to remain viable, then it was important to support creators' rights? If resignation and pessimism can build, so can the sense of self-determination, hope and community that created the punk movement in the first place. Why couldn't passionate music fans lead us out of the doldrums of digital piracy, actively voicing support for the punk ethos that the audience and the performer were part of the same artistic community, one based upon respect and love for creativity and for one another?

It is a tragic irony that so many threw themselves into accepting digital piracy out of a distaste for corporate culture, while engineering the conditions for those same corporations to opaquely influence what bands deserved careers and what bands journalists should cover.

But that is what the lazy acceptance of the illegal exploitation of creators' rights gets us—a whole lot of disempowerment and cultural decline. Piracy is an act of self-destruction.

Whether you view the independent ethos of punk rock as conviction or contrivance, the erosion of that ethos provides a glimpse of the consequences to art and communication when content becomes unbridled from direct consumer support. Without the support of consumer patronage, advertising and branding are left to dominate the realm of incentives, moving deeper and deeper into our essential human need to communicate.

"Ads seem to work on the very advanced principle that a small pellet or pattern in a noisy, redundant barrage of repetition will gradually assert itself," Marshall McLuhan observed. "Ads push the principle of noise all the way to the plateau of persuasion. They are quite in accord with the procedures of brain-washing. This depth principle of onslaught on the unconscious may be the reason why."[20]

If we take McLuhan's analysis, then the consequence of corporate patronage in this respect is that rather than supporting and enjoying the art of our favorite musicians, we are tempting them to help unrelated companies subtly brainwash us in the matter of brand impressions. This is nothing new in our lives. We live with such advertising every day. The question is, do we desire spaces in our lives where such branding isn't welcome, where we have a direct experience with human creativity for its own sake?

The strange thing about True Believers in general is their remarkable blind spot for the loss of real freedom for individuals to influence their surrounding reality in a world of free content. Consumers' self-disenfranchisement is a logical consequence of delegitimizing the sanctity of creators' right to sell their work as they so choose.

Cory Doctorow has written in the past that piracy is a "distant second to the gravest, most terrifying problem an artist can face: censorship."[21] Doctorow admitted in a lecture before Google in 2007 that copyright was preferable, at least, to the patronage system of yore for this reason. "For one thing you got very little art that criticized the king or the Pope under that system," he said. "[Copyright] was a great flowering of expression, because all of a sudden you weren't dependent upon the whim of some plutocrat but rather on the hard-nosed business sense of syndicates of investors. It wasn't perfect, but it sure beat the hell out of 'the king said you can make art so you get to make art.'"[22]

In other words, patronage by concentrated institutions of power, rather than by wide swaths of individual consumers, raises inherent questions of censorship. So, it is strange that Doctorow isn't concerned by the consequences of corporate patronage, as was revealed in his answer to a question after a reading of his in 2006. There, Doctorow was making familiar arguments to his listeners, predicting that, "More people will get accustomed to reading off screens in the future. When that happens, we're going to have to figure out new ways to make a living." On that subject, an attendee asked whether Doctorow would ever plug Pepsi in one of his books. The author lifted his shoulders in embarrassment, and said, "I probably wouldn't plug Pepsi. I would plug someone else, though… I'd be totally transparent about it… I don't mind being a whore. I just don't want to be a cheap whore."

But what is the real difference between an artist being a "whore," either cheap or well compensated, for the Pope or for Citigroup or for the state? In a system in which corporate or government patronage is the only option for creators, overt censorship and self-censorship (or pandering) are inevitable based on realities of power and incentives. In the Renaissance you wouldn't find much art that was unfriendly to the King or Pope, sure. In the emerging reality of corporate patronage, suggested by the music industry, you won't find as many voices that seriously question the status quo of concentrated power. John Lennon, Bob Dylan, Nina Simone, Neil Young…they would never have found an audience under such a system taken to its logical extreme.

"What [people are] missing from a cultural perspective," says *Life, Inc.* author Douglas Rushkoff, "is just because we're not willing to pay for professional journalists doesn't mean that corporations have become unwilling to pay for professional public relations departments."

If we choose to abandon our public or private institutions (as citizens or consumers) in resignation to the self-replicating sign posts of decline, rather than seek to resurrect the health of those institutions, we emerge disempowered and asking to be manipulated.

THE NET FAIL

In Part One, I acknowledged the dreams of Kevin Kelly, that the Internet was destined to merge us into a great and bountiful "planetary soul." That appealing vision has gone on to inspire many activists in their quest to "protect" the Internet from threats to its "openness." The rights of creators (aka the rights of individuals) have been seen as the primary threat to this "open source" digital utopia which will eventually give us more prosperity, democracy and more freedom. In short, this is a belief in the power of networks and the collaboration they allow for. New Media academics like Clay Shirky and Jeff Jarvis have evangelized for this future. For them the future of the Internet should not include paywalls or respect for rights holders because it adds friction to their great wheel of digital life. We will not need professional journalists because the wise crowd knows more collectively than any individual journalist ever could. The wisdom of crowds, through the network effect, is the righteous salvation offered by the Internet.

The incredible effectiveness of the SOPA blackout was seen as the single greatest example of the potential of networks to improve our lives. How could the rights of a few measly artists or old-time corporations justify hamstringing the innovation of *the single greatest advance in human history*!

The technology companies who fought SOPA and participated in the blackout were seen as responding to heartening, grassroots efforts that organically originated from web communities like Reddit. The SOPA blackout was an American Tahrir Square or an offshoot of Occupy Wall Street—normal citizens standing up to defend the freedom of online expression in the face of draconian attempts at censorship that were merely an effort to put money in the pockets of the corrupt entertainment industry.

That's what it was…right?

Right…

When the SOPA blackout was gearing up in January of 2012, a distinct tone of paranoia emerged in the arguments being advanced by critics of the bill. SOPA didn't merely need reform; it needed to be killed. Why? Because it would actually break the Internet. If you posted a single infringing link to your blog, even unknowingly, you could face five years in jail. Were politicians so stupid and in the pockets of the entertainment industry that they would risk passing a bill that would break the Internet and send innocent people to jail for years and result in the mass violation of First Amendment rights? Yes, absolutely they would.

You don't trust politicians and the RIAA, do you?

What's more, SOPA wouldn't even make a difference for rights holders being hurt by piracy. And what would we, the public, be saddled with? Censorship! It was not a copyright bill. It was a censorship bill.

Do you support SOPA? Do you support (clears throat) INTERNET CENSORSHIP?

Due to these talking points, the public was placed in a position where they felt they had to be against the law even if they had never heard of the bill before, read about it or read the legislation itself. The tone and substance of the SOPA backlash harkened back to the heated debate over health care reform in the United States in the summer of 2008, in which ideological lobbying groups pumped an anxious public full of lies that fed their pre-existing biases. The claim that SOPA would break the Internet, I predicted, would go down in history as an infamous piece of propaganda, like the fear mongering warning that President Obama's health reform plan included "death panels" that would "kill Granny."

I took it for granted that the technology industry was viewing SOPA as major new government regulation upon their industry that, all things being equal, they would rather not have to deal with. But why talk about the reasons for or against regulation when you can just as easily scare the bejeezus out of people who weren't terribly well schooled on the issues? Though I suspected the technology industry's influence, I accepted the idea that Reddit had genuinely corralled their digital brethren in the fight against the legislation. With so many eyes on SOPA coming from an established Internet culture that prided itself on openness, transparency and sincere collective actions, it was hard to believe that technology companies like Google would be so daring as to risk being exposed for misleading the public. After following the

Decade of Dysfunction and engaging with a host of bizarre arguments that arose from a need to justify immoral actions, I knew false notions could easily rise up all on their own.

Even if I was appalled by the misinformation being dangerously bandied about, the success of the SOPA blackout was really something to behold. Perhaps it was the genuinely new paradigm of political action that SOPA critics made it out to be, a digital revolution by the consent of the networked. As Tech Crunch declared after SOPA was defeated, "A well-organized, well-funded, well-connected, well-experienced lobbying effort on Capitol Hill was outflanked by an ad-hoc group of rank amateurs, most of whom were operating independent of one another and on their spare time. Regardless of where you stand on the issue—and effective copyright enforcement is an important issue—this is very good news for the future of civic engagement."[1]

On January 26th, PPC Associates CEO David Rodnitzky posted a blog entry that questioned how "grassroots" the SOPA protests really were.[2] He noted, "Google's, Facebook, Twitter, AOL, eBay and many other companies have been aggressively lobbying Congress for months regarding SOPA." The companies had proposed an alternative bill to SOPA and taken out full-page ads in national newspapers on November 16th to express their opposition. Google's spending on lobbying had tripled from the previous year to $3.74 million in the fourth quarter of 2011 as the SOPA battle raged into the winter. Robert Levine, author of the book *Free Ride,* reported that Google's lobbying expenditures jumped once again in the first quarter of 2012, up to over $5 million, covering the run-up to the blackout on January 18th.[3] That was a 240 percent increase from the same period in 2011. Levine wrote, of Google's sudden $5 million lobbying tab:

> That's more than the official lobbying budget of the MPAA ($570,000 for the same time period), the RIAA ($1.67 million), or media companies like Disney ($1.3 million) or News Corp. ($1.57 million). It's more than Microsoft ($1.79 million), Facebook ($650,000), Amazon ($650,000), and Apple ($500,000) combined.

The Board of the Sunlight Foundation, which funded some groups who participated in the SOPA protests, included one former lobbyist for Google. Robert Levine has reported on the financial and personal ties between Google and "open" Internet advocacy groups like the Electronic Frontier Foundation (EFF) and Public Knowledge before. No one could say just how much Google did or did not affect the eventual blackout, but clearly the entertainment industry wasn't the only group flooding Congress with cash. Markham Erickson, who leads the NetCoalition—an advocacy group for tech companies such as Google, Facebook, eBay, Yahoo, Mozilla, Twitter and others—dusted off notions that his group had driven the blackout, telling the *New York Times* that, "The Internet responded the way only the Internet could."[4] In the same *Times* article, Representative Zoe Lofgren said, "Too often, legislation is about competing business interests. This goes way beyond that. This is individual citizens rising up."

David Rodnitzky at PPC Associates was skeptical. He tracked the first big bump in traffic for SOPA searches on November 16th—which happened to coincide with American Censorship Day, a sort of blackout-lite campaign run by the non-profit group Fight for the Future, and also the day of the full-page ads taken out by Google, Twitter, Facebook, et al. The second bump in traffic he saw occurred on December 13th, "when the *Washington Post* ran a story about a 'visual petition' on the website IWorkForTheInternet. com."[5] IWorkForTheInternet was also run by Fight for the Future. When Rodnitzky looked further into the websites run by Fight for the Future, he noticed that the names of whomever had registered their domain names were kept private on the online domain registry. And he found the lack of information provided on the groups themselves, mixed with the obvious professionalism of the websites, suspicious:

> The only names listed on the FightForTheFuture site are "Tiffiniy Cheng" and "Holmes Wilson." I looked up Tiffiniy online and she apparently works for "DownhillBattle," which as best I could tell is a blog that is mad about record labels. But she also lists herself as the "Founder, Executive Director, PPF, Open Congress." PPF is the "Participatory Politics Foundation," a 501-c-3 non-profit that was founded and funded by The Sunlight Foundation, which is also a non-profit… Anyways, I'm not an investigative journalist, but all of this strikes me as quite odd; the sudden launch of some very nicely designed, privately registered, anti-SOPA Web

sites without any contact info other than a woman who once founded a non-profit that gets money from another non-profit that gets money from technology companies? Methinks something is rotten in Denmark.

For most of the millions who signed petitions on January 18th, the day of the blackout, the controversy over SOPA was over nearly as soon as it began. They groggily logged online in the morning only to see Google, Wikipedia, Twitter and a host of other sites they trusted offering alarming information about SOPA. Users were linked to simple websites with petition forms and easy ways to send form letters to representatives in Congress. A couple of days later, users heard that SOPA was dead. These users, we were told, had participated in a revolutionary grassroots movement.

In the days and weeks after the defeat of SOPA, the protest of which had moved very quickly, journalists tried to understand how, exactly, it had happened. Of course, the technology companies and advocacy groups of Silicon Valley were thrilled, and trumpeted the rise of people power. As mentioned above, there were a few voices that questioned how grassroots the protests actually were and whether large companies like Google were truly driving the protests from behind the scenes. Sen. Chris Dodd, the former Senator who was president of the MPAA during the SOPA fight, accused technology companies of using their customers as "corporate pawns."

Mark Stanley, new media coordinator at the Center for Democracy and Technology, told *Macworld* that the notion that the SOPA protests were a top-down affair was wrong. He should have known, seeing as his group had "helped organize" the protest. "That's just such a mischaracterization of what happened. This was definitely the Internet community at large," he said.[6]

The *Macworld* article hewed closely to the conventional wisdom on how the blackout had developed—primarily through "open Internet" luminaries like Reddit and Wikipedia. Wikipedia's Jimmy Wales had mentioned the idea of a SOPA blackout in mid-December and Reddit, an online community in which users can post links or messages and the community has the power to vote them up or down, was the first site to publicly confirm their own blackout on January 18th. They made their announcement on January 10th.

At the time of the blackout, I was so busy trying to understand SOPA that the exact nature of the blackout's run-up eluded me. I accepted the widely-held assumptions about Reddit and Wikipedia. The fact that the "crowd" was so involved explained the poor arguments and misunderstandings emerging as fact in the controversy. Were technology companies and other non-profits involved? Well, of course they were. But without those collaborative online communities and the public rallying around them, the SOPA blackout never would have been possible.

The *Macworld* article cited only "very informal" organizing between outside "open Internet" advocacy groups and Reddit, according to Erik Martin, Reddit's general manager. Martin claimed that it was only after Jimmy Wales came up with the blackout idea that Reddit, and other websites, began to seriously consider a blackout.[7] The truth of the SOPA blackout is quite different from the myth of some wholesome demonstration of mass democracy. To understand how the protest came about, we must look more closely at Fight for the Future—the non-profit group David Rodnitzky called "a bit odd."

"Those guys were amazing," Mike Masnick said of Fight for the Future after the blackout. "They had ideas. Those were two people in Western Massachusetts who came out of nowhere."[8] In fact, Fight for the Future was founded in October of 2011—the same month SOPA was introduced in the House of Representatives—and the group's founders had been running "open Internet" projects like OpenCongress and the Participatory Politics Foundation for years. Founders Tiffiniy Cheng and Holmes Wilson had existed within the framework of non-profit websites and organizations like the Electronic Frontier Foundation and Public Knowledge—groups set against the enforcement of copyright online (because they believe enforcement violates "Internet freedom") and evangelists for "openness" and transparency. This non-profit network has deep personal ties to and funding from Silicon Valley, as shown in the work of Robert Levine.

For their part, Fight for the Future began in October 2011 with a $300,000 grant from the Media Democracy Fund, a foundation that dedicates itself to "free expression on the web."[9] In fact, Fight for the Future is a project of the Media Democracy Fund's Center for Rights.[10] The Center for Rights is described as "a nonprofit

working to expand the Internet's power for good" on the Fight for
the Future website.

Far from a grassroots organization, Fight for the Future was a well-
connected and well-funded arm of the Media Democracy Fund. In
the "about" section of the MDF website, they say the Fund:

> ... partners with funders to make grants that protect and pro-
> mote the public's rights in this new era. We help grant makers of
> all sizes and issue areas amplify their impact...More and more,
> economic opportunity, education, creativity, freedom of expres-
> sion and democracy are intertwined with access to and open-
> ness of our new information and communication technology.
> These connections mean that ignoring this area is no longer
> an option. But this emerging field can be confusing and com-
> plicated. MDF can help you simplify and focus. We understand
> the connections, the policy environment and the landmines. We
> help our partners cut through the noise and make an impact.[11]

The description sounds like MDF is an organization that filters
money from outside contributors, who have specific goals in mind,
to groups and projects that can ostensibly achieve those goals. Was
the $300,000 grant to Fight to the Future the result of one of MDF's
"partners" wanting to "cut through the noise and make an impact"?
If MDF was more or less a middle-man for its donors, then who was
the source of Fight for the Future's considerable funding?

The $300,000 grant was reported in a little read article by the
Boston Globe which revealed other interesting facts of the SOPA
blackout. Elizabeth Stark, a Stanford University Internet activist, is
paraphrased in the article as noting that Fight for the Future "was a
key participant" in the January 18th blackout and that the group built
"much of the technology that made it possible." But Fight for the
Future's "most significant contribution to the effort," according to the
Globe, "may have come during a Nov. 9 meeting about the antipiracy
legislation that was held at the Mountain View, Calif., headquarters of
Mozilla. Taking part that day were tech companies, advocacy groups,
and academics about the antipiracy legislation. Cheng and the group's
other cofounder, Holmes Wilson, 32, said they called in to the session
to pitch the idea of a November 16 protest, which also called for
companies and organizations to close down their websites."[12]

This early November meeting, facilitated by Mozilla, one of Silicon Valley's most visible businesses, never made it into the popular history of the SOPA blackout. Nor was it widely known that both Silicon Valley industry and their complements from the nonprofit world were strategizing so early. It is unclear which organizations were or were not involved, but Elizabeth Stark admitted on a 2012 panel on Internet activism that Google and Reddit joined Fight for the Future and Mozilla in the meeting.[13] So what really happened at this meeting and who was there? Was it true that, far from organically originating from Reddit in January or Wikipedia in mid-December, the idea of a blackout really came from a month-old nonprofit with a questionable source for its hundreds of thousands of dollars in funding?

The obscure website JammerDirect interviewed Fight for the Future co-founder Holmes Wilson for their podcast, The Dose, on January 25th 2012, one week after the conclusive SOPA blackout. Wilson was forthcoming on where the idea for a blackout came from and how that idea was brought to the strategy meeting on November 9th.[14]

"The strike movement itself started in late October—early November, right after SOPA came out," Wilson said. "When SOPA came out it was just way worse than anyone expected" and Fight for the Future started speaking by phone to the Electronic Frontier Foundation and Public Knowledge. Wilson described his reaction the SOPA and what he feared it would mean:

> I thought about it like, 'We were going to wake up and go to the same sites we use every day and see some stupid message from the government telling us we can't visit those sites anymore because we were Americans. Whatever we do for the campaign has to be based off of that feeling'... The idea for the protest was for sites to run one pop-up simulating the site being blocked... We started shopping it around to sites we were close to and organizations saying, 'We think this is the best way to respond to SOPA and are you in?' One of the key moments was—when working with a close friend of ours, Elizabeth Stark who is at Stanford, and has been into the free culture and remix culture movement for ages now—she worked with us to organize a meeting and call at Mozilla, the folks who make Firefox, at their headquarters in Mountain

View a week before the protest. And that was really pivotal in getting the attention of Mozilla and a few other large Silicon Valley organizations... The meeting was basically all these groups in DC being like, 'This is worse than anything we've ever seen and there is nothing we can do to stop it. This thing will pass unless we all band together and do something crazy.' And the folks in Silicon Valley were like, 'This wasn't even on our radar.'... Nobody knew about it. And on that call we said, 'Here's a proposal. We should block out our sites and direct people to email Congress.' Then one of the folks at Mozilla came up with the idea of blacking out your logo as a second-ary ask to sites that can't throw a pop-up on their page the whole day...And we were like, 'That's an awesome idea, we're gonna run with that too.' We put up a page the next day or that Friday, AmericanCensorship.org, and included instruc-tions on how to participate.

Yes, the blackout idea came directly from the MDF-funded organization and was presented to the inside players of Silicon Valley over one month before Jimmy Wales mentioned the blackout idea on Wikipedia. The day after the meeting organized by Mozilla, the veneer of populism was already being applied to the initiative of a handful of dedicated interest groups which derive their funding from Silicon Valley companies. Fight for the Future tweeted: "Internet fights back! PK, EFF, FFTF, FSF, OC to stop #protectip #sopa Join us 11/16 to help to stop worst bill," linking to Fight the Future's website, AmericanCensorship. org. "PK" stood for the group Public Knowledge; "EFF" for Electronic Frontier Foundation; "FFTF" for Fight for the Future; "FSF" for Free Software Foundation; and "OC" for Open Congress, an organization also run by the founders of Fight for the Future.

According to Fight for the Future, these five groups were "the Internet"—and "the Internet" was "fighting back."

As for Reddit, though involved in the Mozilla meeting according to Elizabeth Stark, they couldn't so easily begin advocating for SOPA protests, as they were a bottom-up community of users, predicated on a belief in the wisdom of crowds. As some have suspected, Fight for the Future actively posted articles trying to get the Reddit community involved. Holmes Wilson admitted to placing links on the site. He did so under the username "holmesworcester."[15]

And we got on Reddit that Friday. And it was tricky to get on Reddit even—Reddit is just this beehive of anti-SOPA sentiment but at that point really wasn't woken up to it. I remember sitting down at the keyboard and thinking, 'Okay what will get people's attention?' The post I wrote was something like, 'The MPAA will soon have the power to block American's access to any website unless we fight back'—comma—'hard!' And that was the post—that post got to the top. And that linked directly to the protest site (Fight for the Future's AmericanCensorship.org). So it started going viral. It started going viral on Tumblr at that point with people using the code (provided by Fight for the Future) to black out their titles and a lot of big Tumblr sites doing it. We started to see a lot of sites sign on. I think in the end five thousand sites signed on. And early in the next week we started to get some big sites. I forget exactly what happened with Reddit but at some point they said they would do it. We reached out to the folks at 4chan—4chan is awesome. And Mozilla, the folks who were on the call at Mozilla hustled all weekend—you know, Mozilla is a big organization and for them to take a step that pointed their millions of visitors to their start page to a political action, that's something they never had done before. That was unprecedented and the folks at Mozilla, they took that on and took it up the chain and made it happen… Then BoingBoing and Cory Doctorow there who is kind of an old friend of ours and has worked with us a lot on different stuff and has always been a supporter of projects we have worked on. I mean, he, he—they went above and beyond for us. The Reddit folks did. The conversation started with Wikipedia at that point, too. We said, 'Can Wikipedia do this?' and Wikipedia said, 'We don't control that.'

So, just as they had done to garner viral attention on Reddit, Fight for the Future posted on a Wikipedia forum asking about the site participating in the November 16th anti-censorship protest. "And we did that," Wilson said, "and it didn't go anywhere immediately but then Jimmy Wales restarted that conversation and it started to move forward. That was in mid-December." Some who questioned how grassroots the SOPA protest on January 18th really was point to reports in late December that NetCoalition was considering the "nuclear option" of a blackout. But it is clear that planning between opaquely-funded nonprofit organizations and the very companies represented by NetCoalition were in cahoots long before that date and, more than anyone, Fight for the Future engineered the strategy and organized the blackout. As Holmes Wilson described on The Dose, "The big surprise of that November protest—which was awesome—was that Tumblr called us in the middle of the day to warn us that they were either about to or already sending tons of traffic our way." According to Wilson, Tumblr alone directed 87,000 calls to congress on November 16th and posted an information page on the protest with "perfect talking points." With the success of the November 16th protest, Fight for the Future recognized the need for a follow-up protest:

> And the Round Two will let us go from all the people who participated to an even wider network and say, 'Okay guys, now is the time.' And in the end what really ended up happening was once the idea got out there, the idea itself, sort of took on a life of its own, where the seed we planted at Wikipedia—that started to go—into a real discussion that was engaging the whole community moving forward. There must have been a similar discussion going on at Google, internally. And everybody started talking about, 'When this really gets close to happening, what are we gonna do?' And Reddit called for it. They said, 'We're going dark on the 18th ' and Wikipedia was at the point at which they would almost decide—I think they made the final call the night before. And all the pieces were in place. And we were just like, 'Okay this thing is happening. We're just going to make a website to coordinate, that we can use to list all the sites that are participating and all the tools you can use to participate.' Basically just get out of people's way and give them the tools they need to do this... So yeah, that's the story.

There are some reasons to be hopeful about the future of Internet activism after the SOPA protests. They proved that it was possible to mobilize millions of people thanks to the radical efficiency of digital communication. And though the blackouts would never have happened or had their effects without the dedicated work and organization of Fight for the Future, there were also smaller protests that were more grassroots in nature. But Fight for the Future's deft strategy was to quickly co-opt any genuinely grassroots protest against or criticism of SOPA and then use it for their own advantage. When a long-time user on Reddit wrote to the community saying they were going to transfer dozens of their domains away from GoDaddy, in protest of the company's support of SOPA, the community of users rapidly joined in the boycott, which quickly led to GoDaddy reversing its position.

On December 22nd, the day of the boycott post, Fight for the Future tweeted: "Not an ad, but if u switch from @godaddy to another registrar / host, some companies will give u anti-#SOPA discounts." By December 23rd, they posted a new webpage, GoDaddyBoycott. org which facilitated that protest. That Fight for the Future webpage soon made its way to the original Reddit post, left at the bottom of the post for anyone who wanted to participate.

But the sad truth of the SOPA protests, led for months by Fight for the Future (and enabled by whoever the hell was funding them), was that the actions of millions were fueled by lies and propaganda. As Holmes Wilson said on The Dose, recounting when he was trying to get the Reddit community to run with American Censorship Day:

> 'Okay what will get people's attention?' The post I wrote was something like, 'The MPAA will soon have the power to block American's access to any website unless we fight back'—comma—'hard!' And that was the post—that post got to the top.

We should take note of Wilson's acknowledgement that he was struggling to get people's attention. The more desperate one is to get attention, rather than to accurately communicate what one believes a problem *is*, the more one ventures into the realm of sensationalist propaganda. While it is possible to find attention-getters that are nonetheless truthful, that is not what Wilson did and it is not what Fight for the Future has done or continues to do. Characterizing SOPA as the MPAA (and only the MPAA) having the unequivocal power to block access to "any" website was a misrepresentation (or an outright lie) that Wilson ought to be embarrassed about. Through the Private Right to Action (a provision I did not support), SOPA gave all creators the right to bring forth evidence that a site was "dedicated" to infringement and had reasonable knowledge of the infringement happening on their networks. That isn't "any site," that is a site that may be guilty of illegally exploiting the legal rights of artists or businesses. But such distinctions did not suit the goals of Fight for the Future, so they went on spreading baseless propaganda that frightened well-meaning Internet users into participating in a blackout under false notions.

As Wilson admitted, Fight for the Future was interested in results, not the truth, and they were willing to do whatever it took to sufficiently scare people into actions that benefitted their interests, and perhaps those of whomever was funding them. The slick video produced by Fight for the Future, called "SOPA/PIPA will Break the Internet," a fiction in itself, relied upon conflating the past mistakes of the entertainment industry with a bill that sought to protect all creators' rights. The video presented an entirely false choice between copyright enforcement and popular social networking sites continuing to exist. They presented "Internet freedom" as an inalienable right that the RIAA was trying to strip away, concealing the truth, that the imperfect bill's very aim was to protect human rights and legal rights of artists not be exploited by unsanctioned business. They deceived the public that SOPA was a "censorship" bill, clearly a talking point they had settled on early in the planning of the protest. The SOPA/PIPA video, filled with deception and fear-mongering, was eventually watched by over four million people.

Fight for the Future produced an infographic, also filled with propaganda.[16] It said that "a few infringing links are enough to block a site full of legal material"—an outright lie which provided no support for the claim. The cartoonish digital flyer said that, as a result of SOPA, "Sites' self-censorship increases dramatically," next to a circle-shaped graphic labeled, "self-censorhip on websites." A small, bright red circle labeled, "Today's self-censorship" is overwhelmed by a large, ruddy circle labeled "Self censorship if the bill passes." They provided zero reasoning or evidence for their baseless claim and of course made no effort to draw the distinction between censorship that occurs because someone is breaking the law and censorship that occurs on account of the content of their speech. Nor did they bother to justify a linear chart that purported to show "new startups being launched." A happy, blue upward reaching line represented "before SOPA," with bright red line sinking down "after SOPA." Again, Fight the Future passed a baseless claim off to unsuspecting Internet users as certain fact.

"What sites are at greatest risk?" another text box asked. The answer? "Anywhere people are expressing themselves or finding content: social networks, hosting sites, personal pages." Next to this quote, which didn't even mention piracy or copyright, logos for Vimeo, Facebook, Myspace, Aol Instant Messenger, Twitter and Reddit appeared—even though each and every one of those sites was already liable for "dedicated" infringement under US law. There was no mention of the many sites that, Internet users well understand, exist for no significant purpose other than to facilitate unlicensed downloading or streaming of legally protected works. That's because Fight for the Future had no interest in exploring the nuanced truth of the piracy debate. Their aim was to frighten and mislead and enter themselves into the long tradition of cynical propagandists like Edward Bernays and Ivy Lee.

"Our basic Internet freedoms are on the chopping block," the infographic finished. Sure, if "Internet freedom" means the freedom to exploit people.

SOPA was not a perfect bill by any means, but it could have been fixed and helped us along the path of reconciling the regulation of the Internet with creators' rights. In fact, that's precisely what the threat of the blackout accomplished. The weekend before the blackout, the DNS-blocking provisions were reportedly stripped from SOPA. But Fight for the Future didn't want some watered down version of SOPA to pass. Their irrational and defensive philosophy is based upon the idea that any regulation of the Internet is an attack on the Internet and its "freedom," so any proposed regulation needed to die.

Perhaps the philosophy of "Internet freedom" was truly that of Fight for the Future's donors. Whoever funded the group was apparently pleased after the blackout. As quoted in the same January 26th *Boston Globe* story that revealed the $300,000 grant which seeded Fight for the Future, "[Media Democracy Fund] director, Helen Brunner, said the fund is finalizing another $759,000 grant for Fight for the Future."[17] That's the reward, I suppose, for making a concerted propaganda campaign appear to be a grassroots uprising and duping millions of well-meaning Internet users to suit one's own devices. This was no example of Thomas Jefferson's ideal of an educated public ensuring liberty, but the story of a poorly educated public manipulated by well-funded factions.

As Holmes Wilson admitted to Talking Points Memo, Fight for the Future is a 501(c)4 nonprofit, the designated groups that are known for laundering unlimited amounts of political donations to America's infamous super-PACs."[4] Groups with 501(c)4 status are lobbying and political advocacy groups with no spending limits on their own campaigns and—more relevant to an Internet community that pats itself on the back for their commitment to "transparency"—under no obligation to disclose their donors. Ironically, the Sunlight Foundation itself has publicly campaigned against 501(c)4 groups for their lack of transparency and corrupting influence of the public interest. Fight for the Future could be funded by anyone and will never have to disclose a thing. Who is behind them and how much are they truly receiving? Your guess is as good as mine, and the flip side to hiding sources of one's funding is that any guess become fair.

So much for the grassroots, transparency, openness... and so much for the "planetary soul."

Fear of abuse of the law or civil liberties being infringed upon is entirely valid and should motivate us to be vigilant when our rights are violated. But that is not an argument for failing to enforce the law as it stands, in ways that punish criminals fairly while leaving the rights of innocent citizens unharmed. That is not the conversation Fight for the Future wants to have. They, and other groups like them, will continue to conflate the protection of individual rights (the rights that they would like to wish away, because it violates their naive utopian visions) with some illusory attack on "the Internet."

As Fight for the Future co-founder Tiffiniy Cheng told *TechPresident*, "This is not a copyright issue, this is not about Hollywood. This is about who controls the Internet. And that issue is just so big. People love the Internet, and they want it to be open and accessible to them, and they love the idea of the free flow of information."[18]

They love the idea of the free flow of information, but what about exploitation by the likes of The Pirate Bay? Was that really "so big" of an issue, or one that could be addressed by a combination of enforcement measures (either legislated or voluntary) against such sites mixed with a new conversation about creators' rights, one that embraced the equal rights of citizens while condemning the knowing criminal distribution of unlicensed work?

Cheng said that a bill that related directly to enforcing copyright protections, which Hollywood is based on, had nothing to do with copyright or with Hollywood. She conflated the specific nature of SOPA into being an epic battle over control of the Internet—a characterization that made it easier to trigger people's emotions, including her own. These are the paranoid declarations of someone engaged in selective reality, having imbibed the Kool-Aid of Digital Determinism.

DIGITAL DETERMINISM: DEAD WRONG

In 2009 the United Kingdom Pirate Party excerpted comments of Lawrence Lessig, originally made at a Google event in 2008, and posted the video excerpt to their YouTube channel. Lessig's comments illustrated the sentiments of many in the "Internet freedom" or "open Internet" movements who dismissed or vilified efforts at enforcing creators' rights online[1]:

> If you think about the 'copyfight'—the fight about how copyright law applies—this starts with the recognition that copyrighted data is out of control... The response of many of us in the 'copyfight' is to get people to accept that or... to 'get over it.' That's what we want to tell Hollywood. We want to tell Hollywood, 'Get over it. Get your protection for copyrighted material in other ways.' We want the copyright industry to find a different response to this rather than try to control copying. What they want to do is they want to build technologies to stop this copying. They want to break the Internet. And they'll do whatever it takes to stop this copying... And we 'copyfighters' say, 'You don't need to do that. You don't need to break the Internet. You can protect copyright— or at least the interests of copyright—in other ways. We don't have to stop copying. We can protect it through things like collective licenses that are voluntary or compulsory, through different business models that recognize that free-er might help you in your business. But we don't have to kill the essential character of the Internet to protect this one tiny industry, with this very old... business model.

Lessig's reasoning begins with a trick, of seeing "copyrighted data" as "out of control" rather than recognizing the individuals that lie behind the façade of "data." People created that "data" and invested in it, and did so because of the very protections that copyright provides to incentivize the creative market. What is "out of control," then, is not the data, but people's willful blindness toward creators' rights. Next comes the question of whether something can be done about this.

The Serenity Prayer, credited to theologian Reinhold Neibuhr, may help us to see what fundamentally girds the cult of "openness." The prayer asks, "God, grant me the serenity to accept the things I cannot change; the courage to change the things I can; and the wisdom to know the difference."

The key to believing in an "open Internet," even if it means that openness tramples upon people's basic rights, is that the fundamental characteristic of the Internet is "copying" and one can't fight that inherent nature of the Internet. It is just too powerful and, anyway, it is morally wrong to compromise the Internet's right to be free. "We don't have to stop copying," Lessig says. From that judgment runs a series of reverse-engineered arguments that exist to justify an already sanctified belief, that creators' rights are unimportant when in tension with the rights of the Internet and therefore deserve to be cast aside. Lessig's solution for solving the tension is to wish creators' rights away, to offer nice-sounding but unworkable ideas like collective licenses or the snake oil sales pitch to artists that they can make just as much money if they would just surrender the idea that their creative work is worth anything.

The really dastardly trick is for Lessig to portray protecting copyright, the mechanism for securing rights to all creators, as protecting "one tiny industry" with a "very old" business model. The business model *is* copyright: the idea that creators having a chance to profit from their own creative labor is ultimately a good thing for a culture that values wisdom, communication and progress through greater understanding.

Lessig's arguments are aggressive attacks upon the rights of all artists, but are seen as perfectly realistic by the individual that holds them, once they have accepted the idea that the Internet has its own inherent characteristic of copying, and that if the choice is between "protecting" what the Internet is and "copyrighted bits," we should obviously "defend" the Internet.

Copyright is in need of serious reform in regards to the length of terms and there are valid questions as to whether some music sampling should fall under Fair Use, but it is crucial to remember what copyright fundamentally is: a legal protection against exploitation granted to all individuals who wish to pursue creative ambitions. It is an individual right.

The idea that the Internet (or digital technology) has rights and characteristics that we are obliged to respect, even at the expense of the rights of flesh-and-blood people, is the core sentiment of the great self-destructive, deceitful ideology at the source of those who ultimately support the illegal exploitation of creators: Digital Determinism.

Digital Determinism does not see the people who devise and program computers and software—it only acknowledges the computer and the network as entities in themselves. Digital Determinism doesn't acknowledge art, beauty, truth or communication—only the informational bits that they can be decontextualized and objectified into. Rather than view digital tools as being subject to the laws and rights of the people who create, program and use such tools, Digital Determinism tells us that people now must serve the rights and laws of our digital tools. Because you can't fight technology.

The piracy debate is useful for us as we lay the rails for the 21st century, because it exposes the narcissistic risks of pervasive use of digital tools. We might become numb to reality, be hypnotized by the illusory power of digital tools, believe in the primacy of the images on the screen—even forgetting that the screen *is* a screen—and attack our own interests out of the determination to uphold the "open" values of the machine that gratifies our every thought, desire and emotion.

In embracing the supposed logic and worshipping the power of the machine, Digital Determinism denies reality and denies life on its path to fostering human self-destruction.

"I find death unacceptable."

So said the father of all Digital Determinists, Ray Kurzweil, speaking to *Newsweek* in 2009.[2] Just as determinists used the efficient "copying" of computers to predict that copyright would die, Kurzweil analyzed data and projected exponential growth for the speed and efficiency of digital technology going forward. Relying upon the data-driven projections, and ignoring the mysteries of human choice and free will, left Kurzweil running into the open arms of utopia: "an imagined place or state of things in which everything is perfect," etymologically defined as, "not of this world."

"By 2010 computers will disappear," Ray Kurzweil predicted at a 2006 TED conference without qualification. "[Computers] will be so small they will be embedded in our clothing; in our environment. Images will be written directly to our retina, providing full immersion virtual reality. We will be interacting with virtual personalities."

Kurzweil didn't really mean computers would "disappear," only that their size might dramatically decrease (as they surely have done, and continue to do). Similarly, computer lab technology in 2012 is capable or nearly capable of achieving everything else he predicted. But how many people really want computer chips in their clothing and what purpose would they serve? How many people are interested in importing digital images to their retina? Will we all embrace virtual personalities, or only the loneliest and most depressed among us? Technology is becoming ever more advanced, but we humans are still the only ones who can decide how to use it. This nuance is dead weight for Kurzweil's preoccupation with prediction. In 2009, he outlined a number of new ones to *The Sun*:

> In around twenty years we will have the means to reprogram our bodies' stone-age software so we can halt, then reverse, aging. Then nano-technology will let us live forever.... Ultimately, nanobots will replace blood cells and do their work thousands of times more effectively.... Within twenty-five years we will be able to do an Olympic sprint for fifteen minutes without taking a breath, or go scuba-diving for four hours without oxygen...Nanotechnology will extend our mental capacities to such an extent we will be able to write books within minutes.... If we want to go into virtual-reality mode, nano-bots will shut down brain signals and take us wherever we want to go. Virtual sex will become commonplace. And in our daily lives, hologram-like figures will pop up in our brain to explain what is happening.... By the middle of this century we will have back-up copies of the information in our bodies and brains that make us who we are. Then we really will be immortal.[3]

Does Kurzweil paint these futuristic visions for others or for himself?

As a good Digital Determinist, Kurzweil believes that our "information" makes us who we are. It doesn't. Consciousness and interpersonal communication make us who we are and consciousness is an unsolved mystery of biology. We will grow ever closer to replicating human consciousness in technology—robots will cheaply mimic it but will never achieve it. Our highest consciousness is reflected in our capacities for emotion, inuition and creativity; these human fundamentals are too mysterious to be reverse engineered fully. If you have been programmed to "love," you can never truly love. If you are programmed to "make art" you will never know the wonderous frustrations of creativity. Kurzweil gives little concern to these essentials of life, because he really isn't focused on life or living. He is preoccupied with death and trying to escape it.

Kurzweil is a scientist, inventor and technologist, but more than anything, he is a son who misses the father he loves. His father died of heart disease when Ray was just twenty-two years old, at which point he "became obsessed with developing ways in which his father might be brought back to life," according to *Newsweek* and many other Kurzweil profiles. So the Singularity, a metaphorical sacrifice of our humanity for salvation by the gods of technology, has an emotional core: a son who believes that if he can live long enough, technology will reunite him with his father and they will live together, forever. Kurzweil takes up to 150 pills a day as a part of a regimen he believes will keep him alive until 2049, when he now predicts the Singularity will come and we will achieve immortality by uploading ourselves into digital systems. This is his heaven.

Kurzweil's answers to solving life's problems are really denials of life. If one finds death "unacceptable," isn't that the same as finding life unacceptable? Life and death are intertwined—one cannot exist without the other. Kurzweil seems contemptuous of true consciousness, of reality. His solutions do not mean immortality or good health, but the construction of a spiritual prison that portends suicide. Would we experience the consciousness that defines life in our digital immortality? No. Would we be experiencing life? No. But like other Digital Determinists, Kurzweil has a belief in the Singularity and shepherds his thought in such a way to justify that belief.

The Internet offers us the illusion of selective reality. We can easily filter out the opinions and facts of life that we prefer not to face. But we cannot be so selective in the real world. Kurzweil's

Singularity very clearly is shaped from his fear of death and it may be that the sentiments of Digital Determinism originate from the same common fear. The digital realm will never die and will never disappoint us. Perhaps if we properly serve our digital God, we might evade death and transcend our own humanity thanks to its ones and zeros. But the more we come to believe in our digital illusions at the expense of reality, the more we are controlled by fear—something is missing.

A fear of death translates into a fear of life—the difficult search for meaning that accompanies the realization that *this will not last forever*, that our time on this earth is limited and the end is unpredictable. Conversely, an acceptance of death leads us to an acceptance of life—which brings gratitude for our time and awareness of meaning. A satisfying life is fueled by a basic understanding of one's mortality.

The nanotechnology Kurzweil describes will certainly play a greater role in our health and our lives, but capability does not equal destiny. How many nanobots, no doubt packed with toxins, will we really want coursing through our veins? How many circuits will we really choose to imbed into our skulls? As is the case with technologies we already use in our lives, the law of diminishing returns applies.

There is another inconvenience to Kurzweil's evangelism and that of Digital Determinists: technology fails. Systems fail. As we all know from personal experience, digital technology becomes slow and unpredictable within a matter of a few years. Gadgets wear out, requiring maintenance or replacement. Why would nanobots or mechanisms that "turn off our brain" be any different? Eventually, programming kinks will compromise the nanobots. Rather than "temporarily" turning off one's brain functions (remember Marx's "temporary" dictatorship?), the nanobots occasionally will fail and leave some of our brains turned off… forever. Then it would be clear how suicidal the Singularity is and what self-destructive paths Digital Determinism might lead us down.

———————————

Incredibly, the broad circumstance we face in the early 21st century was prophesied with disarming accuracy over one hundred years ago in 1909, before the popularization of radio, recorded music or television.

In his short story "The Machine Stops," E.M. Forster seemed to have received a vision of the world of electricity to come and its lurking dangers, such as the dangerous utopianism of the Digital Determinists who forget about the dignity of life, humanity and free will.

The story takes place sometime in the future and involves a young man named Kuno and his mother, Vashti. We find Vashti in an empty room, "a swaddled lump of flesh—a woman, about five feet high, with a face as white as a fungus." Kuno calls her in this room by what we today know as video chat, telling his mother he wishes to see her face-to-face.

"I want to see you not through the Machine," he says. "I want to speak to you not through the wearisome Machine."

"Oh hush," Vashti orders him. "You mustn't say anything against the Machine."

By his description, Forster's "Machine" is recognizable as our Internet. He writes of Vashti's empty room, "There was the button that produced literature and there were of course the buttons by which she communicated with her friends. The room, though it contained nothing, was in touch with all that she cared for in the world… Vashanti's next move was to turn off the isolation switch, and all the accumulations of the last three minutes burst upon her. The room was filled with the noise of bells and speaking-tubes. What was the new food like? Could she recommend it? Has she had any ideas lately? Might one tell her one's own ideas?…To most of these questions she replied with irritation—a growing quality in that accelerated age." Via the Machine, Vashti "knew several thousand people," just as we may have hundreds or thousands of "followers" or "friends" through Facebook and Twitter.

But Kuno reminds his mother during their video chat why it is important for her to visit him and share the same physical space.

> I believe that you pray to [the Machine] when you are unhappy. Men made it, do not forget that. Great men, but men. The Machine is much, but it is not everything. I see something like you in this plate, but I do not see you. I hear something like you through this telephone, but I do not hear you.

Man now lives underground, inhabiting their empty rooms fitted only with the Machine, which delivers them whatever they need. In

order to reach the airship that will take her to her son, Vashti must be
transported through a tunnel adjacent to her room. When she opens
her door and views the long dark tunnel, and considers leaving her
room for the first time in years, she is "seized with the terrors of direct
experience," but eventually does venture out to visit her son. Kuno
tells her that he has visited the surface world. He recounts that, as he
escaped the Machine through a series of tubes and ladders, he enjoyed
an epiphany.

> I felt, for the first time, that a protest had been lodged against
> corruption, and that even as the dead were comforting me, so
> I was comforting the unborn. I felt that humanity existed, and
> that it existed without clothes. How can I possibly explain
> this? I was naked, humanity seemed naked, and all these tubes
> and buttons and machineries neither came into the world
> with us, not will they follow us out, nor do they matter
> supremely while we are here…. Cannot you see, cannot all
> you lecturers see, that it is we that are dying, and that down
> here the only thing that really lives is the Machine?… The
> Machine proceeds—but not to our goal.

Vashti travels back across the world to her own room and forgets
about her son, on account of having too little in common. A few
years later, religion is re-established in the society by way of their
technological tool and a new creed becomes central to their culture.

> The Machine…feeds us and clothes us and houses us; through
> it we speak to one another, through it we see one another, in
> it we have our being. The Machine is the friend of ideas and
> the enemy of superstition: the Machine is omnipotent, eter-
> nal; blessed is the Machine.

Vashti hears from her Kuno out of the blue. Though she knows he
has been transferred to a room close to her own, they haven't spoken.
He messages her simply to say, "the machine stops," that he knows the
signs. Vashti dismisses him as ever more the fool and mocks his warning
as she recounts it to one of her friends. Her friend replies, "He does not
refer, I suppose, to the trouble there has been lately with the music?"
The friend refers to distortion in the music playing through the
Machine. The "mending apparatus," which fixes problems with the

machine, had been curiously unable to solve the issue. Eventually, though, Vashti and her friends grow used to living with the imperfections to music and an increasing array of other errors of the Machine. "And so with the mouldy artificial fruit, so with the bath water that began to stink, so with the defective rhymes that the poetry machine had taken to emit. All were bitterly complained of at first, and then acquiesced in and forgotten. Things went from bad to worse unchallenged."

As this dysfunction goes on, a lack of beds, normally provided by the Machine, leaves people to go without sleep and complain more strongly than before. At this point, it is admitted to the public that the "mending apparatus" is itself in need of mending. The people sympathize with the "mending apparatus" and pray for its success. But the Machine continues to gradually fail. The filtered air becomes rank, the lights dim and the communications system breaks down. As she begins to realize what her son meant when he said "the Machine stops," Vashti opens the door to the tunnel, the same tunnel that took her to the airship. She finds that it is filled with people "crawling about, people were screaming, whimpering, gasping for breath, touching each other, vanishing in the dark, and ever anon being pushed off the platform and onto the live rail." So she closes the door again and waits for the end to come as she hears the "horrible cracks and rumbling" from the failing Machine. When her dark room is too fearful for her to endure she manages to re-open the door to the tunnel, where "they were dying by hundreds out in the dark" by a chorus of whispers, groans and tears.

> Ere silence was completed their hearts were opened, and they knew what had been important on earth. Man, the flower of all flesh, the noblest of all creatures visible, man who had once made god in his image, and had mirrored his strength on the constellations, beautiful naked man was dying, strangled in the garments that he had woven. Century after century he had toiled, and here was his reward. Truly the garment had seemed heavenly at first, shot with colours of culture, sewn with the threads of self-denial. And heavenly it had been so long as man could shed it at will and live by the essence that is his soul, and the essence, equally divine, that is his body. The sin against the body—it was for that they wept in chief; the

centuries of wrong against the muscles and the nerves, and those five portals by which we can alone apprehend—glozing it over with talk of evolution, until the body was white pap, the home of ideas as colourless, last sloshy stirrings of a spirit that had grasped the stars.

Incredibly, Vashti hears Kuno dying in their midst and climbs over the bodies in the tunnel to reach him. There, they embrace as their city is "broken like a honeycomb." An airship crashes in from the surface, opening up a hole in layer after layer of the subterranean civilization. "For a moment they saw the nations of the dead, and, before they joined them, scraps of the untainted sky."

Will we also be so overtaken by the power of our technology that we collectively forget to preserve ourselves or the quality of our lives? At issue today is not whether we should be pro-technology or anti-technology, but rather if we can make the effort to place digital tools in their proper place, balanced, in the context of reality and humanity.

Whether you can or cannot fight technology is not in question. We humans invent our own tools (technology). We can use those tools for the benefit of mankind or for its self-destruction. Invent a hammer, and it's just as good for me bashing your nose into your skull as it is to build you a house. An airplane can be used to connect people to the wider world, or used as a hellish explosive device. Humans, believing in the wonders of advanced science, developed an in-depth knowledge of chemistry and chemicals. Such chemicals are used around the world each year to help ensure high food yields that keep the planet fed. The same knowledge of chemicals was used in the 20th century to scientifically—efficiently—kill millions of European Jews and thousands of Iraqi Kurds.

We can use digital technology for individualistic opportunism, trampling upon our fellow man's individual rights, or we can use the same technology to reinforce the individual rights of all men and women, support quality creativity when prompted, build greater communities of thought and subsequently *evolve*. The question posed earlier applies to all of our tools and technologies: shall we use them to create or destroy?

Can we fight technology? The question is beside the point— grasping at air. We humans invent technology and then we go about deciding each day what we want to use it for. Our use of technology is and will always be a choice, determined by the collective wisdom ingrained within our laws and habits. To think otherwise, that we are no longer in control of our technological tools, is to deny a piece of one's own humanity. It is a fundamentally self-destructive attitude.

Digital Determinism may have originated in a genuine hope and enthusiasm for the potential of technology to unite humanity, but it spread to the masses not on the strength of ideals or potential for results; it spread from the pent-up demand of millions of 18-24 year-old young men (The Pirate Bay's overwhelming demographic [4]) around the world who desperately wanted to believe they were entitled to free music and movies. This entitlement was more worthy of protection than maintaining artists' rights, the sanctioned economy, the quality of creative works, or even respecting the rule of law. These young Digital Determinists needn't admit to such entitlement when it was easy to parrot Cory Doctorow and his ilk, arrogantly dismissing critics by saying "Technology giveth and technology taketh away," or "Bits aren't ever going to get harder to copy. So we'll have to figure out a way to charge for something else."[5]

It was the dangerous utilitarianism of Digital Determinism that denied the legal rights of individuals and freed our inner demons to wreak havoc upon our cultural communities and erode our valuation of human creativity. That ideological cover freed us from responsibility as we rampaged and set fire to the streets.

In the near future, we were told, bits would be so easy to copy that only a hopeless Polyanna, who didn't understand technology, could expect people to actually *pay* for digital content. It was the mark of a savvy consumer to see that content was headed towards free, and therefore there was no harm in helping that process along through piracy. But, just as the common assumption that young people would never consider paying for digital content concealed an unreasonably condescending and self-serving worldview, so did this assumption. Digital Determinists could support their theories (or preferences) only by assuming the worst of humanity. Jaron Lanier exposed the flaws in such logic in his book *You Are Not a Gadget*, that the ease of finding free unlicensed copies made obsolete the choice of whether or not we should choose to do so:

[It's] an unrealistically pessimistic way of thinking about people. We have already demonstrated that we're better than that.
It's easy to break into physical cars and houses, for instance,
and yet few people do so. Locks are only amulets of inconvenience that remind us of a social contract we ultimately
benefit from. It is only human choice that makes the human
world function. Technology can motivate human choice, but
not replace it.

But the reality of choice makes Digital Determinists uncomfortable,
for it puts the individual and society back in control of the machine.
Suddenly, the *user* is determining the action and therefore is responsible
for those actions. People must face themselves in the process—
their own fears, hopes, flaws, responsibilities and ideas—rather than
surrendering themselves to what the machine supposedly says is right.
What is the meaning of progress? What is a fair society? What are my
responsibilities as a citizen and what can I influence in the real world?
Digital Determinism, like philosophical suicide, offers an easy way out
from such inconvenient questions.
Just keep the Internet free and everything will solve itself.
Digital Determinists hide behind technological advancement as
objective proof of their philosophy's truth, mocking the moralists and
sentimentalists among us. And it is true that I am making a moral
claim that the rights of creators *should* be respected under the rule of
law. But Determinists are just as guilty of moralism. *The Singularity's*
Ray Kurzweil chooses to believe that humans *should* merge with
technology just as Cory Doctorow believe(d) that bits *should* be free.
These are value judgments. It isn't that you *can't* fight technology, it's
that Digital Determinists don't believe that we *should* fight it. They
don't have the courage to do so and they don't want the courage,
either. Just give them more copies and bits and data, thank you very
much. In Digital Determinism, we greet not a self-evident philosophy,
but a self-fulfilling prophecy that chooses passive determinism over
active self-determination. It is a gospel for true powerlessness.
And if you need proof that Digital Determinism is a self-fulfilling
prophecy, a value judgment and a choice rather than a condition
humans must adapt to, the Decade of Dysfunction has offered plenty
of evidence. History has proven Digital Determinism to be totally,
utterly wrong: an epic fail.

Let's look again at the David Bowie quote from Part One that so captured the spirit, enthusiasm and self-assuredness of Digital Determinism. As you may recall, in 2002 he said:

> The absolute transformation of everything that we ever thought about music is going to take place within ten years, and nothing is going to be able to stop it. I see absolutely no point in pretending that it's not going to happen. I'm fully confident that copyright, for instance, will no longer exist in ten years, and authorship and intellectual property is in for such a bashing. Music itself is going to be like running water or electricity…. So it's like, just take advantage of these last few years because none of this is ever going to happen again. You'd better be prepared for doing a lot of touring because that's really the only unique situation that's going to be left. It's terribly exciting. But on the other hand it doesn't matter if you think it's exciting or not; it's what's going to happen…

I can imagine an Internet user reading this quote anytime between 2002 and 2009 and enjoying a sharp jolt to their nervous system: *Yes! I am living through change. How lucky I am to experience this history up close, no matter what it may mean. How exciting*….

Considering Bowie's deterministic claim that "copyright… will no longer exist in ten years," we imagine an absolutely transformed world in 2012. In this hypothetical world, copyright-based creative industries, unless patronized by the super-wealthy, have failed: recorded music, books, newspapers, and motion pictures. Physical goods and experiences (like concerts) are still paid for, but digital copyright infringement has essentially been decriminalized. In fact, there is a proposal (sponsored by a senator from the Pacific Northwest) to amend the US Constitution for the first time since 1992, so that copyright legally will "no longer exist," just as Bowie predicted. Some senators are promising their pugnacious constituents via Facebook that the sentence, "Music is like water," will be written into said amendment, per the Internet hive's crowdsourced suggestion. Literally no one in 2012 pays for digital music. Because an "absolute transformation" has taken place, no one bothers purchasing CDs either. Vinyl, a relic of pop culture antiquity, is out of the question. Paying for music is but a quaint remnant of the 20th century only the most hard-headed Luddites still fight to keep.

In reality, people purchased dramatically fewer songs and albums through the 2000s, but recorded music remained a more-than-$6 billion industry in the United States and was worth $15 billion worldwide in 2011. The industry was far below its boy-band-and-Britney-fueled turn-of-the-century heights, but far from dead. As for Bowie's "absolute transformation of everything we have ever thought about music," CDs still accounted for about half of all recorded music sold in 2011 in the US, with digital music roughly accounting for the other half of sales. Globally, CDs remained the dominant music format.

It turned out that millions upon millions of people are choosing to pay for their digital music, accounting for worldwide digital sales of $4.6 billion in 2010. And thanks to digital sales, total US record sales actually *grew* by a modest margin in 2011 for the first time since 2004. That point bears repeating: as the decade mark on Bowie's deterministic prophecy came up, recorded music was technically a "growth industry." Glenn Peoples of *Billboard* was so struck by the uptick in digital revenues, that he proclaimed 2011 as "the year digital music broke."[6] He wrote that "there's a common—and incorrect—belief in the music business that nobody pays for music anymore. That claim just doesn't hold water in 2011." Through September 2011, American music consumers purchased 12 million more digital albums and 90 million more digital tracks than in 2010. Peoples projected a total of $300 million dollars of additional digital spending for the year.

Further discrediting Digital Determinism was the resilience of the ten-song, forty-minute album format. That format, invented in the early 1900s, was tied to the technological limitations of the vinyl LP. Such albums held no purpose in the boundless digital era of easy, free copies of individual tracks. Yet sales growth for digital albums consistently outpaced the à la carte singles so many assumed to be the future for digital music. Consumers chose artistic context in spite of the atomization the digital format implied. Human choice overruled digital logic.

What could be more a repudiation of Bowie's baseless prophecy than the resurgence in vinyl record sales? When he made the statement in 2002, 1.2 million vinyl records were sold in the US. By 2011, 3.6 million units were projected to sell—a growth rate of 300 percent!

As music consumption spread out its limbs towards expanding digital possibilities, it simultaneously found steadiness in its analog roots. If there were truly "no point in pretending" that copyright was alive, and that touring would be the only way for bands to make a living, then why did Bowie's own record label re-issue two of his greatest *albums, Station to Station* and *Space Oddity,* in 2009? These re-issues were released on 180-gram vinyl, as two-disc CDs (!) and—you guessed it—as a paid digital download.

Copyright is nowhere close to irrelevant, digitally or otherwise. Record labels (like Beggars Group, Merge, and Secretly Canadian) who focused on maintaining healthy relationships with their fans and developing great artists, rather than litigation, experienced growth, and momentum began to accumulate behind licensed music subscription services like Spotify and Rhapsody, despite the fact that the copying logic of the Internet made such services theoretically irrelevant.

More newspapers strengthened and protected the value of their content by instituting paywalls, rather than continue to "share" their content for free as Digital Determinists told them they must do in 2010 (if quality journalism died as a result, so be it). The *New York Times* paywall drove a massive increase in total subscribers of the publication and paywalls for local US newspapers became normal. *Ad Age* reported on an experiment in Slovakia, in which nine news organizations joined a collective paywall system. Consumers paid a flat fee for universal access starting in May of 2011. Traffic actually increased for half of the newspapers and the subscription services, which operated like a micropayment system. Publishers were paid according to how much time subscribers spent on their respective websites. "What's important for now is that people are learning to pay for the content," said Tomas Bella, CEO of the digital subscription company that facilitated the experiment.[7] The paywall also seemed to scare away the "trolls" who haunted the newspaper article forums. "Once you ask people to pay, it's not a problem," said Bella. "All the idiots leave and the normal people stay."

All content industries faced challenges in adapting to digitization, but none of them had died or even appeared close to dying in 2012. In hindsight, the chaos and confusion brought on by digitization had put all creative industries in a precarious spot, so when the Great Recession hit in 2008-2009 and traditional newspapers, magazines, record labels, and retail locations began to fall, Digital Determinists could point and say, "See! We told you so. You can't fight technology."

But that proved to be a very particular time and place in media and economic history. It turns out that most consumers understood, on some level, that you get what you pay for. These content industries are not saved, by any means. All of them face significant challenges in seeking revenues wherever they can be found. But that the trend toward free content that seemed impossible to fight *reversed* itself proves a critical point for our engagement with digital content. We are *not* following technology. By paying or not paying for it, individuals are gradually deciding for themselves how to use digital content and whether to respect copyright. It is a choice, not fate, and therefore we are responsible for our choices, whatever they prove to be.

As earlier mentioned, Cory Doctorow made waves in the world of New Media by giving his eBooks away for free and telling other authors that they should do so because bits are free and he "[didn't] think it practical to charge for copies of electronic works."[8] His version of Digital Determinism was threatened at its core when Amazon announced the release of its first eReader, the Kindle, in 2007 along with plans to sell eBooks. "Whenever Amazon tries to sell a digital download, it turns into one of the dumbest companies on the Web," Doctorow claimed at the time, his indignation showing through. "Take the Kindle, the $400 handheld eBook reader that Amazon shipped recently, to vast, raging indifference."[9]

Only an "expert" in something so fast moving as digital media could be proven so wrong, so quickly.

Just three years after the introduction of the Kindle, at the tail-end of 2010, Amazon announced that their eBook sales in the US had overtaken paperback sales. How's that for Digital Determinism? In fairness to Doctorow, no one could have predicted the runaway success of eBooks, especially after the struggles of the music industry. From 2009 to 2010, eBook sales rose 165 percent. The following year, in the first quarter of 2011, eBook sales were up another 159 percent. Most month-on-month sales continued to grow at rates between an astonishing 100 to 200 percent. The first Kindle may have been greeted with "raging indifference" according to Doctorow's perspective, but by 2012 no serious person could make such a claim. In 2010 alone, nearly 13 million eReaders, like the Kindle, were shipped worldwide—an increase of 325 percent from 2009.[10] According to figures released by the American Association of Publishers, eBooks already accounted for more total revenue in 2011 than either Adult Hardcover or the Mass Market Paperback formats. After just four years of existence, the eBook was on the verge of overtaking Trade Paperback as the dominant book format. And, most encouraging, total US publishing revenues rose by more than 5 percent from 2008 to 2010, proving that a shift into digitization could potentially lead creative industries to better times.[11]

Perhaps the final nail in the coffin for Digital Determinism was on full display in 2012. All one had to do was sign into Amazon and enter "Cory Doctorow" into the search bar. On the following screen, you would find numerous books of his, offered as electronic editions for the Kindle, his "bits" charged at $9.99. The irony of Doctorow proving his own predictions so wrong would be more amusing if Doctorow hadn't spent so many years selling his fans a false bill of goods, giving them an illusory image of the world to come and making it that much more difficult for musicians to publicly advocate for their exclusive rights as creators. Doctorow was able to gain a few fans and media attention for his policy of giving eBooks away for free, but he sold out his fellow creators in the process.

Another common refrain of determinists is that digital copyright enforcement is pointless for a medium that is so geared toward copying. But, when Google voluntarily began to block certain piracy-related terms from their Autocomplete search feature in 2011, such as "torrent" or "pirate bay," the results were dramatic. According to a post titled "Google's Anti-Piracy Feature is Quite Effective" on *Torrent Freak*, searches for Bit Torrent were cut in half and other searches for infamous distributors of unlicensed content dropped significantly.[12] After Limewire was served with an injunction in 2010, the number of users using Limewire dropped from 16 million to around just three million in the course of one year, according to numbers released by Nielsen and reported by Digital Music News.[13] Half of the users continued file sharing through other sites, but the report concluded that the other half—around five million users— stopped engaging in file sharing all together. When public cyber locker Megaupload was seized the very same week as the SOPA protest, a host of cyber lockers which had been allowing third parties to download or stream the unlicensed files on their network—even paying users who provided the most files for such downloads—rapidly canceled their public "sharing" features and ended the programs that paid users for sourcing illegal files. Traffic to many of the sites that changed their policies plummeted[14] and major torrent index

BTJunkie voluntarily shut down for good the following month. The owner of BTJunkie told *Torrent Freak* that "the legal actions against file sharing sites such as Megaupload and The Pirate Bay played an important role in making the decision."[15] It is important to note that, though the total volume of pirated files has not significantly dropped, voluntary filtering and strong law enforcement actions against the worst of the worst distributors of unlicensed content had the impact of marginalizing the amount of sites offering unlicensed content and made it far less likely that future sites such as these will find investment capital.

Digital Determinism can take its place among other ideologies that seduced its followers with simplicity, but have been proven misguided. Digital Determinism resides in the same realm as Marxism and its foolish "temporary dictatorship" of the proletariat, which misunderstood the human lust for power and persistence of hierarchies. Digital Determinists may also find a sympathetic brother in former Federal Reserve Chairman Alan Greenspan, the most devoted of believers in Randian "free market" fundamentalism, who finally admitted before the US Congress after the financial crisis of 2008 that he was mistaken; his ideology that capital markets were self-regulating and best left alone by government was "flawed." This realization came only after decades of managing the US and world economies under his extreme assumptions, that contributed to eventually running our debt-soaked economies into the ground. Digital Determinists are cousins to the religious fundamentalism of Harold Camping, the American evangelist whose followers believed his prediction that the Rapture would come on May 21st, 2011. They sold their belongings and quit their jobs to prepare for the event, which they were tragically convinced of. For those still drawn to Digital Determinism, it's worth noting that even after May 21st passed *sans* Rapture, many of Camping's believers remained faithful in his prediction. God was merely "testing their faith."

And so the deterministic beliefs, that shroud clear exploitation under the curtain of "defending the Internet," will die hard in some corners. In 2012, the unaccountable 501(c)4 Fight For The Future announced its new project, "The Internet Defense League," an attempt for the group to unleash new SOPA blackout-like mobs to harass congressmen whenever there is a law that Fight for the Future (or a secret donor) doesn't like. Sites like Techdirt will go on serving their anti-copyright audience, cherry picking stories that validate Digitally Deterministic sentiments and ignoring opportunities to find common ground on copyright reform and enforcement. Once you've built an audience and a business on the piracy wars, détente could mean irrelevance and a drop in revenue. Masnick didn't necessarily want to become a copyright gadfly, though. As he explained to *TechPresident*, his digitally inclined audience and the advertising based realities of running a blog pushed him into the role he occupies in 2012:[16]

> A couple of things happened: People started identifying us and me with those issues, and we got more and more of those things sent to us… The other thing is that when we write about the other things people tend to skip over them. People don't have the same emotional connection to it.

Posts that don't engender as much emotion don't receive the same amount of clicks or the deliver the same advertising revenues. Sensationalism and contrarianism pays. Such is the life of a professional blogger.

Some Digital Determinists will hold tight to their faith, that copyright and maintaining a vibrant and free Internet are diametrically opposed ideas. But the further we move away from the RIAA lawsuits in the Decade of Dysfunction, the stranger those arguments that seem to put the rights of the Internet before those of people will sound. Sadly, some in the camp will go on, like an opposition party gunning for the presidency, rooting for failure of both the copyright industries and the artists who continue to execute their legal rights.

Just as Greenspan's markets do not regulate themselves, neither will technology. The battle is as it has been: for ensuring the equal rights of individuals under the rule of law, building fairness and decency in society, and fulfilling the promise of an ongoing (and ever threatened) experiment in self-rule by democracy. The Internet may be used to achieve any of these objectives, but that is no reason to ascribe rights to a machine as a last desperate attempt to hold on to an ill-conceived digital dream. This dream of "openness" and unfettered copying has been used for years to rationalize illegal exploitation of artists in the digital revolution, just as the principle of laissez-faire economics was used to rationalize the exploitation of child labor during the industrial revolution. Then, the labor movement steadily spoke out for the rights of workers and achieved progress for all of society, just as we all can do our small part to accept the rights of artists and communicate that acceptance to the wider world.

We don't excuse serially harmful uses of tools, which is all that digital technology really is, in other areas of life simply because we *really really like the tool.* For those who still want to believe, after all these years, that the need for the Internet to be "open" and "free" justifies obvious cases of illegal exploitation for profit, perhaps they should take Lawrence Lessig's pithy advice.

Get over it.

THE NEW WORLD

Think of those first maps of the New World we see as schoolchildren, illustrated by the cartographers of Europe's Renaissance. North America is an embarrassing ingrown column of crude blotches: the discarded work of a kindergartener, unfit even for the refrigerator door. The true shapes of Florida, South America, and Panama are merely suggested. Bulges and contours hint at the truth. Studying the first attempts at mapping the limits and shape of a new land, it's easy to see that the explorers were mostly clueless as to the fundamental nature of their new landscape. In places, the maps hinted at the true shape of the New World, but by and large they were insufficient aids for exploration.

For hundreds of years, Europe's great explorers lost themselves in utopian fantasy, fixated on the hope of an easy water passage to their trading outposts in Asia. They sailed west across the Atlantic, certain the route would be found. But when they reached their destination, these men of experience repeatedly collided against the unforgiving shores of reality.

Imagine the frustration of the proud Renaissance adventurers as they failed—again and again—to cross through "The New Islands," as the Americas were thought to be. Christopher Columbus believed that Asia was just a short distance past these "islands" and many assumed The New Islands were part of Asia itself, a far-eastern archipelago that buffered the continent. Operating upon these fallacious assumptions, the 1524 expedition of Giovanni da Verrazzano resulted in an erroneous "discovery."

When exploring the coast of present-day Virginia, Verrazzano came across the Chesapeake Bay—and declared it the water route to Asia. In the blank spot between the mouth of the Chesapeake and Asia, Verrazzano's imagination drew in a self-serving, utopian route to riches. His assumptions were reproduced in the form of new maps. When these maps were distributed, his mistaken rendering of the world propagated, multiplied and formed a new conventional wisdom.

Of course the idea of an easily navigable water route struck the explorers' fancy. The idea suggested that they were sailing on the right side of history and were the true keepers of wisdom. But their self-delusion only delayed and amplified their eventual failure; they misunderstood the opportunity before them that lay in a new land of unimaginable resources and beauty. Of course, maps improved over time and explorers learned that the all-water route to Asia was in fact a fantasy—but not until the Lewis and Clark expedition of 1804 proved it so.

It needn't take hundreds of years for humans to correct previously-held assumptions in the Information Age, but it still takes time. And just as the Old World explorers sleepwalked for centuries under the spell of ill-conceived notions, false maps, and intoxicating dreams, today we enter the novel geography of the Internet without a clear idea of where we are or where we're going. Digital Determinists and their New Media brethren may claim to understand the true path of humanity's engagement with technology, just as the explorers of old must have confidently reported back to the monarchies, "Trust me, the water route will soon be found. I understand the true nature of these New Islands."

If we accept the confusion over whether or not to pay for digital content as a proxy for our exploration of the digital age, we see the malformed maps of The New Islands spread out before us. These maps are cognitive in nature. Rather than sketching out coastlines and river mouths, the maps we use come in the form of concepts, words, and symbols. These are the bobbing buoys and pulsing beacons that guide our path into the unknown. We are beholden to them.

As the vaunted American journalist Walter Lippman described in his 1922 treatise, *Public Opinion*, "the real environment is altogether too big, too complex, and too fleeting for direct acquaintance. We are not equipped to deal with so much subtlety, so much variety."[1] We are compelled to simplify the world, for it is the only chance we have to understand its processes and our role within them. "To traverse the world," Lippmann said, "men must have maps of the world." The more comprehensive the map, the better chance we individuals have to chart our own course in this world without losing ourselves in the process.

We require the language of symbols and stereotypes to establish basic landmarks and topography. The most egregious wrong we have perpetrated against ourselves, the reason why our piracy debates so commonly marooned, was our acceptance of the wrong symbols and stereotypes as our guides. Like the 16th century navigators, we find ourselves bumping up against reality, in search of terrain that does not exist.

During my own days of using P2P services like Audiogalaxy, never did I think, "I need to share some music right now."

Digital Determinists rightly point out that humans have a fundamental need to share with others, making "file sharing" appear to be a natural, innocent process of building culture. We are social creatures, so sharing is essential to our being. File sharing, then, must be a net positive.

But, when I used digital services that were supposedly devoted to the utility of "file sharing," sharing itself never crossed my mind. Why would it? I wasn't emailing a friend or using G-chat to offer them the name of a new band I was excited about. My actions had zero relation to sharing something that I felt any sense of ownership over. No, sitting in my dingy bedroom in a slummy house in the same Minneapolis college town where Bob Dylan heard his first Woody Guthrie album, the action more closely resembled, "I want that album… now." After reading an intriguing album review, seeing a hypnotizing music video, or hearing an arresting tune in a coffee shop or on the radio, I purposefully downloaded that artist's work for free rather than purchase it. This choice had nothing to do with sharing. I downloaded because it was so easy, there were no immediate consequences, and best of all, it was free!

Sure, every file sharer knows that somewhere out there on the other end of your wireless connection, some other human's computer—or a number of them, in the case of torrents—is seeding your download. Real people make file sharing possible, but they are anonymous figments of our imagination. In practical terms, they may as well not even exist. You, the file sharer, are engaging with a distributing website, search engine, or torrent tracker—not a person. The process is no different than searching for and purchasing any other item online. Except, in the case of eBooks, MP3s, movies and other creative content, no one can force you to pay if you don't feel like it. Those who knowingly download or stream unlicensed files aren't acting on a deep desire to share, but a deep desire to consume. Their "sharing" is just a ham-handed attempt at denial for their hyper-consumptive actions, nothing more. Over the years, both artists and consumers have misconceived file sharing as a linear extension of familiar, wholesome practices.

"If a friend of yours gave you a DVD of mine for you to watch one night," asks the muckraking American filmmaker Michael Moore, "is that person doing something wrong? I'm not seeing any money from that... See, I think that's okay. That's always been okay. You share things with people. I think information, art and ideas should be shared."

But file sharing isn't a matter of one friend borrowing a DVD, book, or album from a neighbor who has purchased the copy, as Moore suggests. Rather, it is a case of tens or hundreds of millions of consumers being able to permanently borrow (or "take") such works, copied from complete strangers, with commercial distributors like The Pirate Bay openly facilitating the transaction. If an original file is leaked before release, it is possible that none of the copies being shared online even derive from an original sold copy. Searching online for specific files, superficially held by digital simulacra of real people, we're ostensibly accessing a black-market online store where an infinite array of cultural goods are offered for free. The ultimate goal is to get stuff, not to share stuff. Though it is certainly common for friends and colleagues to share files, in the context of unlicensed downloading, "file sharing" is a functionally inadequate term and a self-serving, blithe stand-in for situational reality that sets our journey into the information age off upon false pretenses.

That said, sincere digital sharing manifests a lofty ideal of global human communication. Today, I can write a book or an album, digitize it, and distribute it to anyone I see fit at a negligible cost to either myself or the receiver. Through constructive institutions like Wikipedia, human ideas, knowledge and expressions have fewer barriers than ever to widespread discovery. That is a positive revolution, without question. But as many exciting possibilities as the digital revolution allows, we still must try to control our enthusiasm and maintain perspective. In the widespread adoption of the term "file sharing," we see individuals forgetting that a healthy culture isn't only determined by the degree of shared information, but also shared responsibilities and shared visions of what makes a fair society.

The sheer number of distribution options available to creators today is a testament to all the good that can come from technology. But what do such options amount to when the same technology allows consumers to anonymously disregard creators' rights on a pandemic scale, as is the case with file sharing? To respond by throwing one's hands up in the air, saying there is no choice but to accept the good with the bad and not worry about the consequences, is the moral laziness hiding in clear sight when we accept the term. Consumers aren't sharing; they are fundamentally taking advantage of an artist and ignoring their basic right to distribute their work as they wish.

When I logged on to Audiogalaxy in the early 2000s and downloaded a Shins or Cannibal Ox album, emerging artists on respected independent record labels, I knew the bands were putting the albums up for sale. By signing with their respective labels, the bands had chosen to partner with them and were implicitly asking me—the consumer—for payment if I sufficiently wanted to explore the music they'd worked so hard on. I'd only heard of the Shins (in 2001) after happening upon a music video for "New Slang" on a music blog. The label, Sub Pop, invested their money and time in producing that video and promoting it to online journalists. By that intentional investment of the label and artist, I was exposed to an album that I came to love. And when I hear the album today, I am instantly transported back in time to be reacquainted with an otherwise forgotten self and personal history. That experience is priceless—and no doubt worth $9.99.

But at the time, hitting right-click at my computer, I implicitly communicated to these artists who had made something beautiful for me, "I could care less about you and your choices," as I found some anonymous drone to "share" the full album with me online.

This elemental disrespect between consumer and creator has, surprisingly, been glossed over by most writers of the piracy wars. The early acceptance of the term "file sharing" and the political tones it adopted during the copyright infringement lawsuits of the mid-2000s concealed the brazenness of this social contract violation. Just as erroneous maps of The New Islands amplified misunderstandings rather than corrected them, so too did the term "file sharing."

The innermost mechanisms of commerce may be frustratingly opaque as it applies to creative industries like music, but such mechanisms facilitate a very real exchange between two individual entities—creator and consumer. When I downloaded albums for free, I openly undermined this egalitarian exchange. If the Internet weren't such an anonymous locale, we would never stand for this corrupt concept of sharing. In 2012, both the band Beach House and LCD Soundsystem had songs of theirs closely imitated and used as commercial jingles. In the case of Beach House, they had declined to license a song to an ad campaign for weeks, only to find an obvious copy of the song's style and substance used for a long form car advertisement. When Pitchfork featured these events in their news section, the site referred to the bands getting "ripped off."[2] But is it really much different when a consumer or (especially) an unsanctioned commercial website tries to circumvent an artist's rights to their work for the sake of convenience? Artists have been getting massively ripped off through the Decade of Dysfunction, and we have stayed numb to that fact, in part, because of the term "file sharing."

———————————

In his 2003 book, *The Anarchist in the Library*, NYU law professor Siva Vaidhyanathan fearlessly explored his own habits of downloading from Napster and burning CDs. "Mostly," he admitted, "I download songs to see if I want to buy them."

Seeing as he still buys the music that he likes, Vaidhyanathan says in the book that he didn't see why he would be accused of damaging the music industry or violating any unspoken contract with the creator. Then he read a column by Randy Cohen, formerly The Ethicist at the *New York Times Sunday Magazine*, in which Cohen responds to a letter from a young file sharer. Cohen unconditionally declares that "to download music from the net illegally is theft, depriving songwriters, performers and record companies of payment for their work" and that accusing the music industry of being somehow culpable for such theft was akin to "blaming the victim."

Vaidhyanathan wrote to Cohen to challenge his cut-and-dried approach. Vaidhyanathan reminded Cohen that we couldn't simply use the law as our guide. "Some laws are badly drawn or misapplied, and breaking them under certain conditions is ethical.... Besides... the law is not clear about which actions are copyright violations." The rest of their revelatory exchange in Vaidhyanathan's indispensable book follows:

Cohen responded that while my unauthorized use of copyrighted material might ultimately benefit my favorite artists, the availability of these files should be up to the artists, not me. So I asked him about the pragmatic calculus. "What is the practical difference between listening to downloaded music in the privacy of my apartment and listening to broadcast music in the privacy of my car?" Cohen again asserted that the difference was in the permission. He said the chief concern in this ethical question was the interest of the artist— both financial and moral. "The history of popular culture is a continuous struggle on the artists' part not to get robbed... it seems to be that what MP3 does is democratize the ability to rip off an artist," Cohen wrote to me. "And what's particularly galling is that you not only want to do it, you want to be praised as a social progressive when you do."

When Vaidhyanathan wrote his book just after the millennium turned, there were a plentitude of excuses for such sharing. P2P was still a fresh development. Quite understandably, consumers delighted in experimenting with this new mode of distribution and consumption. At a time when there was no MySpace, Pandora, YouTube, iTunes, or Spotify, the file sharers' insistence that they merely wanted to sample new music held considerable water. They would do so legally, some claimed, but the industry was dragging its feet and hadn't given consumers a reasonable option to do so. It was the industry's own fault for not adapting quickly enough. So goes the basic argument that, for Cohen, amounts to "blaming the victim."

It is crucial to acknowledge that, though there was a time in which more reasonable grounds existed for unlicensed downloading, that time has clearly passed us by. When a plethora of options exist, as they do today, for sharing links to legally streaming full albums or free track downloads offered by labels, the claim that consumers are merely sharing when they knowingly look for unlicensed content is outright sleazy, like a mobster who is merely "borrowing" a semi-trailer full of merchandise.

Music is available to a far larger market than ever before and for far less money per unit. Any music fan in the early '90s would have salivated to hear about what was coming: the $10 album and virtually unlimited access to streaming music for a minimal fee of $10 a month or less. It is important to remember that consumers in the '90s complained that CDs were overpriced, not that they should be free.

But when a searchable online store suddenly exists where any and all music can be quickly obtained for free, why would you ever pay for any of it? Why would you pay, once finished convincing yourself that you're engaging in a victimless act, merely sharing?

Call the unlicensed downloading of digital content what you will, but when we engage in the practice, by no means are we "file-sharing." The term is the defensive expression of a guilty conscience. Breaking new ground in this discussion means putting such transparently self-serving terms to rest, lest we chart a needlessly long and futile path for civilization's journey to digital discovery.

Just as Digital Determinists banked on the fuzzy notions of sharing to bend arguments over unlicensed downloading in their favor, the term "piracy" is used by government institutions and media companies to demonize and frighten consumers into compliance. Like "file-sharing," "piracy" only obscures the truth about unlicensed downloading and hinders our understanding of the new digital world.

When I downloaded files from Audiogalaxy in the early 2000s, I was clearly in violation of the "exclusive rights" of creators guaranteed by copyright law, but was I a pirate? Some, like the RIAA and MPAA, would say absolutely; my unlicensed downloading amounted to theft. The RIAA infamously argued that every "pirated" song represented a "lost sale," in order to buttress their mass lawsuits of the mid-2000s. If only determining the nature and costs of such piracy was that straightforward.

In April of 2010, the United States' Government Accountability Office (GAO) released the results of a national study on the effects of pirated music, movies and books on the economy. Surely the organization could provide some definitive answers on the epochal topic of piracy, a controversy that had chased its own tail for over a decade.

At the conclusion of their study, the vaunted GAO winced, shrugged their shoulders, and scratched their heads in puzzlement. They stated that the "illicit nature" of intellectual property "theft" made it difficult to measure. They said some economic effects may well be positive to related industries, though "research in specific industries suggest that the problem is sizable…efforts to estimate losses involve assumptions such as the rate at which consumers would substitute counterfeit for legitimate products. No single method can be used to develop estimates…. Most experts observed that it is difficult, if not impossible, to quantify the economy-wide impacts."

Would I have purchased the music I downloaded for free online? Maybe, but I'll never know for sure. Neither will the RIAA or the courts. One of the problems with embracing sloppy language like "piracy" is that it fails to draw a distinction between a college student who "pirates" a few albums online (and may very well be later paying for concert tickets, merchandise or the albums themselves), a bootlegger making a few dollars by selling pirated DVDs in your local metro station, and a Somali gang member who pirates an oil tanker in the Gulf of Aden, or the real problem for our purposes—pirate distributors like The Pirate Bay who sell advertising or subscriptions on the backs of exploited creators.

When we accuse someone of being a pirate, don't we normally assume that person is collecting money somewhere in the process? The whole point of pirating goods is to sell them in the black market or collect a ransom. So a pirate isn't simply a person who copies or steals a product, but also someone who seeks to profit financially from this violation of our laws and/or social contract.

Someone who makes illegal copies of cultural goods is engaging in counterfeiting—I don't mean to obscure that fact—but calling that college version of myself a "pirate" fails the test of common sense. Such misapplied terminology weakens the word itself and, therefore, also its meaning and utility. By using the wrong word—the wrong symbol— as the keystone of any discourse, that discourse will eventually collapse from its own shoddy construction, leaving a messy pile of mortar that must be cleared before we can cross over to the gates to progress.

While authorities believe themselves to be playing tough, castigating the consumer pirates, they act out a futile scorched-earth policy with past and potential customers. By accepting the term, we begin a discussion on the terrain of personal attacks and accusation. If someone calls me a "pirate" or a thief, I quite naturally will become defensive.

"I'm not a pirate, I'm just sharing files. Nothing wrong with that. It's not like I stole anything. The original still exists."

Rather than openly engage in a conversation over those subtle, sticky issues of theft and consent, the accuser doubles down.

"Thief!" they continue. "You are pirating my goods. You are engaging in criminal activity and owe me money."

Increasingly offended, my defensive posture shifts into aggression. The dialogue veers out of control into emotional, dysfunctional territory.

"Fine, I am a pirate. Well there are plenty more of us than there are of you and we will gladly destroy you and your old world business models if that's what you really want. You can't fight technology, fools. Arrr!"

If the attack is sustained for even a little while, the accused "pirate" will likely embrace the role. Given the choice, most cagey individuals—young or old—would prefer to be associated with pirates than with average, cog-in-the-machine consumers. The pirate is an archetype for adventure and creativity, ethics aside. When I say "piracy," the murky outline of a ship slowly emerges. It creaks through a soupy fog as sea foam sprays into your eyes. When you open them, you see the skull and crossbones waving on high. The romance of rebellion is visceral and real as Black Beard boards the ferry of some dumb empire. He is a wild-eyed genius; misunderstood and ahead of his time. You don't mind seeing him pillage the ship because, you figure, the crown that owns it has enough treasure as it is. The pirate is a symbol of individuality and vigilante justice—none of which applies to the mass disrespect and laziness that characterize unlicensed downloading. Thus, "piracy" lends an unearned veneer of romance to what is essentially a drab and bloodless practice: numbly violating creators' rights while uploading and downloading bits of data to and from anonymous, isolated computer terminals.

"Arrr!"

You have the same old lawyers, executives, and politicians accusing half the world—it seems—of piracy. As a result, those who have violated the spirit and law of copyright have taken proud ownership of their newfound role, effectively neutralizing the attack. We have The Pirate Bay, the leaders of which have aggressively argued for their right to facilitate widespread unlicensed downloading, giving a pimply middle-finger to the corporations, governments, and supposedly wealthy artists who have tried—and failed—to shut down the site. The Pirate Party fights efforts to enforce copyright, under the pathetic rhetorical guises of free speech and privacy, from Sweden to Germany to Australia.

As time dragged on for the nautical explorers and the Renaissance phased into the Enlightenment, it became abundantly clear that finding an open water passage to Asia would be considerably more difficult than lazily floating up the Chesapeake Bay. They weren't dealing with The New Islands, but with a New World. As this reality sunk in, it must have been a disappointment; difficult for some to accept, as if a great dream had been surrendered. But The New World was a discovery far greater than any water route, because it came with the promise of reality. With corrected maps, the explorers' curiosities, dreams, and goals for the future were finally planted in firm soil, rather than the shifting sands of delusion. They could recognize the geography for what it was, not what they wished it to be.

The words "piracy" and "file-sharing'" have given us a discombobulated map for our exploration of the digital world. One term paints an inappropriately dastardly mask upon unlicensed downloading, while the other applies the grinning face of a town fool. Conversely, the terms downloading or free downloading are too general and imprecise. There is nothing inherently wrong with downloading, and free downloading is fantastic so long as it is being done with a creator's consent. Illegal exploitation is accurate, but sounds shrill upon repetition (apologies, reader). What we are after is fidelity—a word that resonates with the truth.

The downloading of unlicensed digital content for free isn't "piracy" or "file-sharing," it is freeloading.

Freeloading is an ideal term because it describes the technical elements of the practice (free + downloading) while simultaneously exposing its behavioral nature. No more is it necessary to endure a clumsy debate based upon unsubstantiated blanket accusations of theft. No more are individual FreeLoaders so welcome to glibly pat themselves on the back for their digital sharing. The dictionary defines "freeloader" as "a person who takes advantage of others' generosity without giving anything in return," the generosity being that of the content's creators, editors, and investors who have all taken real financial risks to produce the content for your benefit.

In the case of music, it's true that FreeLoaders may end up paying good money at a concert or ponying up for artist merchandise. Neither excuses a fan from owning up to the flat-out disrespect shown to an artist when freeloading an album, knowing full well that an artist has put it up for sale and offered legal means of streaming or sampling the material. The term puts the individual consumer's thanklessness in sharp relief and nurtures a culture of accountability for one's choice of whether or not to pay. Use of the word is an acknowledgement of creators' rights and the importance of their consent. Even if an individual is unable or unwilling to fight the temptation to FreeLoad an album, understanding the action as freeloading accepts the reality of their choice. This shift in perspective may form a foundation upon which the social contract, that respects the rights of creators for our shared benefit, can be reaffirmed in the digital age.

Unlike the term "piracy," the use of freeloading avoids making casual accusations of criminal transgression. Rigid, zero-tolerance ideologies stifle communication and amplify conflict over the long term. So our goal should not be to eliminate freeloading. It will always constitute a particular node of Internet culture; an option waiting for those who seek it out. For every effort at tracking our actions online or encrypting content, someone—probably a highly intelligent, antisocial teenager or college student with nothing better to do—will look for a way to circumvent it. For every freeloading website or service taken down by governments, other services will pop up to replace them. In all likelihood, this cat-and-mouse game will continue, in one form or another, as long you and I go on breathing.

Because we will be living with freeloading—no matter how destructive we may believe it is to the long-term health of democratic, technologically advanced, market-based cultures—our goal must not be prohibition, but marginalization. The further freeloading is pushed to the margins—aided by acceptance of the term itself—the more absurd arguments in favor of freeloading will appear.

We may correct our crude, ignorant maps of The New Islands and find lasting progress, marginalizing misconception and sailing clear-eyed into The New World.

FairLoading

The news media amplifies novelty, conflict, and sensationalism, knowing we can't resist a good disaster, metaphorical car wreck or tribal battle of good versus evil. Such inherent tendencies of media (and ourselves) tempt us into orgies of mass misunderstanding, both of the world and our role within it. We may be entertained. We may watch contentedly and follow along as passive observers. But, in the end, we feel a little more isolated than we started, a bit more pessimistic.

The freeloading debate was nourished by this lust for novelty, conflict and sensationalism. In the case of digital music, consumers were mistakenly led to believe they had to choose between Digital Determinists, who were dismissive of artists' rights yet appeared to be on the winning side of history, and corporate rights holders, who argued on behalf of artists but resembled the greedy relics of an impossible past. The resulting conflict, "technology vs. the man" or "the future vs. the past," rose to increasing prominence in the public mind. Moderates or pragmatists went unnoticed in this polarized debate not because they were missing, but because they had no side to call their own.

And there were perceivable costs to this missing middle ground of opinion. Torrent Freak reported on a study conducted by Lund University in 2012 that found site blocking or graduated response having minimal impact on the 15-25 year old FreeLoaders' attitudes toward creators' rights.[3] "Our conclusion is that repressive actions that lack societal support may still have effects, but that the effects are limited," researcher Marin de Kaminski explained. "Our results show that young people feel no pressure from neighbors, friends, relatives, teachers etc. to refrain from file sharing. A higher degree of pressure or social control would most possibly have a clear impact on habits and practices regarding file sharing." Torrent Freak added that, "Essentially, file-sharers do not believe they are doing anything wrong and while this remains the case the 'problem' is unlikely to go away."

The disengagement and resignation many have offered to freeloading is just as much of a problem as the cat-and-mouse with sites like The Pirate Bay. The disengagement has occurred as a consequence of the haphazard way freeloading was constructed in peoples minds through the Decade of Dysfunction and the notable absence of strong voices from respected artists who are ready to draw a line in the sand for the sake of their fellow creators and a confused public. If a sensible middle ground is to develop, it needs to develop around *something*. If a moderate mind feels isolated in their views, they are much less likely to express them or feel confidence that they are members of a community trying to encourage progress.

Writing a book on freeloading is asking for trouble. Upon studying the issue, I became all too aware of how fast it moves, how quickly one controversy bleeds into another, and how quickly predictions made with absolute confidence are disproven by the passage of time or consumer behavior. For that reason, I am reluctant to draw out specific solutions to freeloading based upon one controversy or another, in the fear (or rather confidence) that the particular conditions of freeloading as I finish this book in 2012 might not apply in five years or ten years.

But after watching both sides of the freeloading debate engage in a seemingly endless war characterized by defamation and distrust, while making no serious effort at clearing out a space for common ground, readers are owed an attempt at solutions. I have spent many pages detailing all that is wrong and self-destructive about our acceptance of freeloading, but how can we pivot this discourse towards a better understanding of copyright and our collective rights and responsibilities? For that, I offer the principles of *FairLoading*.

It is time to unite in service of our linked interests: for consumers, respecting the spirit of copyright as a cornerstone of an open, technological society that values creativity and recognizes that maintaining a diverse creative culture gives us more of the quality art and information we need to understand ourselves and the world around us; for industries and artists, respecting consumers and the spirit of copyright law will help maintain and profit from an engaged market of paying consumers long into the future. Manifesting the principles of FairLoading will require a conscious, good-faith effort on all sides, but our reward is nothing less than economic and spiritual prosperity, as we all benefit from the digital revolution's great potential.

---

1) An independent creator has the right to distribute original works in a manner as s/he so chooses, whether for free or for pay. Consumers have a corresponding duty to respect that right.

This is the core sentiment of traditional copyright. Whatever new technologies or models develop through the 21st century, creators must retain the practical right to describe how and where their works ought to be distributed, lest they be exploited by forever advancing means of copying or evading the rule of law. For every equally held right carries a responsibility to uphold that right for others, and consumers need to keep their duty to respect the rights of creators in mind as they navigate the ever changing terrain of new media.

2) An independent creator can extend the rights to a creative work to a record label, publisher, production company or any other legal business partner as s/he chooses.

Here is another core tenet to understanding traditional copyright. Failure to understand this concept provided an opening for those in the "copyfight" to vilify copyright as solely a mechanism for bloated corporate behemoths. Though it is fashionable to lambast content industries, we are smart to remember the artists who have chosen to partner with such industries of their free will and who have built inspiring creative careers with that industry's help. An attack upon copyright-based industries is really an attack on copyright and, by extension, the multitudes of creators who depend on its legal protections.

3) No individual or business is entitled to knowingly exploit a creator's unlicensed creative works for pleasure or profit.

So long as freeloading is easy and convenient, many will continue the practice. My goal in this book is not to guilt or shame consumers into never freeloading again, but to drive a wedge into the narcotic acceptance of the act. Placing that wedge relies upon individual consumers acknowledging that they are not entitled to content that they know is unlicensed. There are grey areas of copyright, but they shouldn't keep us from acknowledging what is often a black-and-white issue: illegally downloading or streaming free content that one knows is digitally available through licensed means.

Similarly, we can make distinctions for The Pirate Bay and those who advertise the fact that they are engaging in mass exploitation of creators' rights. We can separate the more ethical uses of P2P technology and storage lockers from the egregious violators of creators' human rights. The Pirate Bay itself has proven this point. They trumpet their service The Promo Bay, which provides a home for unsigned artists to host and distribute their work. Why can't we keep the wonderful service that The Promo Bay provides, and do away with the exploitative Pirate Bay? Digital Determinists tell us we have to accept the good and the bad of the Internet, but that is pure laziness. It is merely a question of will on the part of the citizenry, elected officials and the technology sector. In April, the cyber locker service Rapidshare released a paper entitled, "Responsible Practice for Cloud Storage Services," that acknowledged the seriousness of freeloading on storage lockers and suggested concrete policies to establish a foundation for ethics and responsibility in digital commerce.[4] Such steps suggest that a constructive path on addressing the convenience of freeloading is entirely possible, and is in fact already happening.

4) The right to free speech does not entitle an individual or business to infringe upon any person's legal rights as a means of expression and/or speech.

As non-transparent lobbying groups like Fight for the Future dispense propaganda unto the public in cynical means to achieving their own mistaken ends, "censorship" will be trotted out again and again to stiff-arm any attempt at marginalizing the clear cases of artistic exploitation online. It is crucial to keep in mind the distinction between "censorship" that occurs in response to *criminal* activity, which is in accord with the freedom of speech, and censorship that occurs in *response* to speech, such as the Chinese government blocking Internet users from information on the Tiananmen Square massacre or the Iranian government's shutting down of offending newspapers. These are not even remotely the same, and nothing exposes the First World entitlement of Digital Determinists as much as when they portray shutting down criminal enterprises like Megaupload as an injustice somehow related to the oppression Chinese citizens face. And before we put too much trust into Google or any other Internet company on protecting "Internet freedom" we should remember that Google themselves *facilitated* Chinese censorship when trying to enter their market for search engines in the late 2000s. Such companies are businesses with their own profit motives as their primary consideration, not society's health or the preservation of human rights.

5) The traditional principle of copyright, that a creator has exclusive right to the fruits of his/her own labor for a limited period of time, is fundamental to preserving independent free expression in an open, market-based society; and is a Human Right delineated in Article 27 of the United Nations Declaration of Human Rights.

Copyright is dismissed by some Digital Determinists as "unnatural" or "artificial"—and therefore undeserving of respect. But all rights and laws are somewhat "artificial," created by the consent of the governed under the rule of law and the values of society. Creators' rights have gone part and parcel with the rise of modernity and rise of geniuses like Mark Twain, John Ford, Orson Welles, Ella Fitzgerald, The Beatles, Vladimir Nabokov, Bob Dylan, David Foster Wallace, Kurt Cobain…this list could go on for a very, very long time. So it is naïve and self-destructive to pretend that copyright has been anything but a gift to human civilization. It is a human right that demands preservation.

6) In respect to the rights of the public, expressed by the Public Domain, copyright length should be reformed to a retroactive maximum term of fifty years.

The extension of copyright terms far beyond their traditional limit is a violation of the public right to share in the bounty of creative expression; it is as much an abuse as the disregard of copyright shown by the FreeLoaders. At a time when the Pirate Party finds a European constituency and more young people become subject to the propaganda of groups like Fight for the Future, the longer the entertainment industries hold up the sensible return of copyright to a maximum fifty-year term, the more dangers copyright-based industries will face. No one respects the entertainment industries for pushing copyright toward being a near-perpetual right—nor should they. Along with the RIAA mass lawsuits, it is an area in which I wholeheartedly share in the indignation many FreeLoaders express for Hollywood and the RIAA.

Why fifty years? Because it is sensible, easy to remember, and has historical precedent in the United States and around the world. Rights holders in the United States enjoyed a maximum fifty-six-year term for many decades, before our modern acceleration of term extensions began in the late 20th century. As recently as September, 2011, the European Union extended copyright terms for song recordings to seventy years from their original terms: fifty years.[5]

Fifty years is enough time for a creator to exploit his or her own works. I would hold the rights to this book until the age of eighty—this strikes me as perfectly fair and would represent a radical return to traditional principles of copyright. In cases where a rights holder dies before the term is up, it is just that immediate family members be able to reap some rewards for their loved one's labor—but not forever.

If the fifty-year term were enforced retroactively, think of the books that would be available for free electronically and the literary enthusiasts who would emerge online, ready to point readers to free, under-appreciated works of old. Think of the old films that would be made available and the local film societies that would pop up online and off to expose new generations to obscure works and the classics. As for music: well, we already know what it would resemble, don't we? Except in this reality, older songs, from the 1960s on down, could truly be shared, sampled and remixed without fear of law or guilt of violating creators' rights. The abundance of blues, jazz, and early rock 'n' roll could breathe new life into sample-based genres like hip-hop and electronica. It doesn't take much to imagine how this surge of works into the public domain could be quite beautiful. Each passing year, society would have a chance ring in another year of works into the public domain in an annual celebration of our cultural heritage. Don't I sound like the digital utopian?

Of course, the film, music, and publishing industries will be horrified by this idea. But as the Decade of Dysfunction comes to a close, governments are having trouble forcing Internet Service Providers to block websites and torrent trackers that are unapologetic in their violation of creators' rights. Even if they seize website domains, mirror sites pop up in no time. Dealing with the just inefficiencies of due process law, governments are at a distinct disadvantage in this cat-and-mouse game. When governments attempt to better align their powers of enforcement with the swiftness of their enemy, their critics from Silicon Valley erupt with familiar cries of censorship, due process or privacy violation.

Why doesn't Congress explore a fifty-year term that benefits the public domain (and online distributors that might specialize in curating such works, making advertising revenues along the way) in concert with stiff enforcement measures against websites that serve no significant purpose other than infringement, so that creators' exclusive rights still under term have a better chance of being enforced? With sufficient government and ISP cooperation, rights holders could be given increasingly efficient means of being alerted when their copyright-protected works are posted online without their consent, so that they can quickly take down their protected works or leave the content to be casually shared if they so choose.

As it stands in 2012, content companies are treading in dangerous water by continuing to extend copyright terms, while legislating punishments such as temporarily disconnecting infringing FreeLoaders from the Internet. A United Nations report in 2011 called such disconnections a disproportionate violation of human rights, and they are right to raise concerns with the practice.[6] The Grokster decision by the US Supreme Court wisely recognized the problems in too forcefully going after individual downloaders, rather than focusing on distributors. Unless content companies wish to revisit the poisonous history of the RIAA mass lawsuits in the US, they are obliged to work with governments to find proportionate, enforceable punishments for individual FreeLoaders, understanding that nearly any enforcement measure will be doomed over the long term unless copyright terms are returned to a reasonable length.

The fifty-year term also offers an opportunity for digital consumers who feel genuinely oppressed by the length of terms today: civil disobedience. The fifty-year term can be self-enforced by a consumer who wishes to make a statement: simply by counting back fifty years and FreeLoading content released before that year. This is no substitute for pressuring a political representative or organizing a constituency, but such a violation is at least conscientious, based on principle and respectful of creative works under reasonable terms.

If citizens around the world actively rally around the fifty-year term and corresponding enforcement measures, there is real opportunity for progress. But this will take work, time and the frustration of dealing with elected leaders who may not be willing to act.

7) Record labels/publishers and consumers share an opportunity to seek fair treatment of artists in the digital age, embracing a 50/50 royalty split for digital works as an ideal.

There is another opportunity for digital reform that can be powered by consumers and industry on their own: the *FairDeal* model. For the FairDeal model, we look to the community-based ethics of Punk, built on togetherness and mutual respect, epitomized by Dischord Records of Washington, DC. Whether one is attracted to punk or hardcore music, the label presents the communities of independent music and publishing a way to capitalize on the efficiencies of digital distribution, while combating freeloading and revolutionizing their respective industries.

As previously noted, no one in the 1990s argued that music should be free. The staunchest critics of the record industry were found in the punk movement and in figures such as Ian Mackaye, founder of Dischord and member of seminal bands like Minor Threat and Fugazi. The punks' response to the raging commercialism they saw in the music industry wasn't to give everything away, but to respect fans by charging around $10 for albums and keeping concert tickets in the same price range. This is the true spirit of DIY—not that we are all on our own, but that we can build something genuinely better together. Echoing the approach of Todd Patrick in the live realm, Dischord sought to do a "reasonable amount of commerce" to profit as a business, while keeping overhead low to give bands a larger cut of profits while charging consumers less than other labels. But Dischord was marginalized by the stridency of (some of) its music and reliance upon independent record stores and distributors. Thanks to the digital revolution and direct sales, the Dischord model has the chance of exploiting a vastly expanded market of consumers and incentivizing the DIY model on a mass scale. Such is the dream of FairDeal.

Why don't independent labels decide upon a standard of fair business practices that clearly sets them apart from the major labels? For example, that their artists receive a fifty percent royalty on digital sales and at least thirty percent on physical. They could also commit to charging no more than $9 for digital albums, sold directly through their online stores. If the independents were able to decide on such principles and brand them as "FairDeal," or something similar, the stage would be set for radical change in the music industry that benefits independent labels, artists, and fans. Realistically, FairDeal would need to become its own independent organization, charged with certifying that contracts fit its parameters as advertised so that consumers were not deceived. Labels could then use the designation to market themselves individually (FairDeal certified stickers or stamps) or combine their efforts to create a digital wholesale store, where a digital consumer could shop knowing that the participating bands and labels all fell under FairDeal. If some combination of these ideas were initiated by independent labels and found support from paying consumers, the major labels would be forced to take notice. By building such a community of engaged creators, investors, and consumers all treating one another with respect, manifesting shared cultural visions, the Internet would deliver a sustainable consumer revolution. Rather than taking the FreeLoaders' lazy approach to destroy the music industry, the goal would be to participate in creating a better one. Such a course of events isn't as unrealistic as it may at first sound.

Many independent record labels already offer 50/50 deals and would only need to publicize them and organize a FairDeal structure, perhaps through the independent labels' advocacy group, A2IM. As for the digital wholesale store, the basic idea is already being played with. A wide association of labels participated in TheNewRecord.com, which launched in October, 2011. The site served as a center for fans to browse new releases by independent label artists, sample licensed MP3s and link to the labels' respective digital stores to buy directly. Add the FairDeal brand and perhaps some social media features, and the independents have an opportunity to support the wider independent community while profiting individually. Another layer could be added in which physical independent record stores participate by offering promotions or advertising events. The possibilities are exciting and, if successful, could be copied by the book publishing industry with relatively few alterations.

In the capitalist system, any change is possible if consumers perceive value, be it ethical or qualitative, and respond with their wallets. Responsibility can be a truth-based brand, a status symbol, and a signifier of conspicuous consumption. When consumers and industries come together in mutual support of progressive economic practices and can prove such partnerships to be profitable, we have the potential to substantially affect the world, and the internet surely makes this type of change more possible than before.

Finally, resolving the tension of freeloading requires greater awareness of the need for communication between consumers, creators, and editors (such as labels and publishers). The news media in particular has a role to play in this regard, to not be bashful when it comes to reminding readers and viewers of creators' rights when they are questioned or violated; or of the spirit of limited copyright terms if and when additional extensions emerge for legislative debate. The words we use when discussing freeloading, the attitudes we accept and the openness of the conversations we hold on the issue (private or public) all make a real difference in the aggregate—they impact whether we will use the Internet to create or to destroy. The Decade of Dysfunction went on as long and painfully as it did for no other reason than this communication breakdown. For solutions to remain possible, we must not be afraid to listen.

CODA

Remembering that I'll be dead soon is the most important tool I've ever encountered to help me make the big choices in life. Because almost everything—all external expectations, all pride, all fear of embarrassment or failure—these things just fall away in the face of death, leaving only what is truly important. Remembering that you are going to die is the best way I know to avoid the trap of thinking you have something to lose. You are already naked. There is no reason not to follow your heart.

So preached the prophet of the information age when he spoke before Stanford University's graduating class of 2005. Steve Jobs spoke from experience. He had been diagnosed with a rare form of pancreatic cancer two years earlier, and on October 5th, 2011 his body finally succumbed to sickness. Upon his death, Jobs was roundly hailed as a genius, visionary and an heir to Thomas Edison. The attention to detail and aesthetic beauty he brought to his work at Apple was singular and unexplainable, though his obituary in the *New York Times* offered a clue. "Mr. Jobs's own research and intuition, not focus groups, were his guide," it read. "When asked what market research went into the iPad, Mr. Jobs replied: 'None. It's not the consumers' job to know what they want.' "[1]

What could be more out of step with the "open culture" perspective of the time, that preached we could find all the solutions we needed by trusting in the wisdom of the hive and dismissing professional communicators? So long as the designs of technology were trusted to "innovate," cultural progress and creativity was certain.

"Unfortunately," Steve Jobs told *Wired* in 1996, "[creativity is] too rare a commodity. A lot of people in our industry haven't had very diverse experiences. So they don't have enough dots to connect, and they end up with very linear solutions without a broad perspective on the problem. The broader one's understanding of the human experience, the better design we will have."[2]

And how is it that we broaden our understanding of the human experience if not for the full spectrum of communication—if not for the high quality arts that entertain, inform and reveal glimmers of truth in our everyday lives?

Free content ultimately will not give us better books, albums, films, or journalism that improve our mental maps of the world or help us to understand ourselves; it gives us lower quality, lower standards and atomized distraction. As we see in independent music's shift to corporate patronage, "free" means we are more willing to be used for other people's devices, and we surrender our individual influence in the world around us as a result. We dig ourselves a little further underground with the Machine. It is a recipe for decline.

It is impossible to know where technology will take us, or what new ways we may experience culture. If the 2000s are any indication, new digital businesses will rise and fall, surprising models will emerge, false predictions will be made. As we approach the meat of this century—so exciting yet equally uncertain—the best chance we have for avoiding the declinist tendencies of Digital Determinism is to hold on, with passionate fury, to the principle that human creativity is valuable and sacred. When we devalue creativity, when we trample upon the rights of artists to distribute their work as they please, we devalue ourselves and trample upon our own right to a better future.

Art is a bellwether to civilization. Our only hope of approaching the present with honesty and action is through our artists, who alone have the tools to show us the way. Marshall McLuhan, in a televised debate with Norman Mailer in 1968, explained:

> The present is only faced, in any generation, by the artist. The artist is prepared to study the present as his material because it is the area of challenge to the whole sensory life and therefore it's anti-utopian…. There is in IBM a phrase that information overload produces pattern recognition….When you give people too much information, they instantly resort to pattern recognition. In other words, to structuring the experience.

And I think this is part of the artist world. The artist—when he encounters the present, the contemporary artist—is always seeking new patterns, new pattern recognition—which is his task, for heaven's sake! His great need. The absolute indispensability of the artist is that he alone, in the encounter with the present, can give the pattern recognition. He alone has the sensory awareness to tell us what our world is made of. He is more important than the scientist.[3]

If the artist alone has the skills to "recognize the pattern" within the context of his own humanity, and share that recognition with the world, then there is a gulf between the low quality amateur work we find in quantity online and the high-quality professional work that requires far greater investment. It is in the interest of incentivizing "patterns" that are more independent, more truthful and more useful to us in understanding our lives that we recognize the role of copyright in the digital age.

The lies, propaganda and niche-bating of online businesses based upon free expose our need to support high quality information. Rumors and lies spread faster than ever before and pre-existing biases go unchallenged by an infrastructure of selective reality. The quantity of art does us no good. The quality of art and information, however, prompts us to forget about biases and transcend ourselves as we are captivated by fresh and resonant expressions of humanity. We are given accurate patterns of Truth which allow us to understand our actions in the context of the past, present and future. The quality expressions that copyright incentivizes are essential, and we are fools to deem such expressions unimportant out of sloth, praising the false idol of technology.

If we fail to maintain the spirit of copyright into the digital age, what novel expressions of ideas and history will we deny ourselves? What life-changing joys and inspirations originating from our musicians and filmmakers will we stupidly abort, trading faith in our sovereign creativity for that in technology? What uncomfortable truths will go unreported or stolen from their proper journalistic context?

Steve Jobs told *Wired*, "We're born, we live for a brief instant, and we die. It's been happening for a long time. Technology is not changing it much—if at all."

Tucked away in the hills of the Driftless, a space was made where the savanna oaks could grow again under the fullness of the sun. Over time the invasive cedar trees had been recognized for the obvious force of decline they represented. They were methodically cleared away; destructive affronts to Truth.

The grasses and plants of the prairie returned and, one late fall day, a wildfire was set. As the weather warmed, seeds that had laid dormant for many decades sprouted to life amidst the limestone bluffs and the crystal clear spring creeks. Once again, the diversity of life radiated from every field and every tree. Amidst the restored vivacity, the huge oaks towered above all else, as they had for hundreds of years.

But new cedar saplings arose in the grass; reminders that, amidst a world of perpetual change, the work of preserving the beauty of our own nature—our own humanity—is never quite complete.

Acknowledgments

There are many people without whom, and influences without which this book would neither have been conceived of nor published: the GPCH and North Brooklyn community offered a window; Tiny Mix Tapes' Marvin Lin provided space to test early ideas; readers' feedback validated intuition of this project's potential; Mollie Glick and David Hirschman helped workshop the book proposal; interviewees trusted me with their words and provided heart and soul to these pages; the generous participation of Kyp, Ira and Craig was especially critical and appreciated; Connie Rosenblum and James Ledbetter helped me secure those all important clips; the indomitable William Clark of William Clark Associates took on an unknown client and shepherded me through a treacherous process; and John Oakes of OR Books and Henry Rosenbloom of Scribe risked working with an unproven first-time author. To all of the above I am eternally grateful.

Thank you: to my parents and siblings for their bottomless love and support; to family, friends and educators who have guided and/or humored me throughout the years; to the Shorewood School District and the University of Minnesota; to Milwaukee, Minneapolis, Hazleton, Lanesboro and New York City; and especially to my beautiful wife, who shouldered the stresses and risks of this project with grace and grit, and with whom I share its achievement. Love to all.

NOTES

Introduction

1. Cory Doctorow, "Why I Won't Buy an iPad," *BoingBoing*, April 2, 2010, http://boingboing.net/2010/04/02/why-i-wont-buy-an-ipad-and-think-yo.html.
2. Burrows, Peter, "Steve Jobs: I'm an Optimist," *Bloomberg Businessweek*, August 13, 2003, http://www.businessweek.com/technology/content/aug2003/tc20030813_7682_tc121.htm.
3. Billboard Staff, "Steve Jobs: A Collection of His Classic Quotes," October 5, 2011, http://www.billboard.biz/bbbiz/industry/digital-and-mobile/steve-jobs-a-collection-of-his-classic-quotes-1005391302.story.
4. Michael DeGusta, "The REAL Death of the Music Industry," *Business Insider*, February 18, 2011, http://articles.businessinsider.com/2011-02-18/tech/30052663_1_riaa-music-industry-cd-era.
5. Eric Pfanner, "Music Industry Braces for the Unthinkable," the *New York Times*, January 23, 2011, http://www.nytimes.com/2011/01/24/technology/24music.html?pagewanted=1&_r=3&src=twr.
6. Richard Smirke, "Digital Music Sales are Growing," *Billboard.biz*, January 20, 2011, http://www.billboard.biz/bbbiz/industry/digital-and-mobile/digital-music-sales-are-slowing-ifpi-report-1004139657.story.
7. Ibid.
8. "iPad Sales to Double Next Year," *eMarketer: Digital Intelligence,* December 9, 2010, http://www.emarketer.com/Article.aspx?R=1008098.

KYS

1. Emily Friedman, "Florida Teen Live-Streams His Suicide Online," *ABCNews.com*, November 21, 2008, http://abcnews.go.com/Technology/MindMoodNews/story?id=6306126&page=2.
2. Paul Thompson, "Teenager Commits Suicide Live While 1,500 People Watch Online," *The Daily Mail Online*, November 21, 2008, http://www.dailymail.co.uk/news/worldnews/article-1088173/Teenager-commits-suicide-live-online-1-500-people-watch-video-stream.html.
3. "Chatroom Users 'egged on father to kill himself on webcam,'" *The Evening London Standard*, March 23, 2007, http://www.thisislondon.co.uk/news/article-23390052-chatroom-users-egged-on-father-to-kill-himself-live-on-webcam.do.
4. "Warning: Picture of Dead Kevin Whitrick, Britain's First Cyber Suicide," *Celebrity Vivids*, March 27, 2007, http://www.celebvids.co.uk/2007/03/27/warning-picture-of-dead-kevin-whitrick-britains-first-cyber-suicide/.
5. Park Si-soo, "Video Game Addict Kills Mother," *The Korea Times*, February 21, 2010, http://www.koreatimes.co.kr/www/news/nation/2010/02/117_61178.html.
6. Bryan Kay, "South Korea's two million Internet gaming addicts are dicing with death," *The Herald Scotland*, March 21, 2010, http://www.heraldscotland.com/news/world-news/south-korea-s-two-million-Internet-gaming-addicts-are-dicing-with-death-1.1014953?92585.

The Decade of Dysfunction

1. "Special Event: Lars Ulrich, Roger McGunn Testify Before Senate Judiciary Committee on Downloading Music on the Internet," *CNN.com Transcripts*, July 11, 2000, http://transcripts.cnn.com/TRANSCRIPTS/0007/11/se.01.html.

2. Richard B. Simon, "Metallica's Anti-Napster Crusade Inspires Backlash," *MTV News*, June 1, 2000, http://www.mtv.com/news/articles/971500/metallica-scorned-napster-stance.jhtml.

3. Eric Boehlert, "Napster Backlash," *Salon.com*, April 18, 2000, http://www.salon.com/2000/04/18/napster_6/.

4. Christopher Jones, "Metallica Rips Napster," *Wired.com*, April 13, 2000, http://www.wired.com/politics/law/news/2000/04/35670.

5. Steve Albini, "The Problem With Music," *Negativland*, http://www.negativland.com/albini.html.

6. Sarah McBride and Ethan Smith, "Music Industry to Abandon Mass Suits," *The Wall Street Journal Online*, December 19, 2008, http://online.wsj.com/article/SB122966038836021137.html.

7. Electronic Frontier Foundation, *RIAA vs The People: Five Years Later* (Whitepaper), September 30, 2008, https://www.eff.org/wp/riaa-v-people-five-years-later.

8. Victoria Shannon, "One Internet, Many Copyright Laws," the *New York Times*, November 8, 2004, http://www.nytimes.com/2004/11/08/technology/08newcon.html.

9. Lawrence Lessig, "Prosecuting Online File Sharing Turns A Generation Criminal," *U.S. News and World Report*, December 22, 2008, http://www.usnews.com/opinion/articles/2008/12/22/prosecuting-online-file-sharing-turns-a-generation-criminal.

10. Lawrence Lessig, *Free Culture: The Nature and Future of Creativity.* New York: Penguin Books, 2005, p. 256

11. Lawrence Lessig, "Prosecuting Online File Sharing Turns A Generation Criminal," *US News and World Report*, December 12, 2008, http://www.usnews.com/opinion/articles/2008/12/22/prosecuting-online-file-sharing-turns-a-generation-criminal.

12. Patrick Ross, "Copyright Laws Work Well Against Illegal File Sharing, Also Called Online Theft," *US News and World Report*, December 22, 2008, http://www.usnews.com/opinion/articles/2008/12/22/copyright-laws-work-well-against-illegal-file-sharing-also-called-online-theft.

13. Cory Doctorow, Content: *Selected Essays on Technology, Creativity, Copyright, and the Future of the Future.* San Francisco: Tachyon, 2008, p. 27.

14. *Aleks Krotoski, "Cory Doctorow: Publish Books Free Online," The Guardian, May 22, 2010, http://www.guardian.co.uk/technology/2010/may/23/cory-doctorow-my-bright-idea.*

15. Jaron Lanier, *You Are Not a Gadget: A Manifesto.* New York: Vintage, 2011.

16. Doctorow, 46.

17. Doctorow, 21.

18. Chris Anderson, *The Long Tail: Why The Future of Business is Selling Less of More.* New York: Hyperion, 2006, p. 74.

19. Chris Anderson, *Free: The Future of a Radical Price.* New York: Hyperion, 2009, p. 92.

20. Anderson, *Free*, 229.

21. Anderson, *Free*, 230.

22. Mike Masnick, "EMI Kills Off More Innovation: MP3Tunes Declares Bankruptcy Due to 'Withering' Legal Costs," *Techdirt*, May 11, 2012, http://www.techdirt.com/articles/20120511/11203118884/emi-kills-off-more-innovation-mp3tunes-declares-bankruptcy-due-to-withering-legal-costs.shtml.

23. Mike Masnick, "The Future of Music Business Models (And Those Who Are Already There)," *Techdirt*, January 25, 2010, http://www.techdirt.com/articles/20091119/1634117011.shtml.

24. Ibid.

25. Jeff Leeds, "Nine Inch Nails Fashions Innovative Web Pricing Plan," the *New York Times*, March 4, 2008, http://www.nytimes.com/2008/03/04/arts/music/04nine.html.

26. Greg Sandoval, "Trent Reznor: Why won't people pay $5?" *CNet News*, January 10, 2008, http://news.cnet.com/8301-10784_3-9847788-7.html.

27. Amanda Palmer. "Amanda Palmer, Dresden Dolls, MIDEM Interview," *YouTube*, September 16, 2010, http://www.youtube.com/watch?v=Td9r_PVty3c&feature =related.

28. Paul Resnikoff. "Yorke to Artists: Avoid the Music Industry 'Sinking Ship'...," *Digital Music News*, June 9, 2010, http://www.digitalmusicnews.com/stories/060910yorke# mayJNPiNWn7IDfi8pceWtA.

29. Randall Stross, "You, Too, Can Bankroll a Rock Band," the *New York Times*, April 3, 2010, http://www.nytimes.com/2010/04/04/business/04digi.html.

30. Charles Arthur, "Imogen Heap Says Touring's Too Pricy as Record Sales Slump," *The Guardian*, May 26, 2010, http://www.guardian.co.uk/music/pda/2010/may/26/ imogen-heap-twitter-tour-woes.

31. Antony Bruno, "Plugged/Unplugged CwF+RtB=WTF?" *Billboard.biz*, January 29, 2010,http://www.billboard.biz/bbbiz/content_display/industry/news/e3i68e64a3cf 27273505d02d59eabedae01.

32. "Techdirt's CwF+RtB," http://www.techdirt.com/rtb.php.

33. Jen Long. "Michael Gira Interview," *The Line of Best Fit*, September 22, 2010, http://www. thelineofbestfit.com/features/interviews/tlobf-interview-michael-gira-swans-36395.

Onward, Downward

1. Matthew Perpetua, "Amos Lee Breaks Record For Lowest Selling Number One Album," *Rolling Stone*, February 2, 2011, http://www.rollingstone.com/music/news/ amos-lee-breaks-record-for-lowest-selling-number-one-album-20110202.

2. http://www.ice.gov/news/releases/1205/120510norfolk.htm

3. p 27 of SOPA Manager's Amendment HR 3261

4. http://www.guardian.co.uk/technology/2011/may/18/google-eric-schmidt-piracy

5. http://news.cnet.com/8301-31921_3-57349540-281/sopa-opponents-may-go- nuclear-and-other-2012-predictions/

6. http://blog.reddit.com/2012/01/stopped-they-must-be-on-this-all.html

7. http://techcrunch.com/2012/01/19/sopa-scorecard-Internet-lobbyists/

8. http://pogue.blogs.nytimes.com/2012/01/19/put-down-the-pitchforks-on-sopa/

9. http://popuppirates.com/?p=1454

10. http://www.theatlantic.com/magazine/archive/2010/03/the-freeloaders/8027/

The Laziest Rebellion

1. Mike Masnick, "Label Complains that Amazon Devalues Artists by Making Music Cheap," *Techdirt*, September 23, 2010, http://www.techdirt.com/articles/ 20100922/04284311111/label-complains-that-amazon-devalues-artists-by-making- music-cheap.shtml#comments.

They Don't Have a Choice in the Matter

1. A somewhat obscure baroque-pop Brooklyn band.

This Is about Creativity and Art

1. "If it's allowed to happen," said former Beatle George Harrison of the Nike deal in November 1987, "every Beatles song ever recorded is going to be advertising women's underwear and sausages. We've got to put a stop to it in order to set a precedent. Otherwise it's going to be a free-for-all. It's one thing when you're dead, but we're still around! They don't have any respect for the fact that we wrote and recorded those songs, and it was our lives." By February 1988, as Nike continued to use the ad and its music while the court fight proceeded, Paul McCartney said: "[T]

he most difficult question is whether you should use songs for commercials. I haven't made up my mind. Generally, I don't like it, particularly with the Beatles stuff. When twenty years have passed maybe we'll move into the realm where it's okay to do it." "Nike and the Beatles," *The Pop History Dig*, last modified December 13, 2011, http://www.pophistorydig.com/?tag=the-beatles-vs-nike.

Angry Armchair Quarterbacks

1. A renowned, mid-sized rock club in Hoboken, NJ.

Common Ground

1. Lead singer of the Swedish orchestral pop group, Sigur Ros.
2. A 1,400 capacity venue in Manhattan, NY.
3. Lead singer of the folk rock group, Mountain Goats.
4. Cost Per 1,000 consumer views or impressions.

Hope

1. Andrew Orlowski, "Public: Whack Freetards Harder (most 'pirates' agree)," *The Register*, May 17, 2011, http://www.theregister.co.uk/2011/05/17/wiggin_entertainment _survey/.

A Failure of Memory

1. http://pitchfork.com/news/36594-lily-allen-quits-piracy-debate-possibly-quits-music-business-as-well/
2. Fred Goodman, *Fortune's Fool: Edgar Bronfman, Jr., Warner Music, And an Industry in Crisis*. New York: Simon and Schuster, 2010, p. 129.
3. Steve Knopper, *Appetite for Self-Destruction: The Spectacular Crash of the Record Industry in the Digital Age*. New York: Free Press, 2009.
4. Goodman, 146.
5. "Right Before Napster Got Buried, This Happened..." *Digital Music News*, July 29, 2011, http://www.digitalmusicnews.com/stories/072911napster#P5JZhQQ5uIOT JcyyZao47A.
6. Brad King, "Napster May Not Matter Anymore," *Wired*, May 15, 2000, http://www. wired.com/culture/lifestyle/news/2000/05/36315.

Creators' Rights and the Slippery Slope

1. http://www.copyhype.com/2011/11/copyright-and-the-first-amendment-the-unexplored-unbroken-historical-practice/
2. http://www.copyhype.com/2012/05/myths-from-the-birth-of-us-copyright/
3. http://www.copyhype.com/2012/05/myths-from-the-birth-of-us-copyright-part-2/
4. http://www.bbc.co.uk/news/technology-17894176#TWEET134932

Markets, Morality and Incentives

1. Adam Smith, *The Theory of Moral Sentiments* (1790; Library of Economics and Liberty), Chap 5, http://www.econlib.org/library/Smith/smMS5.html.
2. Mike Masnick, "Interview With Will Page, Music Industry Economist," *Techdirt*, April 29, 2010, http://www.techdirt.com/articles/20100429/0116199232.shtml.
3. http://www.nationalreview.com/articles/292088/piracy-not-competition-robert -verbruggen?pg=1
4. Smith, *Theory of Moral Sentiments*.

5. Dan Pink, "Drive: The Surprising Truth About What Motivates Us (Video),"
    RSA Animate on YouTube, April 10, 2010, http://www.youtube.com/
    watch?v=u6XAPnuFjJc.
6. http://theoatmeal.com/comics/game_of_thrones

Tragic Irony

1. Lanier, 86.
2. Lanier, 82.
3. http://www.nytimes.com/2010/10/10/arts/music/10brand.html?_r=3&adx
    nnl=1&ref=music&pagewanted=all&adxnnlx=1337749767-/pvdadzL9Thg/
    EzDRxmyFw
4. http://blogs.villagevoice.com/music/2010/10/is_it_possible.php
5. http://www.youtube.com/watch?v=oERzcGqZKT0
6. http://gawker.com/5313306/bloggers-just-selling-out-all-over-the-place
7. http://blogs.suntimes.com/music/2008/03/pitchfork_founder_and_indieroc_1.html
8. http://www.youtube.com/watch?v=4CObiu40qSI&feature=related
9. http://www.youtube.com/watch?v=LayMnnNekd8&feature=related
10. http://www.youtube.com/watch?v=FrgqsliR7NI
11. http://www.arthurmag.com/2008/12/03/
12. http://www.pitchfork.com/news/28256-camel-rolling-stone-under-fire-for-indie-
    rock-ad/
13. http://www.pitchfork.com/news/34497-bob-dylan-to-sing-with-william-for-pepsi/
14. http://pitchfork.com/news/34412-matt-kims-matt-talks-selling-out-joy-rick-
    rubin/
15. http://pitchfork.com/news/39247-watch-wavves-perform-new-song-live/
16. http://pitchfork.com/news/38020-neon-indian-teams-with-mountain-dew/
17. http://pitchfork.com/tv/daytripping/149-wavves/271-daytripping-ruined-my-life/
18. http://www.theFADER.com/2009/04/29/strike-FADER-strike-pitchfork-
    tv-daytripping-with-wavves/
19. http://www.SPIN.com/articles/backstage-pass-fucked-wavves
20. Marshall McLuhan, *Understanding Media*. New York: McGraw Hill, 1966, p 227.
21. Doctorow, 55.
22. http://techcrunch.com/2012/01/19/sopa-scorecard-Internet-lobbyists/

The Net Fail

1. http://www.ppcassociates.com/blog/analytics/lobbyists-1-Internet-0-an-
    alternative-take-on-sopa/
2. http://www.fastcompany.com/1836709/why-no-web-blackout-for-cispa-google-it
3. http://www.nytimes.com/2012/01/19/technology/web-protests-piracy-bill-and-
    2-key-senators-change-course.html?_r=1&pagewanted=all
4. http://www.ppcassociates.com/blog/analytics/lobbyists-1-Internet-0-an-
    alternative-take-on-sopa/
5. http://www.macworld.com/article/1165221/who_really_was_behind_the_sopa_
    protests.html
6. http://www.macworld.com/article/1165221/who_really_was_behind_the_sopa_
    protests.html
7. http://techpresident.com/news/22165/voices-net-meet-mike-masnick-accidental-activist
8. http://articles.boston.com/2012-01-26/metro/30667660_1_wikipedia-editors-
    advocacy-groups-tiffiniy-cheng/3
9. http://techpresident.com/news/21600/geeks-gear-fight-sopa
10. http://www.mediademocracyfund.org/about
11. http://articles.boston.com/2012-01-26/metro/30667660_1_wikipedia-editors-
    advocacy-groups-tiffiniy-cheng/2

12. http://www.youtube.com/watch?v=i3eA7H4wdtY&feature=relmfu
13. http://www.jammerdirect.com/Jammunity/JamNouncements/tabid/156/
    EntryId/139/Holmes-Wilson-One-of-the-Creators-of-the-SOPA-Strike-
    Movement-is-this-weeks-special-guest-on-The-Dose.aspx
14. http://www.reddit.com/user/holmesworcester
15. http://americancensorship.org/infographic.html
16. http://articles.boston.com/2012-01-26/metro/30667660_1_wikipedia-editors-
    advocacy-groups-tiffiniy-cheng/3
17. http://techpresident.com/news/21600/geeks-gear-fight-sopa

Digital Determinism: Dead Wrong

1. http://www.youtube.com/watch?v=KEYbD-TFlxs
2. Daniel Lyons, "I, Robot," *Newsweek Magazine* on *The Daily Beast,* May 16, 2009,
   http://www.thedailybeast.com/newsweek/2009/05/16/i-robot.html.
3. Duncan Begg, "Why in 2029, We'll Start Living Forever," *The Sun,* October 8,
   2009, http://www.thesun.co.uk/sol/homepage/features/2648937/Why-in-2029-
   scientists-believe-well-have-technology-to-live-forever.html.
4. "Girls Are Not Into The Pirate Bay, Or Bittorrent," *TorrentFreak.com,*
   September 19, 2011, http://torrentfreak.com/girls-are-not-into-the-pirate-
   bay-or-bittorrent-110919/.
5. Doctorow, *Content,* 74.
6. Glenn Peoples, "Business Matters: Why 2011 is the year Digital Music Broke, By
   the Numbers," *Billboard.biz,* September 29, 2011, http://www.billboard.biz/bbbiz/
   industry/digital-and-mobile/business-matters-why-2011-is-the-year-digital-
   1005378032.story.
7. Emma Hall, "Slovakian Publishers' Paywall Appears to Be Success," *AdAge.com,*
   July 5, 2011, http://adage.com/article/global-news/slovakian-publishers-paywall-
   appears-success/228483/.
8. Doctorow, 74.
9. Ibid., 65.
10. "Nearly 18 Million Media Tablets Shipped in 2010 with Apple Capturing 83%
    Share; eReader Shipments Quadrupled to More Than 12 Million, According
    to IDC (Press Release)," IDC, March 10, 2011, http://www.idc.com/about/
    viewpressrelease.jsp?containerId=prUS22737611&sectionId=null&elementId=nul
    l&pageType=SYNOPSIS.
11. "New Publishing Industry Survey Details Strong Three-Year Growth in Net
    Revenue, Sales (Press Release)," Association of American Publishers, *Publishers.org,*
    August 9, 2011, http://www.publishers.org/press/44/.
12. http://torrentfreak.com/googles-anti-piracy-filter-110712/
13. http://www.digitalmusicnews.com/permalink/2012/120508limewire
14. http://torrentfreak.com/megaupload-shutdown-inflicts-pleasure-pain-on-
    cyberlockers-120330/
15. http://torrentfreak.com/btjunkie-shuts-down-for-good-120206/
16. http://techpresident.com/news/22165/voices-net-meet-mike-masnick-accidental-
    activist

FairLoading

1. Walter Lippmann, *Public Opinion.* New York: Wilder Editions, 2010, p. 11.
2. http://www.pitchfork.com/news/46637-lcd-soundsystem-ripped-off-by-tgi-
   fridays-ad/
3. http://torrentfreak.com/file-sharing-prospers-despite-tougher-laws-120522/
4. http://torrentfreak.com/rapidshare-publishes-anti-piracy-manifesto-for-
   cyberlockers-120419/

5. Richard Smirke, "EU Extends Copyright Term To 70 Years," *Billboard.biz*, September 12, 2011, http://www.billboard.biz/bbbiz/industry/publishing/eu-extends-copyright-term-to-70-years-1005348552.story.
6. Stan Schroeder, "United Nations: Disconnecting People from the Internet is a Violation of Human Rights," *Mashable*, June 6, 2011, http://mashable.com/2011/06/06/un-Internet-access-human-right/.

Coda

1. John Markoff, "Apple's Visionary Redefined the Digital Age," the *New York Times*, October 5, 2011, http://www.nytimes.com/2011/10/06/business/steve-jobs-of-apple-dies-at-56.html?pagewanted=all.
2. Gary Wolf, "Steve Jobs: The Next Insanely Great Thing," *Wired*, http://www.wired.com/wired/archive/4.02/jobs_pr.html.
3. CBC Summer Way, 1968.